Victorian Divorce

Victorian DIVORCE

ALLEN HORSTMAN

ST. MARTIN'S PRESS
New York

First published in the United States of America in 1985

Library of Congress Catologing in Publication Data

Horstman, Allen, 1943-
   Victorian Divorce.

   Bibliography: p.
   Includes index.
   1. Divorce—Law and Legislation—Great Britain—
   History.   2. Divorce—Great Britain—History.   I. Title.
   KD764.H67   1985   346.4201'66   85-14491

   ISBN 0-312-84156-6   344.206166

50,803

Contents

Tables

to Nan

Preface

My interest in Victorian divorce began about ten years ago when, as a budding legal historian, I sought another way to examine Victorian society. Ater an initial burst of activity, however, other things took precedence and only in the last year have I been able to return to the topic and also to widen my original focus to all divorce before 1900. In that decade the field of family history exploded with much theory and some work, the historiography of which is briefly discussed in the Appendix, but few used the vast resources of the law courts. From that lode, my diggings followed other veins to produce the work here.

This book was made possible by grants from the American Bar Foundation's Program in Legal History and the Albion College Andrew Mellon Faculty Development Fund. Also I received a year's leave from Albion College which enabled me to complete the research and writing of the work. During that year I was a Visiting Research Fellow at the University of Bristol and the recipient of numerous acts of hospitality from the Department of History there. I thank the University of Bristol Department of History for the opportunities provided, and I also thank members of the department, especially Professor John Vincent, for comments and suggestions on my work. I express my gratitude to Professor Sheldon Rothblatt and Joan Annett for comments on portions of the text and to Professor Thomas G. Barnes who undertook the task of converting a lawyer into a legal historian. Help and courtesy have always come from the staff of the British Library, Public Record Office, House of Lords Record Office, University of Bristol Library, Bristol Library, Bristol Record Office, Somerset Record Office, Gloucester Library, University of Michigan Law Library, University of California at Berkeley Library, and, the one which should be first, Albion College Library.

Two final thoughts. In the book which follows I have adopted the posture and tone of a respectable Victorian gentleman, perhaps a tutor in history. The meaning of this will become clear as you go along. Secondly, I mention that this work has been of no relevance to me at all. Like respectable Victorian gentlemen, I am not divorced. That, of course, is the result of being married to Nan. Her help and patient listening to my discussions of Victorian divorce have aided immensely in the formulation and production of this book; hence the dedication.

Albion, Michigan

Abbreviations

DNB	*Dictionary of National Biography* (Leslie Stephen and Sidney Lee, eds)
Hansard	*Hansard Parliamentary Debates. Hansard* has several series, all of which are cited in the notes as *Hansard*. The exact series can be found by checking the date in the text and consulting the following:

First	1–41	1803–20
New	1–25	1820–30
Third	1–356	1830–91

Law Reports	*The Law Journal Reports.* Reports of cases in the Court for Divorce and Matrimonial Causes, etc., change title as they are lumped with reports of other courts, sometimes Probate or Admiralty, sometimes common law. Also a new series is introduced and the publisher changes several times. The volumes proceed sequentially despite these variations.
Lords Journal	*Journals of the House of Lords*
PRO	Public Record Office, Chancery Lane

A Note on Language

In the text the words 'divorce' and 'judicial separation' are used as we use them today. A note of caution, however, to readers who seek nineteenth-century materials about divorce. Many Victorians, especially those who opposed the Act of 1857 (Gladstone, for instance), frequently used 'divorce' to mean the judicial termination of a marriage without the right to remarry: the partners had no further rights or obligations in relation to each other but neither could remarry during the lifetime of the other. In the late twentieth century this situation does not commonly exist in the laws of Western countries, though it may pertain if the partners are members of churches which prohibit the remarriage of the divorced. Additionally, many Victorians preferred 'dissolution of marriage' to 'divorce'. The quotations used in the text have been chosen so as to conform to our usage, not Gladstone's.

1 The Origins

Lustful or conscience-stricken, or both, Henry VIII, the king with six wives, never did obtain a divorce. Nor did anyone else, royal or no, during his reign or for 130 years after, as divorce was unknown in England. John Manners, Lord Roos, future Earl and later Duke of Rutland, has the honour of the first English divorce. In 1670 his wrecked marriage with Lady Ann Pierrepont, daughter and co-heiress of the Marquis of Dorchester, came before Parliament. Two years earlier he had obtained a private Act of Parliament which declared the three sons Lady Ann bore, after leaving him in 1659, to be bastards; this would keep the boys — 'spurious issue' — from inheriting his titles and lands. Parliament favoured him with a second private Act, divorcing him from Lady Ann and permitting him to remarry so as to attempt to maintain his line and titles.

Politicians saw in Roos's divorce a stalking horse for the king. Charles II, childless by his wife, Catherine of Braganza, though father many times by his mistresses, would be succeeded by his brother James, Duke of York and a Roman Catholic. Bishops, on the other hand, worried about the theological propriety of Roos's request as most thought divorce prohibited by the Bible; but the Church of England, with its bishops nearly unanimous against divorce in the 1670s, failed to dissuade Parliamentarians from passing the first divorce. Members of the House of Commons sought, unsuccessfully, a Bill making divorce widely available, echoing calls by the maritally unhappy John Milton over two decades earlier. Roos remarried twice; Charles II did not. Roos finally had a son who succeeded to his titles, though this son died childless. The Roman Catholic Duke of York succeeded to the throne of England but was thrown out of the kingdom during the Glorious Revolution of 1688.[1]

That Revolution, the crowning achievement of the aristocracy in its efforts to subdue the crown, offered another kind of hope to another aristocrat, Henry Howard, seventh Duke of Norfolk. The premier peer of the realm, Norfolk had watched helplessly since 1685 as his Duchess, Lady Mary Mordaunt, the daughter of the Earl of Peterborough, carried on a liaison with Sir John Germaine. Norfolk, failing in his efforts in 1691 and 1692, returned to Parliament for a divorce in 1701. Lady Mary fought the divorce all along and, as she had been discreet and had produced no children, much evidence had to be presented to prove her adultery. She had lived at Vauxhall under the name Lady Beckman and Sir John had, when visiting, pretended to be her brother. Whenever Lady Mary went to Sir John, she wore a mask. But the Duke and his agents had scoured London to catch her out and eventually they found a French footman and a Dutch cookmaid who would testify about seeing Lady Mary and Sir John in bed together. There followed a display of all the dirty linen to the public, which took a prurient interest in it all. The maid saw them in bed, the footman undressed Sir John, an apothecary brought Sir John a clyster (enema) while they were abed together — all circumstantial evidence necessary to prove the adultery.

After Norfolk failed in 1692, he sued Sir John in a common law court for taking his wife. The Duke, not necessarily more sinned against than sinning, had a mistress, a Mrs Lane, and their conduct so affronted sensibilities that, when he gave a ball in Norwich, no ladies attended for fear of being compromised. Norfolk signed a separation agreement with the Duchess's family who supported her throughout until she quarrelled with them over a political intrigue; Norfolk then saw his chance and took it in 1701. In that year the decade-old evidence was hauled out and supplemented by new discoveries. Also, in a period when religious passions inflamed easily, the childless Duke claimed his Bill was 'not only for the benefit of the duke, but of the public, as a means to preserveth inheritance of so great an office and honours to persons of the true religion' — a not subtle reminder that the Duke, a staunch Protestant, would be succeeded by someone from his family, the Howards, long notorious for their Roman Catholicism. Why throw out James II for his religion and then let the premier peerage fall to one of his co-religionists? Upon obtaining his divorce, the 47-year-old Duke promptly died of a fever, childless. His Roman Catholic brother became the eighth Duke of Norfolk.[2]

While the Duke of Norfolk followed the fortunes of politics before getting his divorce, the Earl of Macclesfield obtained a private divorce Act in 1698. The marriage of Charles Gerard, Lord Brandon and second Earl of Macclesfield, and Anne, daughter of Sir Richard Mason, hit troubled waters immediately and they separated two years after the ceremony, in 1685. Lady Anne married to escape her parents and had a sharp tongue, while Charles was violent — when only 17, he killed a footboy with a blow to the head while drunk — and deeply involved in political intrigue. In 1685 he wrote to his wife:

You have more reason to wonder at my forbearing so long to express the resentment of your behavior to me, than to be surprised that I now resolve to ease both you and myself of so unpleasing a conversation . . . You have long since spoke with scorn and contempt of me and my family to my face, and expressed that you did not care to have any children by me . . . This show to [your parents] for I will never live with you so long as I live.[3]

Imprisoned in the Tower in 1683 for Whig political activities, Charles, after his release, soon saw Traitors' Gate again after the Rye House plot against the king. Condemned to death for treason, he was saved by the money, jewels, and pleading of Lady Anne. Despite her efforts, he would not have her back and she eventually took up with Earl Rivers, having two children by him in 1695 and 1697. Charles, now Earl of Macclesfield, and childless, sued for divorce and, after obtaining it, died of a fever on Guy Fawkes Day in 1701 without having remarried. He was succeeded by his bachelor brother who died in 1702 and the title became extinct. The Countess married again, though not to Earl Rivers, and lived until 1753.

Three noblemen, all anxious to end their marriages and remarry, exposed aspects of divorce which remained part of English divorce until well into the twentieth century. Religion, with its twin problems of Roman Catholicism and the church–state relationship, publicity and the public's prurient interest, spurious issue, the double standard, marital unhappiness — matters not easily, if ever, solved, matters which make divorce an integral part of English history. Some issues remain volatile today as the Church of England continues worrying about divorce and nothing sells newspapers like a spicy divorce trial. Nobles, however, led the way in the seventeenth century because of their concern over their lineage and their titles.

Roos and Macclesfield, confronted with children of their wives which they had not fathered, raised the probability of their lands and titles being inherited by 'spurious issue'. All three men sought a new mate so as to continue their lines, but Norfolk and Macclesfield died childless while their former wives remarried and lived happily ever after. Roos's son was the end of his line and, in the 1850s, collateral descendants of Norfolk and Roos, the fourteenth Duke of Norfolk and Lord John Manners, both vigorously opposed divorce reform. The ironies of divorce history!

The first century and three-quarters of English divorce, long ignored by historians, followed the procedures and rules established by these three seventeenth-century nobles because, in English law, practices quickly become rigid — as the twig is bent so the tree doth grow. Already in 1701 when the first two commoners — Ralph Box, grocer, of London and Sir John Dillon of Lesmullen, Ireland — sought divorces, the only problems raised in Parliament concerned the wives' finances, not the procedures, grounds, or even the possibility of divorce. Future generations conformed to the original pattern which lasted to 1857, the year of the Matrimonial Causes Act, commonly known as the Divorce Act.

Divorce meant adultery and adultery remained the only grounds for a divorce until the twentieth century. To obtain a divorce a man — no woman obtained a divorce before the nineteenth century — followed the procedures pioneered by the three nobles in the seventeenth century. Going to a church court, the aggrieved husband sought a divorce *a mensa et thoro*, a divorce from bed and board. In modern terms this was a judicial separation — the couple could legally live apart — and the wife often received permanent maintenance from the husband at about one-fifth of the husband's income. Neither party, husband or wife, could remarry. Many unhappy couples proceeded no further than this court as they lacked money or were content with the results this court afforded. Handling other matters — annulments, probate, clergy discipline — church courts used procedures from the Middle Ages. Witnesses' evidence was taken by the centuries-old technique of written deposition by a court official; witnesses had questions put to them by the official, not by lawyers, months before the trial, not at a trial where a nervous manner or red face might suggest a liar. The entire proceeding remained, despite the Reformation, in the hands of civilians, a group of lawyers trained in church, not common, law. They cited St Augustine and Eusebius, not Bracton and Coke, in their briefs. As late as 1857, fewer than 300 civilians still had a monopoly of church court business and their own separate inn of court (Doctors' Commons), as well as opportunities for selection to the bench of the various church courts. Divorce was not a staple of the church courts but its existence in those courts at a time when most church court business — probate — was decidedly secular, accustomed men to viewing divorce as a secular, not a religious, matter.

Following success in the church court, the cuckolded husband proceeded to a common law court and sued his wife's lover. The suit, an action of trespass, assault, and criminal conversation, was referred to by everyone as 'crim. con.'. As the suit's object was to collect money from the lover for the husband's loss of his wife to the lover, crim. con. came to look uncomfortably near to setting a price on the wife's virtue. The defendant, the lover — if he opposed the suit, and many did not — denied that he was an adulterer or claimed that the wife's reputation was so low, due to prior affairs, as not to be worth much. Many of these suits were shams as husband and lover agreed beforehand as to the amount, which the husband then returned to the lover for not obstructing the other steps to a divorce. Whatever the situation, the wife, not directly a party to a crim. con. suit, saw her actions paraded before a 'grinning jury' and her reputation ruined. After a crim. con. suit, few men, other than the lover, would ever consider marriage to her.

Finally, if a husband wanted a divorce which permitted him to remarry — a divorce *a vinculo matrimonii*, from the bond of wedlock — he needed to obtain a private act from Parliament. The private Bill began in the House of Lords which usually (after 1798, always) required the husband to prove previously successful verdicts in his suits of crim. con. and divorce *a mensa et thoro*. Notwithstanding those previous trials, the House of Lords reheard all the evidence. Once the Lords had satisfied themselves that adultery had occurred and no other impediment existed, the Bill moved to the Commons which usually took little interest, other than in provisions for the wife. The bill, besides divorcing the couple, unscrambled the marriage settlement with its many provisions governing money for children, dowry and pin money, lands, jewels and inheritances. When the royal assent was received to the private Bill, the couple was divorced and each free to remarry, after perhaps three years of litigation and legislation!

That divorce became an adversary proceeding was inevitable so long as Parliament avoided any systematic approach to the matter. With estates, settlements, and the like all at stake in an aristocratic divorce, lawyers would soon appear. The curious procedure, however, of the three courts can only be explained by the combination of seventeenth-century notions about the supremacy of Parliament and the ability of nobles to get Parliament to allow them their wishes. In the eighteenth century not all divorces contained all three steps but, by 1800, any deviation from the pattern required justification before the House of Lords would proceed. So long as divorce remained rare, the unusual process attracted no attention; by the time people believed divorce was becoming too common, the three-step proceedings had been sanctified by a century of use.

The chief part of any divorce trial — evidence of the adultery — came from witnesses, sometimes to the act itself, sometimes of circumstances suggesting the act. As husband and wife could not testify about such matters, other witnesses had to be sought. Servants, ever present in the households of the rich, saw much and knew more:

Admiral Knowles's wife, in the 1750s would often 'pull off her stays against the usual time' of her lover's coming, said her maid, and she would 'sigh, coo, and smile' at her lover.[4]

In the 1770s Elizabeth Campbell's servants, suspecting things amiss, stayed up one night when the lover visited and the husband was absent. They 'heard kissing very distinctly', 'heard a noise, as of panting of breath', and 'plainly heard the bed crack for a little time'.[5]

Anna, a maid of a Mrs Daly, hiding behind a settee, saw that the Earl of Kerry 'after kissing and toying with her for some time, laid her down upon the chairs, and — —'. Another servant saw that Kerry's 'Breeches were down and that Mrs Daly's Petticoats were up, so that he saw her naked Thighs'.[6]

Mrs Wilson's servant, in 1798, testified he viewed her and her lover from 'Outside of the House upon a ladder, which raised me as to look over the Shutters of the Window'.[7]

The Duke and Duchess of Grafton spoke French during their disagreements to frustrate prying servants.[8]

Already in the 1690s, the Duchess of Norfolk warned of the dangers when the marriages of the great depended on the testimony of their servants: 'Masters are already too much in the power of their servants'. Who would serve whom?

In addition to the problem of proving the adultery, the husband faced the serious obstacle of cost, an obstacle high enough to keep all but the rich from divorcing. The Duke of Norfolk spent much over the course of his decade-long struggle and rumour had it that a late-eighteenth-century merchant went through £10,000 when his wife resisted. More often, disputes were not very protracted, if resisted at all, and cost perhaps £1,000 — a sizeable amount but not more than a few months' income to those getting divorces.

The law, not the purse, raised the greatest obstacle to the parting couple, especially if they both behaved as their class is commonly portrayed. Mutual guilt — if both husband and wife had been adulterous — stopped the divorce as the church courts and later the House of Lords deemed such behaviour a bar to a divorce.

Richard Lord Grosvenor, owner of London lands that were later to make his family the wealthiest in England, married Henrietta Vernon in 1864 and they had one son. In 1770 Richard decided that Henrietta's conduct with the king's brother, Henry, Duke of Cumberberland, attracted so much notoriety that a divorce was necessary and he spared no horses in gathering and presenting the evidence. Cumberland and his equerry, Captain Foulkes, had travelled to and from Cheshire, where the Grosvenors had their country house, with the Duke, 'his hat pulled so low over his face, that [the innkeeper] could see only his nose and cheeks', passing himself as a foolish heir in one inn and 'Squire Jones' in another. Visiting the pleasure parks of Vauxhall and Ranelagh as well as the palace of St James almost daily, Henrietta often reappeared with her clothes 'tumbled and disordered' and her hair 'rumpled and loose'. Richard's steward and some servants, trailing the adulterous pair to a St Albans' inn, broke into their room, catching them undressed. Lady D'Onhoff, a confidante of Henrietta, testified she saw them 'in the very act of carnal copulation', 'his body was in motion'. One landlady testified, when Henrietta was pregnant, their lovemaking was done standing up.

Henrietta fought back, using Cumberland's gentleman-porter to give long testimony explaining away all the events. Her sister, a maid of honour to the queen, also provided alibis for her. Then, pulling out the stops, Henrietta accused Richard of 'a vicious, lewd, and debauched life' especially with prostitutes. One prostitute, frequented by Richard, testified how he 'r——d' her, further describing the punch they drank and the tips to the innkeeper, as well as the time Richard had her take off all her clothes and sit on his knee.

Richard received a judgment for £10,000 against Cumberland in the crim. con. suit but Henrietta's recriminations kept Richard from obtaining a divorce.[9]

The law's other major obstacle, in legal terms 'collusion', reflected the desire of many that divorce be neither common nor easy. Couples co-operating to obtain divorces regularly found their efforts thwarted and their marriages intact.

David Moreau petitioned for a Parliamentary divorce in 1755. The evidence revealed David married Susannah in 1737. After one child, he disappeared abroad, leaving her in great distress. He lived at Minorca and Gibraltar while she went into service and eventually lived with George Smedley, a harness-maker. David's mother, wanting her son rid of Susannah, signed articles of agreement with Susannah and George to facilitate the divorce. (David was coming into an inheritance.)[10]

Mr Chisim, a drysalter, sought a divorce in 1779 from Mrs Chisim, daughter of Mr Roberts who 'lived upon his fortune at Boarshall, in Sussex'. The co-respondent, William Greaves, also 'a man of property' did not resist the crim. con. suit and the House of Lords soon discovered that Mr Roberts's fortune was financing all so his daughter would be free to marry in her own rank. Collusion.[11]

Captain Thomas Edwards wanted rid of Judith Edwards in 1779. He signed a bond promising her £45 a year if she did not delay or oppose the divorce. Collusion.[12]

Mr Esten's efforts for a divorce from Harriet Bennet Esten in 1798 failed when it became apparent the Duke of Hamilton was the force and the finance behind the scenes. Harriet was Hamilton's mistress and mother of his child.[13]

In a related matter separation deeds could be a bar to divorce if it appeared the deed was signed at a time when the husband knew of the wife's misconduct or if the deed surrendered all the husband's control over the wife who then misbehaved. Also, a separation without 'adequate' cause could bar a divorce. The law required that the couple do all within their power to keep their marriage together.[14]

The only rule facilitating divorces declared that the birth of a child at a time when, due to absence, the husband could not have been the father, was sufficient evidence of adultery. Lady Anne Hope Weir (1757), Mrs Scott (1766), and Lady Colleton (1772) were all divorced when they produced such a child.[15]

As the entire proceedings depended on outward appearances, not inner feelings, the legal system demanded evidence of acts and accepted no excuses about outrageous behaviour driving a wife to seek solace elsewhere. Though Jane Austen might make much of the disparities between mind and manners — misunderstandings tumble from her novels — the law courts concerned themselves only with the appearances. Marital unhappiness was not an issue in divorce. The law's emphasis on acts coincided with society's concern for appearances and nowhere more than in the affairs of the couple, despite the image projected by much of eighteenth-century society.

Robert Rochford, Baron Bellfield and later Earl of Belvedere, was the grandson of Hannah Handcock, to whom Swift wrote 'Advice to a very Young Lady upon her Marriage'. With his Irish title and lands, Robert married Mary Molesworth, daughter of Viscount

Molesworth. Though she brought 'only' £6,000, 'her accomplishments and sprightliness were the conversation of everyone'. Within two years of her marriage in 1736 she was conducting an affair with Arthur Rochfort, her husband's brother, who was also married. Testimony was presented that she planned to poison her husband and her lover's wife so she would be free to marry her lover. Bellfield sued his brother but stopped the case when Arthur promised to leave Ireland. When Arthur violated the understanding, Robert proceeded, obtaining a judgment of £20,000 which sent Arthur, unable to pay, to King's Bench prison for debt. Mary was shut up in a country house the rest of her life. When Mary's father was told of her affair with Arthur, he muttered 'Damn the whore!' and never mentioned her name the remaining 20 years of his life.[16]

Other men, more tolerant than Mary Molesworth's father, still might find themselves seeking a divorce, and not merely because of spurious issue. The eighteenth century had not the highest standards of morality, be they political, personal, or sexual, found in English history, yet the bounds could be exceeded. In matters of adultery, a husband, who long knew the facts, felt compelled to seek a divorce if his wife's conduct became too notorious or if she 'eloped' with her lover. Even this convention, which pushed divorce beyond the titled, did not govern all as the Countess of Oxford's many affairs — her four children by four different lovers were called the 'Harleian Miscellany' — never provoked her husband into divorcing her.[17] While Lord Grosvenor found his wife's attentions to the Duke of Cumberland covered by the press, which forced his hand, the Duke of Grafton simply never cared for his wife's numerous card parties (which meant gambling), and Lord Bellfield was outraged at being made a cuckold by his own brother — quite diverse reasons for seeking divorce. Although the records are too sparse and divorce too rare to discover what provoked husbands to act, no man wished to look the fool, and that wish was the father to many a divorce petition.

Gossip governed appearances. England had a small ruling class and annually they gathered in London for the 'season' when gossip was intense. The 'people who count' — and who constituted the group from which most divorces came — were few enough that they knew of, if not knew, everyone. Even as late as 1814 gossip found its way into all corners. Sir John Burke, quietly enjoying a dinner party in 'St James, close to the Palace', heard the guests discussing the elopement of an adulteress unknown to the guests but, from their comments, identifiable to Sir

John as his sister. He promptly fled to Paris and his anger and embarrassment still burn from the pages of his testimony in the later divorce.[18]

Gossip was joined by the press in governing appearances in the course of the eighteenth century. Politicians, early in the century, suffered mightily for their actions, physical characteristics, and sins. Printers also soon discovered the value of sex in increasing sales. They often printed the seventeenth-century trials of the Countess of Essex who, with her lover, poisoned Sir Thomas Overbury, and of Lord Audley who forced his servant to have intercourse with Lady Audley while he simultaneously committed an 'unnatural crime' on the servant. Adultery trials also constituted a continuing source of like material and a part of the printing industry devoted itself to reporting lawsuits involving sex and violence. The year 1779 saw the publication of *Trials for Adultery*, a seven-volume collection complete with prints of scenes from the lives of the lovers, enough to gratify even habitual followers of such suits. The press reported the scandal of Lady Grosvenor and the Duke of Cumberland even before the trial.[19]

Wives and lovers maintained appearances as adultery could become a desperate game, not a joyful or loving tryst. A duel, while adding spice to life, also added the chance of ending that life. But less glamorous results were more feared.

In 1750 Admiral Charles Knowles married. Fourteen years old, Maria was (by court testimony) the daughter of an innkeeper at Aix-la-Chapelle or (by Burke's peerage) the daughter of Henry Francis, Comte de Bouget, Council of the Elector of Cologne, and the sister of Ferdinand, General Count von Bouget, Lieutenant-Colonel Austrian Imperial Guard. When Knowles was sent to Jamaica as Governor in 1750, Maria began a secret affair with Captain Gambier there. Gambier, married with two or three children, and Maria, with three children, hoped for another as 'a token of their love'. When Maria was to return to England, Gambier's ship was chosen and the couple cavorted across the Atlantic. In England Maria had a closet in her bedroom fitted for Gambier to hide in if her husband ever surprised them. When the Admiral learned of the affair, Gambier lost his command, went badly into debt, and suffered an award of £1,000 against him in the crim. con. suit. A lifetime in debtors' prison awaited him.[20]

Lord Bellfield's brother also viewed life from inside debtors' prison after losing a crim. con. suit for £20,000.

Wives faced considerable risks, besides divorce, for adultery. Lovers locked up in prison lacked usefulness, and many women underwent pregnancies, never a safe event in the eighteenth century, as a result of their affairs. Certainly, the literature of the day would make any woman's skin crawl when it described the effects of pregnancy and childbirth. While Lady Morrice fought her husband, saying she 'would not be buried in the countryside', Baroness Bellfield, less fortunate, was shut up in an Irish country house. In 1829 Mrs Tyrell, who brought £45,000 to the marriage but who committed adultery with an impecunious clerk, was left nearly destitute when her husband divorced her.[21]

These problems and risks for cuckolded husbands, wayward wives, and adventuresome lovers meant that divorce, in the eighteenth century, could not be lightly undertaken, a fact which kept the number of divorces low. The other legal possibility of escape from a marriage — annulment — was, in England, not much of a possibility at all. When Henry VIII shed his queens, making himself head of the English church and breaking with the rest of European Christendom, he made two contributions to English marital history. Studies of his problems clarified the rules about annulments as he so ended three of his marriages — Catharine of Aragon, Anne Boleyn, Anne of Cleves. In those three instances, Henry and his advisers claimed the marriages were never valid as Catharine had been married to Henry's brother (violating a rule against consanguinity); Henry had been intimate with Mary Boleyn, Anne's sister (violating another rule against consanguinity); and Henry and Anne of Cleves, 'the Flanders mare', never consummated their marriage. An effect — and the reason why Henry sought annulments rather than divorces — of this procedure was to make bastards of the children of the unions, the future Queens Mary and Elizabeth. Despite Henry's example, annulments never became a popular means of escape from an unwanted spouse because few couples could allege non-consummation and the prohibited degrees of relations had little applicability as most observed the rules at marriage.

Divorces difficult, annulments rare — careful marriage became more necessary as many worried about misalliances. Fewer thoughtless or improvident marriages became a goal as the scarcity of divorce brought home to people the permanence of marriage, and steps were taken in the eighteenth century to reduce the ease of marriage. The medieval Western church had laid down the rules for a valid marriage: consent of the parties and sexual intercourse. Various impediments — consanguinity, youth, prior contract — could lead to annulments but, overall, people could marry easily. Too easily for some as intent plus intercourse — no church ceremony required — led to lots of marriages. A man or woman might wake up after an evening of drink to find a person sharing the bed who, after drunken professions of intention, had consummated the marriage during the night. If the unwitting, but reckless, partner was young and the heir or heiress to a fortune, the circumstances had a sinister face, but the result remained the same — they were married. However, by the seventeenth century, church courts came to require a ceremony officiated over by a clergyman to establish validity. Parliament also tackled the problems, with little result. Lovers, seeking to avoid the publicity of banns read at the church or the licence from a bishop, resorted to clergy who were prepared to officiate without such procedures — the participants might be breaking the law but the marriage remained valid as it had consent, consummation, and clergy. Avoidance of family objections, desire for speed, evasion of the stamp tax on marriages, all led to the growth of a 'clandestine' marriage industry in and around London. Churches at Lincoln's Inn, the Southwark mint, and Newgate Prison specialised in instantaneous marriages. Suppression of those sites shifted the trade to Fleet Prison where clergy, imprisoned for debt, officiated, the fees helping alleviate their condition.

In 1754 Lord Hardwicke's Marriage Act required marriage after banns in the parish church of one of the parties. Not everyone thought of the Act as progress and the day before it took effect 217 marriages were 'solemnised' in the Fleet. To young bloods seeking heiresses, the Act represented a plot to ensure that nobles' children, denied the hasty marriage and therefore subject to parental wishes and pressures, would marry only other noble children — the caste would close. In fact, the Act lacked those extreme consequences and went far to clarify and regulate marriage procedures. Few problems remained — Dissenters obtained their own procedures in 1836 — and the Act threw the mantle of the state over the institution of marriage. To say that it changed the nature of marriage from a sacrament to a contract overstates the case, but thereafter the state regulated marriage at its beginning and at its end.[22]

Royalty, after 1772, lived under special, more stringent, rules about contracting marriage due to to George III's fury over the marriages of his brothers, the Dukes of Gloucester and Cumberland (Gloucester married an illegitimate daughter of Sir Edward Walpole and Cumberland a young widow of no social position). The Royal Marriage Act laid down that a member of the royal family could not marry before the age of 25 without the monarch's permission or after 25 unless twelve months' notice was given to the Privy Council or Parliamentary approval obtained. As George III, a serious, respectable, and faithful husband, and Queen Charlotte had fifteen children, twelve growing to adulthood, the Act governed a sizeable brood. To the king's disgust, however, the marital life of the royal offspring flaunted appearances and provided examples of all variations of trouble:

> In 1793 the Duke of Sussex, ignoring the Royal Marriage Act, married Lady Augusta Murray (he was 20, she was 30) in Rome, though with a Church of England rite, but, after much browbeating, he agreed to seek an annulment. Thereafter, Sussex lived with several women but only married again in 1831. The Prince of Wales, future Prince Regent and, as George IV, king, secretly married Mrs Fitzherbert, ignoring the Royal Marriage Act, and later, without disowning his wife, married Princess Caroline, a disastrous match that nearly ended in divorce. William, Duke of Clarence and future king, cohabited with the actress Mrs Jordan from 1791 to 1811, fathering ten children, before marrying Adelaide of Saxe-Meiningen. Princess Sophia had an illegitimate child. And so on with the royal family.

Royal behaviour, always an influence on much of English society, did nothing to encourage marital faithfulness in the rest of the populace. Stiffer marriage laws produced not greater obedience in the royal family, but greater evasion.

That eighteenth-century spouses might turn a blind eye to marital unfaithfulness, given the few remedies available, should not surprise. Others, cynicism overwhelming them and with the royal examples before them, never worried overmuch in any case. Viscount Molesworth's 'Damn the whore!' represented one attitude about unfaithfulness, and religious strictures governed many, despite the rationalism of the intellectuals. With all these considerations governing couples, the complicated three-step procedure yielded, by 1800, 128 divorces, including three dukes, one marquess, one earl, five barons, five baronets, and numerous sons, daughters, and relations of the peerage (see Table 1.1 at end of chapter). Countless other couples quietly separated or simply waited for the release of death. All in all, eighteenth-century marital life, due to the vagaries of divorce law, had variety.

Adultery and the family, the moral problem and the practical one, were the problems of divorce. The three seventeenth-century peers began the tradition of noble concern with the descent of titles and honours within the family but, as the peerage was not very numerous in England, this always remained a minor theme in divorce. However, armigerous gentry also brooded over family lines and, besides worrying about continuance of the family line by spurious issue, the rest of society, less wealthy than a duke, faced the problem of the expense of raising and educating children, plus finding them jobs.

The law of England, however, was not receptive to desires to protect the class from the vicissitudes of life. The Duke of Norfolk, before his concern about the Duchess's behaviour led him to a divorce, had been a litigant in the most famous lawsuit in English land law. *The Duke of Norfolk's case.* He attempted to tie up his lands forever — in perpetuity, as the lawyers said — so his heirs could not sell or give it away. His goal, to marry his land and titles for eternity, would maintain future Dukes of Norfolk at the head of the English peerage. If imitated by others — and it would have been had not the House of Lords struck it down — his device would have removed the land of all England from the market. No new nobles, no jumped-up merchants or pettifogging lawyers could rise to challenge the old order, led by the oldest and highest dukedom, Norfolk.

Divorce, therefore, represented a middle position between the extremes of a closed caste, as attempted by the Duke of Norfolk with his lands, and the extinction by death of noble and gentle lines. This fear of the extinction of their lineage created another legal change in the late seventeenth century — name changes. Adoption not being legal in England until the twentieth century, name changes dealt with the future of the family name. Childless and wealthy Englishmen and Englishwomen wrote wills stipulating that a nephew — usually a sister's son — or a more distant relative or in-law would inherit all if he changed his name to that of the testator. Even without such incentives, Jarrit Smith, a prosperous Bristol solicitor and Member of Parliament, when his wife Priscilla Smyth inherited her father's properties at Ashton Court, soon blended into his new surroundings — Smith became Smyth. Name changes involved, like divorce, a private Act of Parliament; they became common in the last quarter of the seventeenth century, when divorce originated, and declined only in the nineteenth century, when divorce became more available. After the seventeenth century, with the development of both divorce and name changes, few men, noble or not, made much of a desire to remarry in order to continue the family; adultery now loomed larger.

Adultery, with its two dimensions — spurious issue and appearances — was the focus of divorce for most eighteenth-century men and so it remained into the twentieth century. Punishment of adultery by the law, never very effective, became less so with the decline of the church courts after the Reformation. Adultery — its moral taint was traditional, its reprehensibility biblical — was never justified or questioned. The Seventh Commandment settled the matter but, as eternity lacked immediacy to many, the problem of adultery became the province of divorce. Divorce came to be seen as both a deterrent and a punishment for adultery. Already by 1700, after only two divorces, writers sought to make divorce 'less chargeable and difficult' so it could better function as a means to punish wives. Few doubted that divorce deterred — the expense, the scandal — and interest shifted to whether further deterrence could be introduced by forbidding the wife and her lover to marry after the Parliamentary divorce. If the adulterous pair could not marry, the wife would hesitate before taking a lover — so the argument went — because, as all agreed no one but a lover would marry a divorced adulteress, her alternatives after discovery and divorce would be disgrace, poverty, prostitution, death — usually in that order. A wife should, therefore, pause before embarking on a course which led down such a dark path.

Deterrence became urgent in the years after 1770 and again after 1790 when contemporaries discerned a 'divorce epidemic' raging in England. The Parliamentary session of 1772–3 produced seven divorce Acts and the decade of the 1770s saw 20 couples parted by Parliament, whereas the previous century had witnessed only 46 divorces. In the late 1790s — the excesses of the French Revolution before their eyes — men saw 31 divorces in three years. In efforts to stem the tide the House of Lords established a standing order in 1798 requiring men to show success in the crim. con. suit and in the church court— previously this had not always been insisted upon— and investigated more closely the possibilities of collusion among the parties, husband, wife, and lover. Bills appeared in Parliament in 1771 and 1779 to ban the marriage of the lovers and, with the persistence of Lord Auckland, a strong supporter of Pitt and a barrister who wrote *Principles of Penal Law*, the matter became one of considerable public discussion around 1800. The Bishop of Chichester wanted adultery punished with a five-year imprisonment but the Duke of Bedford opposed this — he was 'very eager against it' — as it would make lovers too desperate. (The Bishop told this to Lord Holland, the lover, and later, husband of Sir Godfrey Webster's wife, who 'was, of course, puzzled how to answer'.) Whether the erring wife should be treated with compassion or as a criminal was a difficult decision, but in 1801 the House of Lords passed a Bill forbidding the remarriage of the lovers; the House of Commons threw it out. No one sought to abolish Parliamentary divorce — the need for it was too clear, the resulting injustices would be too great. *The Times* wished Parliament had never started giving divorces, but there was no going back now. Legal tradition, spurious issue, the family name, punishment, deterrence — all combined to keep divorce available.[23]

In 1801 with the grounds, procedures, and rationale of divorce securely in place but with a divorce epidemic near at hand and Napoleon rampaging over Europe spreading ideas spawned by the French Revolution about women and equality, a woman petitioned the House of Lords for a divorce!

Table 1.1: Parliamentary Divorces before 1800

Year of Act	Name of Husband
1672	Lord Roos
1698	Earl of Macclesfield
1701	Duke of Norfolk
1702	Sir John Dillon
—	Ralph Box
1713	Francis Loggin
1714	William Young
—	Francis Annesley
1733	Sir John Rudd, Bart.
1744	Duke of Beaufort
1745	Daniel Mathew
—	Corbyn Morriss
1747	Samuel Rush
1751	Godfrey Copley
1752	Daniel Lascelles
—	Thomas Benson
1753	John Ennever
—	Samuel Low
1754	Charles Wymondesold
—	Peter Henley
—	John Maydivell
1755	Richard Morgan
1756	Richard Glover
1757	Charles Hope Weir
—	Thomas Nuthall
1758	Godfrey Wentworth
—	George Foster Tussnell
1759	John Cooke
1760	Exuperius Turner
—	Mark Goodflesh
1763	William Hazeland
1764	John Weller

Table 1.1: (continued)

1765	John Nixon
1766	John Matthews
—	Charles Aldcroft
1767	John Scott
1768	Thomas Brooke
—	Viscount Bolingbroke
—	Charles Daly
1769	Duke of Grafton
—	John Worgan
1771	Henry Knight
1772	Viscount Ligonier
—	Sir John Colleton, Bart.
—	Hugh Lewis
—	Ambrose Godfrey Harckwitz
—	Richard Draper
—	William Skinn
—	George Collier
1773	John Featherston Bowerbank
—	John Gordon
—	John Green
—	Philip Cade
1774	Robert Heatley
—	Stephen Popham
1775	Robert Green
1776	John Williot
—	Charles Horneck
—	Thomas Williams
—	Sir Thomas Bunbury, Bart.
1777	John Potter Harris
—	John Braithwaite
1778	John Hooke Campbell
—	Sir Patrick Blake, Bart.
—	Thomas Darby
—	George Christopher Degen
—	Clotworthy Dobbin
1779	Lord Percy
—	Lord Osborne
—	Henry Sealy
—	Thomas Bailey Heath Sewell
—	Charles Bromfield
—	Charles Francis Damergue
1782	John Newton
1783	John Williams
—	John Hankey
—	Andrew Bayntun
1784	Walter Nisbet
1785	John Inglis
1787	William Fawkener
—	Edward Foley
1788	George Errington
—	John Twiss
1789	Henry Fortick Sheridan
—	William John Arabin

Table 1.1: (continued)

1790	Francis Thomas Rybot
1791	John Parslow
—	John Walford
—	Henry Cecil
1792	William Raybould
—	John Larking
—	John Wilmot
1793	Alexander Stewart
—	John Street
—	Richard Marten
—	Edward Brown
—	Calverly John Bewicke
1794	Bernard Edward Howard
1796	Henry Wakeman
—	William Townshend Mullins
—	Lancelot Shadwell
—	Henry Farrer
—	William Brook Jones
—	Richard Morrson
—	Joseph Seymour Biscoe
—	James Christie
1797	John Opie
—	William Bright
—	Lord Cadogan
—	John Henry Cooke
—	James M'Gauley
—	Sir Godfrey Vassall (Webster)
—	Sidenham Teast
1798	James Fozard
—	Samuel Boddington
—	Thomas James Twisleton
—	James Woodmason
1799	Edward Jervis Ricketts
—	William Williams
—	William Henry Ricketts
—	Marquess of Abercorn
—	John Stanton
—	Shuldham Peard
—	John Thoroton
—	Sir Hyde Parker
—	John Buller
1800	Edward Henry Columbine

Source: *Statutes of the Realm.*

Notes

1. Architell Grey, *Debates of the House of Commons* (D. Henry & R. Cave, London, 1763) vol. 1, pp.251–63; Gilbert Burnet, *History of My Own Time* (Oxford, 1897) vol. 1, p.471; J. S. Clarke, *The Life of James the Second* (Longman, London, 1816) vol. 1, p.438; 19 Charles II, no. 21; 22 Charles II, no. 14.
2. T. B. Howell, *Cobbett's Complete Collection of State Trials* (R. Bagshaw, Lon-

don, 1809–26) vol. xiii, cols 1283–1369; *DNB*, Henry Howard; E.M. Thompson (ed.), *Letters of Humphrey Prideaux, sometime Dean of Norwich* (Camden Society New Series XV, London, 1875) p.184.

3. *DNB*, Charles Gerard; W.M. Thomas, *Notes and Queries,* 2nd series, vol. 6 (1858) pp.361–5, 385–9.

4. Francis Plowden, *Crim. Con. Biography* (London, 1830) vol. 1, pp.109 et seq.

5. Ibid., vol. 2, p.9.

6. Ibid., vol. 1, p.138.

7. *Lords Journal*, vol. xli, p.550.

8. Plowden, *Crim. Con. Biography*, vol. 1; *Trials for Adultery* (Bladon, London, 1779) vol. 3, p.90.

9. *Trials for Adultery*, vol. 4; Plowden, *Crim. Con. Biography*, vol. 1, p.241.

10. John Macqueen, *A Practical Treatise on the Appellate Jurisdiction of the House of Lords & Privy Council* (A. Maxwell, London, 1842) p.578.

11. Ibid., p.582.

12. Ibid., p.583.

13. Ibid., p.588.

14. Ibid., pp.588, 589.

15. Ibid., pp.580, 581.

16. Plowden, *Crim. Con. Biography*, vol. 1, p.21.

17. A. Aspinall (ed.), *The Letters of King George IV* (Cambridge University Press, Cambridge, 1938) no. 263n.

18. *Lords Journal*, vol. lii, p.295.

19. Peter Wagner, 'The Pornographer in the Courtroom: Trial Reports about Cases of Sexual Crimes and Delinquencies as a Genre of Eighteenth-century Erotica', in Paul-Gabriel Bouce (ed.), *Sexuality in Eighteenth-century Britain* (Manchester University Press, Manchester, 1982) pp.121–40.

20. Plowden, *Crim. Con. Biography*, vol. 1, p.109

21. John Macqueen, *A Practical Treatise*, p.644.

22. 26 George II, c. 33; John Bossy, 'Challoner and the Marriage Act', in Eamon Duffy (ed.), *Challoner and his Church* (Darton, Longman & Todd, London, 1981), pp.126–36.

23. The Earl of Ilchester (ed.), *The Journal of Elizabeth Lady Holland* (Longman, Green, London, 1909) pp.79, 77; *Hansard*, vol. 35, cols 280, 1248, vol. 17, col. 185, vol. 20, col. 601; *The Times*, 20th May 1801.

2 Before The Act: Victorian Divorce, Part I

Jane Addison married Edward Addison in 1788, three years after her sister Jessy wed James Campbell. By 1793 Edward and Jessy, his sister-in-law, had taken to travelling together in Scotland; their adultery produced two divorce Bills — Jane's and James's — in 1801. James Campbell's Bill, usual as to form and substance, excited no controversy in the House of Lords, but the Upper House dithered, debated and delayed when Jane's Bill appeared. As a daughter of Sir James Campbell of Inverneild, hereditary usher of the white rod for Scotland and strong supporter of William Pitt's government, Jane Addison had the usual family connections found in a Parliamentary divorce. The English legal tradition of similar treatment for similar people similarly situated meant Jane and James should both obtain their divorces. But Jane was a woman. The double standard confronted!

Because divorce had long — for over a century — been only for husbands, one rationale already existed for differing treatment of husbands and wives: 'spurious issue'. The wife's adultery, by introducing children of doubtful paternity into the family, provided one of the grounds for the first divorces in the seventeenth century and nineteenth-century Englishmen still accepted it, almost as axiomatic. The husband's adultery could, but rarely did, burden the family with the financial obligation of supporting the offspring, if his paternity could be established — this possibility rarely occupied anyone's mind in the public discussions. History contributed further to the inequality of the spouses as English law had a tradition growing out of feudal custom — medieval law protected warriors, not wives — which affected such areas of married life as control over property and earnings and custody of children. Women also had a greater power of forgiveness, so said a long tradition of thought and teaching in the West. Gibbon, in *The History of the Decline and Fall of the Roman Empire*, declared the wife's offence greater, even among fabulously rich Roman aristocrats. A century earlier, Mary Astell, whose many writings about proper education and the behaviour of women coincided with the first divorces, had claimed: 'Husband's Vices may become an occasion of the Wife's Vertues.'[1] Certainly forgiveness was, as a Christian virtue, theoretically encumbent on men as well as women — but the long history of the concept of honour still lingered. Duels continued, the last as late as the 1840s, and the divorce process had honour and its own version of the duel in the crim. con. lawsuit. Honour overrode forgiveness as adultery touched a husband's honour at its prickliest spot. John Milton's belief that marriage was made for man but woman was made for marriage captured a common attitude to the genders. All these strands combined to make a wife's marital reputation and faithfulness more important than a husband's, though behaviour in the easygoing days around the turn of the century did not always agree with the ideals.

By 1801 when Jane Addison sought her divorce, a new type of individual had appeared in English life. Called 'Evangelicals', these were members of the Church of England who emphasised sin, the conversion experience, and service — things the eighteenth-century church had often ignored. God-fearing, serious, and conservative, Evangelicals sought, and gained, adherents from the rich and powerful in the years after 1790. Founding such new organisations as the Society for the Suppression of Vice, they attacked obscenity, violations of the Sabbath, the theatre, and the like. Much of eighteenth-century conduct was indicted and English life assumed a new seriousness. Beau Brummell and other Regency dandies would still have their innings, but the attitudes and behaviour we call 'Victorian' had made their appearance, a generation before Victoria herself.

Believing that life had a purpose, a moral purpose, Evangelicals set out to spread that doctrine, aided by the events of the French Revolution which had convinced many aristocrats that selfishness and fecklessness had disastrous consequences. Evangelicals made great gains early in the century and had carried the day by 1840, establishing their beliefs as dominant. Long before that date, however, their success meant English society at its upper reaches divided into two groups: the serious and the fast.

As to the double standard, Jane Addison's obstacle, Evangelicals did not condone adultery whether committed by husband or wife. Evangelicalism, despite the roles of Hannah More and other women in its success, brought no equality for wives. The shame of an eighteenth-century aristocrat about being a public cuckold joined the Evangelical shame of being married to a sinner who flouted God's law. The sin of a wife's adultery merely joined all the historical reasons for her inferior condition before the law.

A practical objection flowing from the practice of divorce and the double standard then increased the difficulties facing a wife. As a man's reputation suffered less — far less — from an accusation of adultery, unhappy couples might connive together for the wife to bring the Bill. Perhaps the wife, by prior agreement of the couple and their lawyers, would seek the divorce, which the husband would not oppose; adulteresses could then get divorces and, perhaps, even couples when no adultery had occurred but who were merely unhappy together. Divorce by consent! The floodgates open! The argument had validity — it describes a practice occurring after 1900 — but which was 100 years before its time. Moreover, even if a husband committed the adultery, a wife's reputation suffered — 'she wasn't a good wife' — and most women would have avoided the risks of collusion. The argument, rather than describing any present reality, reveals an awareness that people might be so unhappy in a marriage that they would take desperate steps to escape the tie that bound them. This idea — divorce on the grounds of marital unhappiness — never made much public headway as most Victorians were not clear that the primary purpose of marriage was happiness: marriage was for children, family, economic benefit and spiritual uplift; it provided the basis of organised society. But happiness? Well, yes, but among well-matched couples happiness would exist in all sorts of forms.

The Times opposed Jane Addison's petition, believing all divorce was a mistake. Though there was no taking back husbands' opportunities (now almost rights) for divorce, wives should not obtain similar opportunities — two wrongs do not make a right. The Duke of Clarence, George III's son whose marriage to Lady Augusta Murray had been annulled in 1794, believed too many divorces occurred. To permit wives to petition would exacerbate an already unwieldy problem. The divorce epidemic of the last three decades of the eighteenth century affected his, and others', thinking.[2]

Jane Addison got her divorce. The Lords also decided that, in the future, a wife might seek divorce only when her husband committed an incestuous adultery. Incest was the key as it added great stigma to the husband's adultery and it also touched a deep-seated psychological fear of the aristocracy about family. For a century already, and for a century to come, Bills to permit marriage with a deceased wife's sister had agitated Parliamentary opinion. Incest — the great Western Taboo — tipped the balance and gave Jane Addison freedom from her husband.[3]

Four years later, Elizabeth Teush petitioned the House of Lords for a divorce:

Frederick Teush and Elizabeth Utterton married in 1790. By 1800 he had three children by his mistress while both of his children by Elizabeth had died. Frederick's counting-house was bankrupt and in 1801 Elizabeth obtained a divorce *a mensa et thoro* in the Consistory Court of London. Her father died, making no provision for her, but, despite all, her behaviour remained irreproachable. A witness testified he had visited her 'with his children' so spotless was her reputation. Despite strong support from the Earl of Caernarvon, Elizabeth's petition failed. Frederick and his mistress went to Scotland and, Elizabeth following, a divorce was obtained.[4]

The double standard, safely settled as to divorce, was not to be changed and Elizabeth Teush's efforts stirred little debate and were almost routinely dismissed. Thirty years elapsed before another woman, Louise Turton, obtained the second English divorce by a woman, again when the husband committed an incestuous adultery:

Louise Browne and Thomas Turton married in 1812. In 1822 they went to India, taking Louise's sister Adeline with them. It turned out Thomas and Adeline had committed adultery in England and she was pregnant. Louise took Adeline with them to the East to conceal the mess from gossips, hoping 'something might be done to save the Misery of the Situation'. (Louise's father, General Gore Browne, forbade any discussion of the matter in his house.) After Adeline's baby had been born and nothing improved in India, Louise returned to England though her husband and sister stayed on, having a second child, until 1829. Divorce Bill passed.[5]

A second front for wives appeared only in 1840 when Ann Battersby's situation generated outrage sufficient to modify the double standard, though only slightly:

Ann and Arther Battersby married in 1826 after the briefest of courtships and lived together for only three weeks, during which time he openly visited brothels. Having venereal disease before marriage, and knowing it, he gave it to her during their three weeks together. After their separation, he joined the First Regiment of Life Guards under the assumed name of Disney, deserted six months later, and resurfaced only in 1838 in Newgate prison (minus an arm, an occurrence never explained). By 1838 he had married again and, after a conviction for bigamy, was transported to Australia for seven years. Divorce granted.[6]

Ann's situation — adultery compounded by bigamy — was not duplicated in the House of Lords for another decade when Georgina Hall obtained a Bill — technically, it was an annulment as she and her husband never cohabited — in 1850.

That was all! In 186 years of Parliamentary divorce, only four women successfully braved the legal and social obstacles of English society to find permanent relief by legislation. Though wives could receive a separation and permanent maintenance in a church court for a simple adultery by their husbands, the legal requirement for a Parliamentary divorce that the husband's adultery must be coupled with incest or bigamy was so difficult to meet that it continued to deny Parliamentary divorce to women — the nineteenth century brought no substantial change from the eighteenth. Evangelical efforts to improve society's manners and morals had brought no help to wives in the area of divorce but did set other forces moving which changed the lot of women, and men. In the years after 1790 Evangelical labours changed the tone of English life, setting standards of behaviour for husbands and wives much different from those of the eighteenth century.

The old met the new, the serious faced the frivolous, in 1820 when George IV, at last king after the death of his insane father, set out to shed his queen, Caroline of Brunswick. George, Victoria's uncle, never loved his wife; not that kings were expected to love their spouses, but George actively despised Caroline and had done so since the beginnings of their marriage. Many, including her father, thought Caroline indiscreet — she said the wrong things and acted with too little regard for appearances and consequences; George came to believe that she diminished his dignity. When George became king, he determined, against the advice of his ministers, to divorce Caroline. A Bill of Pains and Penalties, which would also declare Caroline no longer the queen, was introduced in the House of Lords in June 1820.

The resulting spectacle entertained the kingdom for four months. Politics entered as the Whigs, annoyed with George, took up Caroline's cause. Caroline became the heroine of the hour with the populace — her purity contrasting with George's history of lechery, her suffering innocence with his prideful selfishness:

The Prince of Wales was unpopular for most of his life. His profligate habits — heavy drinking and recurring money troubles — combined with petulance to make a man many disliked. His political and personal differences with his father and his grabs for power whenever his father had a bout of illness made political enemies. Secretly marrying Mrs Fitzherbert in 1785, he violated two laws, the Act of Settlement (she was a Roman Catholic) and the Royal Marriage Act (no permission or notice). Leaving Mrs Fitzherbert, he took up with Lady Jersey, nine years his senior, even sending her to conduct his future bride, Caroline, to London. Despite his marriage in 1795, he continued his liaison with Lady Jersey until 1799 when he returned to Mrs Fitzherbert, staying with her until 1809. Miscellaneous affairs broke the monotony of these women from time to time.

Caroline, on the other hand, seemed blessed, at least as to popularity. An ill-educated daughter of the duke of a small German land, she was indiscreet, personally dirty and dishevelled, and occasionally coarse, yet popular adulation followed her.

The marriage, a failure before it began, resulted in a separation after only a few weeks. During that few weeks, however, Princess Charlotte was conceived. Thereafter, the Prince never failed of an opportunity to belittle or harass Caroline and she returned as good as she got. Caroline's behaviour at her separate establishment at Blackheath led to the Delicate Investigation of 1806. Nothing illicit could be proved — though strongly suggested — but much impudent talk, indecent language, and dubious conduct was unearthed. After the report, former Lord Chancellor Thurlow recommended a divorce to the Prince, advice not taken for a decade and a half. As political society increasingly ignored her, Caroline decided Continental travelling — her own Grand Tour and Crusade — would be preferable to the boredom and ignominy of her small establishment on the outskirts of London. Her motley travelling entourage was managed by Bartolommeo Pergami, a handsome Italian. However, it soon appeared to many that the relationship between the Princess of Wales and her courtier was closer than the disparity of rank required. At the trial for her divorce in 1820, Caroline's past proved unsavoury. A maid testified about stained sheets in a German hotel, sailors described the sleeping arrangements under a tent on board ship during hot Mediterranean nights, travelling Englishmen gave details about the state of dress, or undress, at Italian masquerades. Retaliating, Caroline's Whig lawyers hinted that the king's past was not above reproach. (Lord Melbourne, talking with Queen Victoria

years later, said of George that 'Considering the way he lived himself, he should never have attacked her character.')

George did not get his divorce as the government withdrew the
Bill, fearing it would not pass both Houses of Parliament but Caroline was disgraced by the public parade of her life. Not invited to the
coronation in 1821, she tried to force her way into Westminster
Abbey but was turned away amid cries of 'Shame'. Dying soon after,
she was buried in the cathedral in the Duchy of Brunswick whence
she had ventured forth to marry George more than a quarter of a century before.[7]

The widespread belief that the reputation of a husband could receive
more slings and arrows than that of a wife proved true. George, whose
private life had been far more scandalous than Caroline's, suffered
much less. Indeed, cheers greeted him at his coronation whereas Caroline heard only abuse.

The old way of life lingered in various corners of British society as
not everyone accepted seriousness and the Evangelical outlook. The
British army remained old-fashioned, especially in its code of conduct.
Officers were drawn largely from landed society and, even if from other
backgrounds, were men who accepted the values of landed society.
Jane Austen's characters were drawn from life and none more so than
the army officers. Duelling lasted far longer in army life than in the rest
of society; the Earl of Cardigan, known to us for his part in the charge of
the Light Brigade, duelled as late as 1840. Similarly, the attitude of 'an
officer and a gentleman' toward other men's wives resembled that of a
Regency dandy long after the end of the Regency:

> John and Caroline Trelawney, married in 1813, resided in a Bristol
> rooming house in 1816. Also there, recovering from an illness while
> on half-pay, was Captain Thomas Coleman of the 98th Regiment of
> Foot. Soon Caroline and Thomas were exchanging notes, hiding
> them in books they passed to and fro. Despite his illness and her
> pregnancy, their mutual attraction led to their landlady seeing them
> in bed together. Caroline, begging on her knees that 'her life was in
> [the landlady's] Hands', then fled to Boulogne, while Thomas
> suffered a judgment of £500, which he could not pay, against him in
> the crim. con. suit.[8]

John William Dunn and Knightley Musgrave Clay had been brother
officers in the Dragoon Guards. John married Eliza Papps in 1813

but she eloped with Knightley to St Omer. Eliza's mother, learning of her daughter's misconduct, promptly went to France, located the pair, and brought Eliza back. One month later Eliza ran off again and travelled around England with Knightley under assumed names, once changing names between towns, to the great confusion of her maid.[9]

Pownoll Bastard Pellew married Eliza, daughter of Sir George Barlow, Bart., KB, President and Governor of the Council in Madras, at Fort St George in 1808. (Sir George was to get a divorce in 1816.) After two sons and a daughter, they separated, and she, by the time of the divorce in 1820, was in Bantry, Ireland, with Alexander Tennant of the 35th Regiment. Pownoll's father was created Viscount Exmouth in 1814 and, when father and son received the news that Eliza 'may be in a family way', speed became urgent as they feared the Exmouth title might be affected in the future — 'spurious issue' again. The divorce Bill, with Viscount Exmouth attending the House of Lords, passed the Upper House in three weeks and the Lower in three days. Pownoll and his son duly succeeded to the viscountcy and all was as it should be.[10]

In the Parliamentary session of 1819, three of the five divorce Acts involved army officers, a figure typical of the four decades before the Divorce Act of 1857.

In England officers posed enough of a threat, but in India they were a terror. The debilitating heat, the scarcity of fellow-Europeans, the loneliness of the stations — all were bad enough for the civilian administrators of the East India Company and their wives; army officers, with the chivalrous code and shortage of women, added burdens to an already difficult existence. The absence of clergy in many areas led inhabitants to forget all about religion, observed Emily Eden, the sister of the Governor General of India, during her travels around the subcontinent. Outside the cities of Madras, Calcutta, and Bombay, administrative centres for the East India Company and the army, Englishwomen were often outnumbered ten or 20 to one by Englishmen. The veneer of English life was thin; Thomas Turton, whose wife took her sister to India to avoid scandal, and the sister continued to receive visits after Louise went back to England from 'Respectable people', despite their illicit union.

Sir George and Elizabeth Barlow were married in 1789 at Calcutta. While Sir George, as Governor of Madras, provoked a mutiny of his own officers over a perquisite, Elizabeth was committing adultery with Major Barlow, a relative of her husband. When all the Barlows, including the Major, returned to England, Sir George discovered the adultery and that he was not the father of his wife's youngest son. Elizabeth fled to Edinburgh, the Major lost £2,000 in a crim. con. suit and Sir George obtained a Parliamentary divorce.[11]

James Perry and Elizabeth Margaret Reed married in 1826 in Madras. At the time of the divorce James had risen to the lieutenant colonelcy of the 31st Regiment of Light Infantry and Elizabeth's father was also a lieutenant colonel and the Deputy Quartermaster General of HM Forces in India. In 1837 Elizabeth, returning by ship from a sojourn in England for her health, discovered a third lieutenant colonel, Scudamore Steel. The pair went directly to his house when their ship came in. James recovered 3,000 rupees in a crim. con. suit in India and obtained a Parliamentary divorce in 1840.[12]

William Hough married Sophia Raikes at Kurnaul in 1835. In 1838 servants caught Major Thomas Skinner leaving Sophia's room. Ten days later she decamped to join Thomas, and William contemplated a duel but found his religious scruples prevented him. Sophia and Thomas lived openly together and had a daughter. Thomas, author of *Excursions in India* in 1832 and *Adventures during a Journey Overland to India* in 1836, received the Cross of the Bath during the campaign to relieve Kabul in 1842. He also paid William 5,000 rupees after the crim. con. suit. By the time William got his Parliamentary divorce in 1844, Thomas was dead and Sophia's whereabouts uncertain.[13]

With much leisure — servants numbered by the dozens — and frequently absent husbands — officers on campaign, civilians on other duties — the temptations overwhelmed 'grass widows'. Small wonder that about 20 per cent of Parliamentary divorces originated in India. By 1820 the demand became so great that Parliament enacted special procedures to facilitate recording and transporting evidence from India to Westminster.

The Grand Tour and the fluid English society it produced on the Continent also proved beyond the reach of the new standards developing at home. The anonymity of living in a foreign land and the large numbers of travelling English — already estimated at 40,000 a year in 1785 — produced small pockets of English life, often a refuge for the tourist. Life was not made any easier for Respectable travellers, however, by the numerous English couples passing as husband and wife who were, in fact, a wife and her lover:

In 1784 William Frederick Wyndham married Frances Mary Harford, a natural daughter of Lord Baltimore, after her first marriage had been terminated by an annulment. In 1794 they went to Florence where William was the British envoy to Tuscany. In 1799, as the French revolutionary armies were rampaging through Italy, William wrote frantic letters from a besieged house where he had fled. His letters, amidst the turmoil of the day, requested that he be allowed to return to England so he could seek a divorce as Frances had eloped with Lord Wycombe, an English aristocrat touring the Continent. 'I think it is a duty I owe to my family, to my Children & to Myself to get rid of this woman, to obtain the fortune she has forfeited for her children who would be marred by her scandalous & unprincipled conduct & to obtain from Ld W some recompense for having disturbed my domestic peace & ruined the comfort of my whole family.' When William did return, his lawsuit was non–suited as he could not serve process on the guilty pair, still on the Continent.[14]

Henry Pelham, Earl of Lincoln and future Duke of Newcastle, married Lady Susan Harriet Catherine Hamilton Douglas, the only daughter of the tenth Duke of Hamilton, in 1832. Lincoln, a Peelite and High Church in his religion, was Chief Secretary for Ireland in 1846, Secretary of State for the Colonies 1852–4 and again in 1859 and Secretary of State for War in 1854–5. The Countess, after the birth of four sons and one daughter, eloped to the Continent with Lord Walpole, eldest son of the Earl of Orford, in 1848. Lincoln's friend, W.E. Gladstone, the future Prime Minister, went to Italy to, he said, attempt a reconciliation of the Earl and Countess, or, as his enemies said, gather evidence. At any rate, Gladstone found the Countess in Italy, pregnant by Walpole. As she would not receive him, Gladstone hid behind a pillar to observe her leaving her house in a pregnant condition. Subsequent investigators discovered the baby was baptised in Italy as Horatio Walpole Lawrence, Lawrence being the Countess's travelling name. When the divorce came before the House of Lords in 1850, Lincoln was travelling in the Levant. Moreover, he had not sued Walpole for crim. con. as Walpole remained on the Continent, out of reach of the arm of English law — the House waived the requirements of a crim. con. judgment and the husband's attendance. The Countess's solicitor accepted service on her behalf and, with her family co-operating fully, the divorce Bill passed.[15]

The cities along the routes from the Channel to Paris teemed with adulterous couples. Among the divorces of 1819, wives and their lovers were found in Boulogne, St Omer and Paris.

In all of these areas — the army, India, the Continent — people lived further from the controls and guidelines of English society. They also hoped their mistakes might be hidden in the midst of a foreign and fluid population, but news usually spread in even the most distant corner of the world:

William Jervis, Captain in the 42nd Regiment of the Bengal Native Infantry, and Mary Amelia Jervis often were apart as she lived in the hills of India all the year round due to her health. Eventually, she formed an attachment to Henry Vansittart, Assistant to the Commissioner in the Jullunder, and became pregnant. She disappeared without explanation in 1845 but her letters to William discovered her whereabouts and her problems.

My dear William,   25 April
I am determined now to write you an Explanation of my long Illness, though by doing so I shall inflict a Wound I can never heal. Painful, most painful, is the Task; I hardly know how to begin. I shrink from causing you the great Distress of the Communication, and yet I must force myself at once to throw aside all Deception; and though I cannot ask Forgiveness, I solicit your Forbearance. Your unhappy Wife is not worthy of that Title; and it rests with you to expose me to the World, and bring Disgrace on your Name and my Family, for as yet by no open Act have I compromised either. I have delayed writing till now, as it was my earnest Wish that your Father should go to his Grave in Peace, and not have his last Days embittered by a Knowledge of your domestic Sorrow and my Fall. This Wish has been granted, and I will deceive you no longer. I feel I have much to explain, but I attempt no Excuses; I must bear the Penalty of my Conduct, and be wretched the Remainder of my Life. After Months of Suffering I went through a difficult and dangerous Confinement Four Weeks ago. I thought, for many Reasons, that I could not have passed the Seventh Month, and hoped all would have been over in January;

not that if it had I would have eventually deceived you, but I might have saved my Name with the World, that is, if such had been your Desire. When Jan[uar]y passed my Distress was so great I could not write. I remained entirely in my Room, and saw no one; I hired no Nurse; I lived in perfect Seclusion; so if you choose to save me from public Exposure and Degradation and your own Name from Disgrace, it is in your Power to do so, and I will go where you please to direct, and live no Burden upon you; but otherwise I shall have no Alternative but to seek his Protection for whose Sake I have forfeited all that makes Life dear. Oh, William, call to your Mind what I once was; think of my happy and innocent Days, when I was full of Hope and Smiles and Merriment; contrast this with my present Position, — forsaken by the World, an Outcast from my Family. I cannot write any more. Let me hear from you, and let me implore you to spare me Reproaches and Upbraidings.

I cannot feel my own Disgrace or your Grief more than I do. I do not ask you to write kindly, I do not ask you to forgive me, you cannot do either.

I only pray for Mercy, — a little Gentleness. I have no Right to ask this, but it will be generous in you to have Pity.

I alone am to blame; there is no one but me who should suffer; I alone deserve Punishment. Have I not already suffered enough? I know I must bear much more, and be miserable for ever. Farewell, my dear William; I trust when the first Shock is over that you may be happy, happier than you would ever have been with me. Farewell; I have still much to write about, but will wait till I have heard from you. Perhaps you will not write to me. May I still sign myself,

Yours affectionately,
M. A. J.

My dear William,   Saturday, 26th April
Captn Morkler came down Yesterday before the inclosed Letter was sent to the Post. He told me that I was much talked of at Mussoorie, that my Reputation was gone, that it was supposed I was living a Life of Infamy, that all Hope of being saved from Exposure was passed. I have taken the last Step: Yesterday Evening I came over to Mr. V's House, and by doing so have brought Ruin on him, Misery to you, and Destruction on myself.

Do not think I am happy; I am far more wretched than you can be.

I have lost all beyond all Recovery. You may still be happy; and earnestly do I pray that you will be so. You will cast me from your Breast, as one unworthy of a Thought; you will accuse me of Ingratitude, Deceit, and Falsehood; I am not ungrateful.

I own I have deceived you, but I did not intend to continue doing so, and every Word I have written in all my Letters to you have been true. Again, dear William, I write that I do not look for, expect, or desire Forgiveness, but I intreat your Forbearance. I must not write more. Pity me, William; remember I am now an Outcast, separated for ever from all my dearly loved Family. I brought Misery on you, but will you add to the Bitterness of my present Position?

Farewell. Believe me when I say how truly I grieve for the Distress I have caused.

I remain yrs affectly,
M. A. Jervis[16]

Even India was being affected by the 1840s by the changes in outlook.

While seriousness and the Evangelical approach to life were continually challenged by the remnants of the eighteenth century, be they in India, the army, or the Continent, the spread of these new attitudes, symbolised by the defeat of Queen Caroline, continued unabated until, in the 1830s, that outlook dominated and the old-fashioned lives were just that — old–fashioned. Regency dandies died slowly — Lord Palmerston lived into the 1860s — but they no longer set the tone for 'those who count'. The future Prime Minister W.E. Gladstone, with his strongly held religious views, impressive intellectual range, mastery of the minute detail of government budgets and a personal crusader among prostitutes, represented the new age.

Despite the leisure, wealth and temptations of the upper classes, despite the appearances given by the Parlimentary divorces, few marriages, in fact, broke up openly. In the nineteenth century, in the years between Jane Addison's petition in 1801 and the reforms of 1857, Parliament dissolved 190 marriages. Couples obtaining divorces *a mensa et thoro* in church courts numbered, on average, fewer than 50 per year in the early 1840s, with London accounting for a majority of those. In Ireland fewer than 15 couples received divorces *a mensa et thoro*, two–thirds of those in Dublin. Scotland, with different laws and divorce *a vinculo matrimonii* available in the courts, produced another 50 divorces per year (see Tables 2.1 and 2.2).[17] In all of the British Isles each year about 50 marriages ended in divorce and another 100 or so in judicial separation — when the total population at mid-century approached 18 million and over 150,000 marriages were celebrated annually. Obviously, numbers alone could not make divorce an issue of national concern. Yet few domestic issues of the 1850s exceeded divorce in the attentions of the political nation. Why?

Divorce touched the family, and the family became the central concern of lots of people as seriousness permeated much of English life. Unfortunately for historians, the 'Victorian family' did not exist. No single description could cover a nation with 6 million married couples as the mix of ideals with reality provided nearly limitless variety. John Bright, the manufacturer and MP representing the thrusting business and professional classes, like a satrap viewed his family as the focus for his despotism, at least after his second wife died. G.H. Lewes, critic and populariser of science, played at the game of spouse-swapping, before settling down in an illicit union with George Eliot, while many women combined successful marriages and feminist political work. Children rebelled — the Evangelical William Wilberforce produced a Roman Catholic priest; and children imitated — the writing Brontë sisters succeeded a writing father. Out of this *mélange*, several dominant strands do emerge, though more often visible in imaginative literature and *Punch* cartoons than in the lives of people.

The usual images of husbands, in literature anyway, focused on the owner of broad acres (often a baronet) with relations in the church, the army and landed society; and the urban professional or manufacturer, busy about his occupation. The former might be a despot (Sir Thomas Acland the elder), patiently tolerant (the Earl of Minto), or painfully inept (Sir Edward Clark's father); the urban dwellers had less range, often being Dissenters, but were too occupied with their work to find time for the scrapes so necessary to novelists.[18] Further down the economic ladder, lower-middle-class husbands, with still less time and money, fade into a uniformity — faceless clerks concerned with the outward appearances of gentility and the like. Wives similarly varied from the ministering angel to the shrew to the frivolous butterfly to the efficient manageress. Once the working class join the throng, Dickensian variety explodes as imitators of the other classes mingle with the hopeful and the hopeless.

Table 2.1: Matrimonial Suits in England, Wales, Ireland and Scotland, 1840–3

Diocese	Number	Cost		
		£	s.	d.
England				
Canterbury	37	168	7	5
Carlisle	1	17	16	9
Chester	8	52	11	3
Durham	1			
Exeter	4			
Gloucester and	3	9	13	0
Bristol	2	45	0	0
London	87	120	0	0
Norwich	5			
Winchester	4			
York	8			
	160			
Wales				
St Asaph	1	16	19	9
St David's	1			
	2			
Ireland				
Andagh	1	1	6	8
Armagh	0			
Cashel	0			
Clogher	2	25	0	0
Clotert	0			
Cloyne	2	33	13	3
Cork	4			
Derry	0			
Down	2			
Dronion	1	99	7	4
Dublin	40	14	0	0
Elphon	1	120	0	0
Fehr	0			
Kildare	0			
Kilmore	0			
Killala	0			
Killaloe	0			
Limerick	1			
Meath	0			
Ossory	no return			
Raphoe	0			
Tuam	2	25	0	0
Waterford	1	30	0	0
	57			
Scotland				
All areas	169			
Total	388			

Source: *House of Commons Parliamentary Papers*, 1844, xxxviii, 155–7.

Table 2.2: Matrimonial Causes in Ecclesiastical Courts of the Diocese of London

Years	Divorces	Nullities	Restitution of conjugal rights
1787–9	8	7	1
1807–9	12	11	0
1827–9	28	9	7

Note: All the other dioceses of England had a total of 41 causes during the three periods.

Source: *House of Commons Parliamentary Papers*, 1831–2 (199), xxix, 311.

Further complications arose from, to use the modern term, sexuality, as medical knowledge, tradition and religion produced varying attitudes to genetics (perversions lead to weak descendants), mental health (women have more 'nervousness') and personality (masturbation destroys moral fibre). Still another layer of variety came from the relationship between husbands and wives and the nature of their marriages. Tennyson, the future poet laureate, mingled many ideas of the 1840s in *The Princess* and, after setting mankind atop the pyramid of God's creation, made marriage mankind's ultimate destiny:

> either sex alone
> Is half itself, and in true marriage lies
> Nor equal, nor unequal. Each fulfils
> Defect in each, and always thought in thought
> Purpose in purpose, will in will, they grow,
> The single pure and perfect animal,
> The two-cell'd heartbeating, with one full stroke,
> Life.

As together the couple travelled life's highway, the 'like must they grow', 'He gain in sweetness and in moral height . . . She mental breadth . . . ' People grew in marriage.[19]

The paramount role of religion produced Coventry Patmore's *The Angel in the House*.[20]

> This little germ of nuptial love,
>   Which springs so simply from the sod,
> The root is, as my song shall prove,
>   Of all our love to man and God.

Putting marriage at the base of all society, as Patmore did, could be found throughout Victorian thought. Gladstone, himself happily married though scourging himself whenever temptation reared its ugly head, said marriage was 'a powerful instrument of discipline and self-subjugation, worthy to take rank in that subtle and wonderful system of appointed means, by which the life of man on earth becomes his school for heaven.'[21]

Chivalry provided images from the Middle Ages, curiously re-produced in the nineteenth century. Commencing with the Eglinton tournament in 1839, chivalry, with knights protecting ladies, added an unusual strand to ideas about marriage. Concerns with purity became so pronounced by the 1850s that several aristocratic marriages — those of Lady Waterford and her nieces, Ladies Pembroke, Brownlow and Lothian — remained unconsummated as the couples imitated medieval stories.[22]

Truth, for some, could be experienced, not merely sought intellectually. Like knowledge in general, truth was the province of masters. Within marriage, husbands had more experience due to their age and prior activities and wives learned from them. The couple, together, then pursued the 'truth' of marriage. Even Utilitarians, approaching issues rationally and calculating the total of happiness in all events, relied on experience as the ultimate test. Marriage, not a contract alone, grows, with cohabitation, into something beyond description. The father of Utilitarianism, Jeremy Bentham, who tolerated easy divorce, thought married couples would remain together after the children were raised — the Utilitarian reason for marriage — because of the 'thousand little habits binding them together'. Similarly, the church and the common law, with talk of the 'union of bodies' and 'the two become one', created imagery of marriage as beyond analysis and description. All is debased if reduced to mere words.

For those not poetically or chivalrously inclined, nor intellectually interested, money governed much as couples needed each other's work or income. Not everyone had myriad servants or lived separately from ageing parents. While the rich still worked out marriage settlements, those with less, delayed marriage until financial security was achieved — by the 1860s, professional men averaged age 30 at marriage, their brides 26.[23] For all, marriage, whether romantic or economic, settled into habit with the couple fighting and forgiving, boring and ignoring, loving and growing. Separate spheres for the sexes, the double standard for sex, 'nor equal, nor unequal' — Victorian marriage, like a cloth with a warp and woof of many materials, produced variety of colour and texture.

Divorce became of crucial importance to one part of this *mélange* of marriages, a part that called itself 'Respectable society'. Respectability, like all such terms, was hard to define and never static, anyway. Not exclusively an economic classification, Respectability included aristocrats and extended down the economic scale to the working class, though barely, as at some point people lacked money to behave Respectably. Thackeray, whose novels analyse the concept, defined Respectables as 'the class of lawyers and merchants and scholars, of men who are striving on in the world, of men of the educated middle classes of the country'.[24] His definition, really of the upper middle class, excluded too many — peers and engineers could be Respectable — but his emphasis on 'striving on in the world' catches an important economic element. Respectables saw themselves as the pillars of future Britain, whether as owners, managers, or workers.

Not a religious category either, Respectability required the earnestness associated with the Evangelicals but not necessarily the beliefs. Attending church or chapel, while a part of Respectability early in Victoria's reign, became less important after waves of doubt swept over the educated classes after 1860, but maintaining a religious outlook remained. Life mattered, in a moral sense. Even geography played its part as some neighbourhoods facilitated Respectability while the challenges of others made it difficult. Respectability came easier in London's Bayswater and Birmingham's Edgbaston than it did in Hackney or Salford.

Most often, Respectability, depending on values and attitudes, hinged on the treatment of others (be they inferiors, superiors, or equals) and appearances — in other words, behaviour. A Respectable master paid his servants decent wages, encouraged their religious beliefs, and expected traditional morality, be it about property or people. A Respectable worker gave an honest day's work for an honest day's pay and, when not working, associated with kith and kin in Respectable activities. Self-improvement and education, pursued throughout life, combined discipline and seriousness.

Knowing what was unRespectable and avoiding it constituted the other side of the coin. Three activities — drink, gambling, and sex — came to be the focus of Respectable hates and fears. They represented the bad, old ways of the eighteenth century against which Respectables were fighting and, as wasteful, not serious, and with no moral purpose, they could not lead to a future that was safe, happy and prosperous. Dissipation had no place in Respectability.

And Respectable society proselytised — by example, by talk, and by law. UnRespectables, be they aristocrats or commoners, could be ostracised. Servants, an obvious target, proved challenging but their lack of money posed problems. Where proselytising ceased, the drawing of lines began as distinctions were made to define Respectable behaviour. Money created a problem. The masses, lacking money and education, were seen as recalcitrant, perhaps evil, and, though efforts to convert never ceased, Respectables made certain that workers remained separate — economics crept in the back door, having been shut out allegedly at the front. Nevertheless, the attractions of Respectability proved so great that workers constantly sought to acquire the trappings and outlook. By the end of the nineteenth century, a large part of Respectable society resided in working–class housing.

Challenges to Respectability came from more than just the working class without adequate income. As Respectable society never embraced all of any part of English society, Respectables had to mingle with unRespectables — the cheating solicitor, the lecherous curate, the drunken lord. Moreover, contradictions occurred — paying workers 'too much' jeopardised a business — and if a Respectable could not harmonise the discordant themes, at least an appearance of Respectability could be maintained. Was it humbug or charity to dine with the banker who squeezed debtors dry? Should the peccadillos of an aristocrat be ignored on a round of visits — after all, civilised society depended on hierarchy. If classes divided English society horizontally, Respectability divided that society vertically. At the fringes Respectability, like all such ideals, had problems; but it guided the lives of many Victorians for the better part of the nineteenth century and, for some, into the twentieth.

At the core of Respectability lay the family. Whatever the marriage, chivalrous aristocratic or lower-middle-class humdrum, Respectables shared one attitude to divorce — it was bad. That kings, unRespectable ones at that, had sought divorces, and that aristocrats, idle and probably dissipated, had obtained divorces did not give them a patina of elegance — divorce was bad. Divorces originating in India, the army, or the Continent emphasised the consequences of the failure to consider appearances as well as the lack of seriousness and discipline. Divorce, with its oft–accompanying problems of gambling and drink, became the ultimate unRespectable event. Moreover, all divorces involved adultery, and adultery meant abandoning the family, forsaking the spouse, placing today's pleasure ahead of tomorrow's responsibilities, and sinning against God's commandment. Other challenges to the family — drunkenness, prostitution, violence, poverty — paled into insignificance against adultery. Respectability meant marriage, and marriage required faithfulness.

By 1850 the publicity surrounding divorce proceedings offended Respectable sensibilities. Victorians were always of two minds about publicity. Was there virtue in publicising lapses in virtue? Spreading the details of a divorce in the press had the beneficial effect of deterring others from imitating bad behaviour. On the other hand, certain evils were intractable, and newspaper stories helped no one and pandered to all the wrong instincts. Details of adultery injured the morals of children and the working class, both groups which Respectables sought to educate to their own standard. Worse, divorce occasionally portrayed Respectable society in the wrong light — as when William Gladstone, a Respectable if ever there was one, was found sneaking around Italy collecting evidence for the divorce of his friend, the Earl of Lincoln. Respectables should not 'sneak' and catch people out; they should be open, and expect others to be as well, for they had nothing to hide.

Crim. con., the special joy of newspapers, aroused the special disgust of Respectables. Thackeray, known today for his novels, thundered against a particularly ludicrous crim. con. suit in a poem of 1850, 'Damages, Two Hundred Pounds':

He by counsel and attorney there at Guildford does appear,
Asking damage of the villain who seduced his lady dear:
But I can't help asking, though the lady's guilt was all too clear,
And though guilty the defendant, wasn't the plaintiff rather
    queer?

First the lady's mother spoke, and said she's seen her daughter
    cry
But a fortnight after marriage: early times for piping eye.
Six months after, things were worse, and the piping eye was black,
And this gallant British husband caned his wife upon the back.

Three months after they were married, husband pushed her to the
    door,
Told her to be off and leave him, for he wanted her no more.
As she would not go, why he went: thrice he left his lady dear;
Left her, too, without a penny, for more than a quarter of a year.

Then the honest British Twelve, to each other turning round,
Laid their clever heads together with a wisdom most profound:

And towards his Lordship looking, spoke the foreman wise and
  sound:—
'My Lord, we find for this here plaintiff, damages two hundred
  pound.'

So, God bless the Special Jury! pride and joy of English ground,
And the happy land of England, where true justice does abound!
British jurymen and husbands, let us hail this verdict proper:
If a British wife offends you, Britons, you've a right to whop her.

Though you promised to protect her, though you promised to
  defend her.
You are welcome to neglect her: to the devil you may send her:
You may strike her, curse, abuse her; so declares our law renowned;
And if after this you lose her, — why, you're paid two hundred
  pound.[25]

Thackeray's distaste for the process of setting a price on a woman's virtue, or lack of it, reflected a widespread criticism of crim. con.
Moreover, whatever value divorce had as a deterrent or punishment
was lost by 1850 because its incidence was too unsystematic. Divorce,
dependent upon lots of money, could not be sought by many Respectables. And even the innocent partner hesitated before running the
gauntlet of the three-step divorce procedure, with its humiliating
publicity. Parliamentary divorce simply did not work to serve
Respectability.

Newspaper coverage of divorces became increasingly a concern in
the 1850s as circulations mushroomed, especially outside London.
Economic prosperity, technical advances in printing, and elimination
of the stamp tax in 1855 led to phenomenal growth. The *Daily
Telegraph*, soon the world's largest paper, multiplied from 27,000
copies a day in 1856 to 141,700 in 1860. The Union for the
Discouragement of Vicious Advertisements and the Obscene
Materials Act were two reactions to this growth, divorce reform a third.
The national press had been born, and the double-edged sword of
publicity made divorce a problem in Respectable thinking.[26]

The problem of divorce grew also because few alternatives were feas-
ible for Respectable society. Living apart required sufficient money to
maintain separate households — beyond the reach of anyone below the
upper middle class — or a family available and willing to receive a
grown child back into the home. Separation deeds, formalising the

arrangement of couples who could not live together, set forth the sums of money and conditions of contact involved. Thackeray, ever the observer of marriage law detail, had Becky Sharp and Rawdon Crawley execute a separation deed towards the end of *Vanity Fair*. Separation deeds, sufficiently common for legal handbooks to have forms for the usual situations, survive from the eighteenth century and continued to be used in the twentieth century but were mainly for the rich.

Desertion occurred regularly. William Cobbett, farmer, journalist, politician, agitator, and Tory Radical, advised this remedy to the cuckold. Divorce records in the late 1850s suggest that the huge emigrations to the United States and Australia in the late 1840s contained large numbers of fleeing husbands, as well as the occasional eloping wife. Charles Dickens in *Hard Times*, pleading for cheaper divorce, painted a common scene as Stephen Blackpool, Respectable though a power-loom weaver, suffered from a drunken wife who repeatedly deserted him, only returning to extract money.

At the lower end of the economic ladder many drew up papers themselves, legally ineffective but often believed to be official divorces. Bigamy was not uncommon. *The Times,* in its casual manner of selecting items of news from the assizes, catalogued 15 bigamy prosecutions in 1845 and reported a judge saying he had been too lenient on numerous bigamists in the past. The sale of a wife in the marketplace occurred in settings other than Thomas Hardy's *The Mayor of Casterbridge* and printers saw enough profit in such events to produce newssheets describing the transaction. Violence surfaced often and poisonings and rumours of poisonings floated through discussions of marital discord. The occasional murder was always widely noted.[27]

With all these problems focusing on troubled marriages, small wonder that solutions began to be suggested. However, criticisms of the law of divorce, except for those mooted by the law reformers discussed in Chapter 4, foundered on the rock of English Respectability. Divorce was so unRespectable that talking about it tainted the speaker. Even radicals steered clear of the issue so as not to distract from their other proposals. Robert Owen, the socialist visionary who founded New Harmony in the United States to test his ideas about property and profits, condemned marriage because it made people too selfish and reinforced their isolation and privacy rather than encouraging them to work and join communities. He also thought marriage was used by priests to control people. But Owen's desires for marriages based on affection and easy divorce kept his books out of Respectable book shops. G.J. Holyoake, a life-long agitator, secularist, and articulator of ideas for the 'aristocracy' of the working class, wrote on nearly every issue to appear on the Victorian scene, but not divorce. Minor flurries about divorce occurred in 1801 due to Jane Addison's petition, in 1821 due to Queen Caroline's trial, and around 1830 due to reformers' disgust with the Church of England and its unrepresentative institutions as well as the publicity surrounding Lord Ellenborough's divorce.

No fuel to stoke the fires of criticism came from English knowledge of European divorce practices either. The late-medieval church settled on the principle of no divorce but some annulments. With the Reformation, Protestant countries ended the sacramental status of marriage and usually permitted divorce for adultery and desertion. Roman Catholic countries, after the reforms of the sixteenth-century Council of Trent, prohibited divorce and made annulments difficult to obtain. The eighteenth-century Enlightenment supported divorce by mutual consent, a practice adopted in only a few German states. The era of the French Revolution produced easy divorces but the changes did not survive the fall of Napoleon. Closer to home, Scotland, after its Reformation, permitted divorce for adultery, without differing standards for the sexes. (Desertion as a ground for divorce appeared in 1573 in order that the Duke of Argyll could obtain a divorce.) By 1840 fewer than 50 Scottish couples divorced yearly, and throughout Europe, regardless of the laws and the differing religions, people did not divorce. The single exception — widely believed in England though never documented — was a few years in the midst of the French Revolution when Parisians swarmed into the courts under Revolutionary laws. The exception confirmed English fears and prejudices so, when French ideas about women, derived from Saint-Simon, appeared in English intellectual circles in the 1830s, they met Respectable resistance. So did divorce.

The most powerful criticisms of English divorce practice arose, not from foreign sources or radical thinkers, but from the history of English divorce itself and it was directed at the disabilities of wives. Elizabeth Teush's petition to the House of Lords in 1805 received scant support but the efforts of Ann Dawson in 1848 had more impact, especially on the lawyers in the House of Lords:

In 1833 at the age of 15 Ann, Respectable daughter of a Respectable and wealthy Manchester merchant, secretly married John Dawson, an artisan of no great means. By the time she bore him two children, John had progressed from 'cross words' about her father's pusillanimity to physical violence. He broke a riding whip over her back, pushed her down the stairs, threw his morning coffee and noontime beer on her, drank and gambled excessively, fathered two children on two other women (giving one venereal disease in the process), beat his son until the flesh putrefied, and failed in his business. He also hunted Ann out wherever she moved to hide from him. Despite John's cruelty, desertion and adultery, Ann's petition failed as he had committed neither incest nor bigamy, the only two grounds available to a wife. Additionally, Lord Campbell, one of the Law Lords in the House of Lords, said her Bill did not show anything which 'would prevent the parties once more living together as good Christians'.[28]

After its brief impact on a few Law Lords, though not Lord Campbell, Ann Dawson's situation, being ignored by reformers, politicans and the press, disappeared from the public eye. However, another woman, better connected with the elite and a skilled writer as well, soon made the problems of wives widely appreciated:

A granddaughter of Richard Brinsley Sheridan and consequently a member of the 'Whig cousinhood', Caroline Norton was an aristocrat by birth, though a poor relation after her father's early death. Her sister, Lady Seymour, portrayed the Queen of Beauty in the Eglinton tournament of 1839, so chivalrous, as well as feminist, blood ran in the family. Though a striking beauty, poverty forced Caroline to marry in 1827 George Norton, a barrister of no great fortune or prospects; she quickly bore him three sons. The Nortons were mismatched as she enjoyed the spotlight and he was, to many, too dull and, to himself, too poor to join London society. Caroline's liveliness and intellect attracted Lord Melbourne, Victoria's first Prime Minister, who enjoyed her company, though, he swore to his dying day, not her body. Their behaviour — long hours together discussing politics, life, and society — flouted conventions, and in 1836 George, perhaps urged by Melbourne's political opponents, sued Melbourne for crim. con. The jury acquitted Melbourne of wrongdoing without leaving the box although the evidence showed, as a wag observed, 'Melbourne had more opportunities than any man ever had before and made no use of them.' The Nortons never reconciled. They fought about the custody of their children. George was niggardly in supporting her so Caroline took up literary work as her livelihood. Once called the 'Byron of poetesses' she earned enough to survive but George, as he was by law entitled to do, claimed her earnings. Their disputes continued over decades, flaring up periodically — he lied about his support of her, her earnings problems — keeping their situation in the public eye.[29]

Caroline Norton, besides writing fiction, often turned her attention, and her pen to her problems and those of other similarly situated women. Her child custody fight produced *A Plain Letter to the Lord Chancellor on the Law and Custody of Infants* in 1838, which contributed greatly to a change in the law. After that year, mothers in most circumstances had custody of children up to the age of seven.

When changes in divorce law loomed as a real possibility after 1850, she wrote *English Laws for Women in the Nineteenth Century* (1854) and *A Letter to the Queen on Lord Chancellor Cranworth's Marriage and Divorce Bill* (1855). Both were credited at the time with making the differing treatment of women, and wives, difficult to sustain. After 1850 politicians, enlightened by her writings, rarely believed inequality of the sexes was intellectually justifiable; they did, however, continue to believe it was the political will of the nation that inequality be maintained.

The Divorce Act of 1857 did not permit Caroline Norton to divorce George, nor he her — both lacked the necessary grounds. Nevertheless, in the House of Lords — the scene of so many divorces over the years — stand two frescos by Daniel Maclise, symbolising the role of aristocracy and the Upper House — *The Spirit of Chivalry* and *The Spirit of Justice.* Caroline Norton, the fighter for the rights of wives, modelled for Maclise; Caroline Norton is Justice! And Caroline Norton, with her great powers of publicity, demanded justice.

Notes

1. Mary Astell, *Some Reflections upon Marriage, occasion'd by The Duke and Duchess of Mazarine's Case* (J. Nutt, London, 1700) p.18; Keith Thomas, 'The Double Standard', *Journal of the History of Ideas*, 20 (1959) pp.195–216.

2. *The Times,* 20th May, 1801; *Hansard,* vol. 35, cols 1429–36.

3. *Lords Journal,* vol. xliii, pp.75, 101–4, 190, 290.

4. *Hansard*, vol. 5, cols 1805, 428; *Lords Journal*, vol. xlv, pp.307, 296; John Macqueen, *A Practical Treatise on the Appellate Jurisdiction of the House of Lords & Privy Council* (A. Maxwell, London, 1842) p.604.

5. *Lords Journal,* vol. lxiii, pp.782, 327.

6. *Lords Journal*, vol. lxxii, Appendix 6.

7. Christopher Hibbert, *George IV: Prince of Wales* (Longman, London, 1972) p.160; W. D. Bowman, *The Divorce Case of Queen Caroline* (George Routledge, London, 1930).

8. *Lords Journal* vol. lii, pp.137–42.

9. *Lords Journal* vol. lii, pp.148–54.

10. *DNB* Pownoll Pellew: *Lords Journal*, vol. lii, pp.155, 163, 283, 300; See generally Gwyn Harries-Jenkins, *The Army in Victorian Society* (Routledge & Kegan Paul, London, 1977).

11. *Lords Journal*, vol. 1, pp.484, 518. For Indian life, see Emily Eden, *Up the Country* (R. Bentley, London, 1866) and J. S. Stanford (ed.), *Ladies in the Sun* (Dent, London, 1962).

12. *Lords Journal*, vol. lxxii, Appendix 6.

13. *Lords Journal*, vol. lxxvi, p.432; *DNB* Thomas Skinner; I George IV, c. 101; *Lords Journal*, vol. lii, pp.214, 300.

14. H. A. Wyndham, *A Family History* (Oxford University Press, London, 1950) pp.226–7; Somerset Record Office, DD/WY Box 186.

15. *Lords Journal*, vol. lxxxii, pp.143,146 168; *The Times*, 29th May 1850.

16. *Lords Journal*, vol. lxxx, p.279.

17. *House of Commons Parliamentary Papers*, 1844, vol. xxxviii, pp.155–7; *House of Commons Parliamentary Papers*, 1831-2 (199) vol. xxix, p.311.

18. David Roberts, 'The Pater Familias of the Victorian Governing Classes', in Anthony Wohl (ed.), *The Victorian Family* (Croom Helm, London, 1978) p.71.

19. Alfred Tennyson, *The Princess* (Ticknor & Fields, Boston, 1868) VII, 285; see John Killham, *Tennyson and The Princess* (Athlone, London, 1958) p.259.

20. Frederick Page (ed.), *The Poems of Coventry Patmore* (Oxford University Press, London, 1948), *The Angel in the House*, Canto VI: 'Love Doubtful'.

21. *Quarterly Review*, vol. 102 (1857), reproduced in *Gleanings of Past Years*, (J. Murray, London, 1879) vol. 6, p.102.

22. Mark Girourard, *Return to Camelot* (Yale University Press, New Haven, 1981) p.200.

23. Charles Ansell, Jr., *On the Rate of Mortality, the Number of Children to a Marriage, the Length of a Generation, and other Statistics of Families in the Upper and Professional Classes* (National Life Assurance Society, London, 1874) p.45.

24. William Makepeace Thackeray, *Letters*, vol. iv, p.105n. (Harvard, Cambridge Mass., 1945), quoted in W. L. Burn, *The Age of Equipoise* (George Allen, London, 1964), p.315.

25. William Makepeace Thackeray, *The Works of William Makepeace Thackeray*, (Scribner, New York, 1903-4), vol. xxv, pp.205-7.

26. G. A. Cranfield, *The Press and Society* (Longman, London, 1978), p.207, Ch.8.

27. Mary Hartman, *Victorian Murderesses* (Schocken, New York, 1977); Bristol Library, Miscellaneous Broadsides, 22nd November, 1822, 29th May, 1823; S. P. Menefee, *Wives for Sale* (Blackwell, Oxford, 1981).

28. *Lords Journal*, vol. lxxx, pp.206–16, 238–44, 261–4; *The Times*, 10th March, 22nd April, 1848. To be fair to Lord Campbell, he was merely stating the law, though awkwardly. Wives obtained divorce when reconciliation would be illegal under church or English law (i.e. incest and bigamy).

29. David Cecil, *Lord M.* (Constable, London, 1954) pp.62–72, 154–68, 304–9; Abraham Kriegel (ed.), *The Holland House Diaries 1831–1840* (Routledge & Kegan Paul, London, 1977) p.345.

3 Resistance: the Church of England

Religion dominated Victorian life at mid-century though great diversity characterised that religion. When divorce, pre-eminently a matter of religious doctrine to many, came before the public eye in the 1850s, the strongest opposition to reforms came from segments of the Church of England, but the rich variety of religious life produced a diffuse response from the religious community as a whole. While history since the Reformation of Henry VIII convinced many Englishmen that, in politics, men could disagree and the kingdom still survive, indeed prosper, in religion, many came to accept that men differed but were not agreed that this was a good idea. Truth still existed in religion, if not in politics, and the confusion among Christians about divorce confused others about any possible reforms. Besides, not all thought divorce reform a religious issue and they did not want to hear the opinions of the churched. Mid-Victorian religion had many aspects and many themes, and divorce affected different men differently.

The divisions in the Christian community emerged from the English past which had cobbled together a strange *mélange* in the United Kingdom, perhaps the strangest situation in Europe. When Henry VIII took the English church out of the European church, he forgot, or neglected, the Irish portion of his realm which thereafter gave its loyalty to Roman Catholicism. Also, a few Englishmen, such as the Dukes of Norfolk, maintained their allegiance to the old forms. Roman Catholicism, as a group rather than a political issue, re-emerged in England towards the end of the eighteenth century when Irish emigrants appeared in England. With the continued growth of their numbers, the matter became more pressing in the nineteenth century. The Scots, in a separate kingdom until the death of Henry's daughter Elizabeth, had their own Reformation, establishing a Reformed Church. Finally, the English, after executing Charles I in 1649 and frightening away James II in 1688, emerged with an established Church of England and a group of, more or less tolerated, Dissenters, largely Baptists and Congregationalists. The cooling of passions, both political and religious, in the early eighteenth century produced the inevitable reaction, the fire and excitement of George Whitfield and John Wesley. Enthusiasm proved catching and both the Church of England and Dissent soon contained serious and committed souls, Evangelicals, dedicated to improving the world. The abolition of the slave trade in 1807 remains the greatest public work of those industrious people. All of these religious groups, with their conflicting histories and practices, flowed into the nineteenth century when population growth, urbanisation and the Industrial Revolution profoundly altered the society in which the religious found themselves.[1]

By 1851, the year of the Great Exhibition in Hyde Park which proclaimed Britain's industrial greatness to the world, about 40 per cent of all English citizens professed enough interest in organised religion to attend church on Mothering Sunday and be counted. The religious census of 1851 (see Table 3.1) revealed two facts — that large numbers of working people were not in any church and that the numbers of Anglicans and non-Anglicans in churches were about the same; the latter discovery, sadly, interested and shocked more people than the former.[2]

Table 3.1: The Religious Census of 1851

	Estimated number attending	Per cent of total population	Per cent of attenders
Church of England	3,773,474	21	52
Nonconformist	3,007,348	17	42
Roman Catholic	305,393	2	4
Sectarian	174,817	1	2
		41	

Source: *House of Commons Parliamentary Papers*, 1852–3 (1690), lxxxix

The relative strengths of the religious bodies uncovered by the census produced another thunderclap in the long storm of the nineteenth century over the place of the Church of England in English life. Claiming combined numbers equal to that of the established church, Dissenters and Roman Catholics saw no reason for the Church of England's privileged position and redoubled their efforts to alter that situation.

Attacks on the Church of England, therefore, came not from atheists — who were not organised systematically and who were not very thick on the ground or influential, anyway — but from the Christians in the various sects grouped under the label 'Dissent'. Including Baptists, Reformed Churches, Unitarians, Methodists of various connections and many local groups, Dissent flexed its muscles from the 1820s onwards and especially after 1851 when the census revealed its strength. Moreover, the census information further discomfitted many because Dissent, except for Methodism, was a phenomenon of the cities, cities where the growth and power for the future lay. Yet cities generally had proportionally fewer church-goers than the countryside, and London, 'The Great Wen', came last even among cities with only 21 per cent of its population enfolded in the various churches. This patchiness of membership around the country meant Dissent's impact on politics was erratic and Dissenting gains uneven.

Dissenters obtained civic equality in 1828 when Parliament gave them the right to hold office, nationally and locally, but major grievances remained: the necessity of marriage by Anglican rites, payment of church rates (taxes to support the Church of England), taxation of Dissenting church buildings, registration of births and deaths by the Church of England, burials by Anglican rites, and the necessity of accepting Anglican beliefs before graduating from either Oxford or Cambridge. From 1833, Parliament repeatedly saw Bills to eliminate one or another of these problems but, on the whole, change came slowly. By 1857, the year of the Divorce Act, most of the personal annoyances of the old system — births, marriages, burials — had fallen before the Dissenting attack but some lingered. Church rates, long a major sore, were not abolished until 1868.

As Dissenters came from cities and cities produced many of the reformers of the day, a great number of Dissenters combined demands for change in religion with other matters — law, economics. Victorian politics rarely coalesced into only two groups but the polarities often saw Dissenters, reformers, progressives and Liberals pitted against the Church of England, conservatives and Tories.

As to divorce, Dissent offered little contribution. Speakers in the House of Commons occasionally referred to the *Reformatio Legum*, a compilation of various changes proposed by Archbishop Cranmer and others in the mid-sixteenth century which represented the English church in its most Reformed state. Periodic references to the practices of other Protestant nations occurred but aroused little interest. In the heady reforming days of the early 1830s an occasional Dissenter, influenced by Benthamite ideas, dabbled with ideas of easier divorce; but during most of the nineteenth century Dissent produced preachers, not theologians. Charles Haddon Spurgeon, the London preacher whose audiences were surpassed by no one, combined hymns, a dynamic style and a confident demeanour to entrance crowds of 15,000, but he spoke not about divorce. *The Baptist Magazine*, a monthly periodical, maintained silence throughout the debates over divorce in 1857. *The Noncomformist*, a radical journal with the motto 'The Dissidence of Dissent and the Protestantism of the Protestant

Religion', mildly supported the reforms in 1857, though considered divorce 'not a pleasant topic'. Generally, Dissenters took the position that divorce was permissible and ought not to be restricted to the rich but that Respectable, God-fearing people — Dissenters — would never seek a divorce so the issue was irrelevant to their beliefs.[3]

A red thread had run through the fabric of English religious history since the Reformation: Roman Catholicism. Englishmen long nurtured a hate and a fear of 'the Popish religion', commencing with Henry VIII's break with Rome in order to get rid of his wife, continuing with Elizabeth's valiant resistance to the intentions of Spain with its Great Armada, and culminating in the eighteenth-century 'No Popery' riots in London. In the eyes of the English, as their nation moved into the clear sunlight of Protestantism, another part of the British Isles languished in the darkness of Popish superstition. The Irish, despite and because of the conquests, rebellions and reconquests of the sixteenth and seventeenth centuries, clung to the faith of their fathers. The hardening of hearts during all this bloodletting made Ireland an ever-feared cauldron, despite the presence of a largely Protestant ruling class, and Roman Catholicism a foreign and a threatening menace. The menace crept continually closer as the Irish, during the Industrial Revolution, moved to the factories and construction sites of England in increasing numbers, numbers much greater than the church-going 4 per cent recorded in the census of 1851. Thought to be ever-susceptible to priestly or papal agitation, the Irish, whether in Ireland or England, provided a substratum which might erupt if encouraged, and concessions to their religion were few and hard won. Catholics obtained freedom of worship in 1791 and in 1828 the right to vote (though the property requirement in Ireland was simultaneously raised from 40s. to £10, thereby keeping the 'Irish hordes' from 'slavishly' following their priests to the polls). Further efforts to change the conditions of Catholics focused on Ireland, not England, and only resulted in minor prunings of the Church Establishment in 1833. The basic attitude to the Irish as superstitious Catholics led by their priests remained unchanged, however, and contributed to the slow response of the English and their government to the potato famine of the 1840s when half a million of the Irish died and 1 million emigrated. Three centuries of hatred and fear reaped a terrible harvest.

The Pope, the other half of the Catholic fears of many English people, appeared as a new problem again in the 1840s. After the wars of blood and propaganda in the sixteenth century, the English and the

Pope settled into postures of ignoring one another. With the Pope's declining importance in European politics and England's internal upheavals of the seventeenth century, the relationship mattered little in any case. Things began changing in the 1840s when both the Pope and the English government under Lord John Russell sought to use each other. The growing numbers of Catholics in England, largely due to Irish immigration, needed more religious administration than that existing by 1847 when the Pope approved, unbeknownst to the English, a scheme for an archbishop and seven bishops in England. The English government wanted to make concessions to Catholics — as liberal men, they saw little sense in many of the laws irritating Catholics — and a co-operative Pope would make governing Ireland less troublesome. Unfortunately, a third side to the negotiations appeared when French troops were needed to return the Pope to Rome in 1850 following a revolt and temporary republic there in 1848, the year of revolution in Europe. Pius IX returned to Rome with less sympathy for liberal governments, such as Russell's, and more desire to strengthen the Roman church's hierarchy and obedience to Rome.

When Pius publicly announced in 1850 his plan for a Catholic hierarchy in England, Russell labelled it a 'Papal aggression', playing on English prejudices. Russell, and many Englishmen with him, saw the Pope proceeding with a blatant disregard for the established relationship between religion and the English state. Toleration was fine, but no church should so act without consulting Parliament and the government. To assume titles duplicating those of English bishops and to see a cardinal in England affronted English sensibilities and memories. The ten new bishops joined the Pope and Guy Fawkes that Fifth of November, and Parliament banned the use of titles which duplicated those of the Church of England. This dispute slowly simmered down but the decade of the 1850s, the decade of the divorce debate, still had some of the excitement raised by the 'aggression'.

The Roman Catholic Church, unlike Dissent, had a clear and known position about divorce — it was not permitted. European countries still dominated by the Roman Church banned divorce and the Catholic churches of England took the lead in sending petitions to Parliament protesting against any law permitting divorce. But Catholics had little political power as few members of the Commons were Catholics or courted Catholic votes and in the Upper House the only Catholic to speak repeatedly was the Duke of Norfolk, not a political heavyweight. Nevertheless, the position taken by Catholics of opposing divorce convinced many Englishmen, conditioned by centuries of enmity, that divorce might be permissible to true Protestants.[4]

The Church of England, having separated itself from the Roman Catholic Church and separated Dissenters from itself, still lacked internal unity. Anglican Evangelicals, concentrating on personal piety and salvation, formed a group which, in the late eighteenth and early nineteenth centuries, sought social amelioration. Largely at Evangelical instigation, the Church of England built new churches and renewed its efforts in urban areas, producing growth matching that of Dissent. By 1850, however, Evangelicalism often hardened into concern about things — observance of the Sabbath, dislike of theatres, strict sexual behaviour — which kept 'puritanism' alive in the language. The strand of genial tolerance, against which Evangelicals rebelled in the eighteenth century, reposed in the Latitudinarians in the church who minimised theology, downplayed differences over liturgy or politics, and maintained as all-encompassing a church as possible. A third group, attracting most of the clergy as the nineteenth century wore on, emphasised ritual, tradition and the sacraments. Low, Broad, High — the names attached to these various tendencies — all lived together uncomfortably in the Church of England after 1840. While Evangelicals resembled Dissenters in ignoring doctrine in favour of personal action and Broad Churchmen minimised doctrine so as to attract Dissenters to the church, High Churchmen increasingly emphasised the uniqueness of the Anglican tradition. Many, of course, merely thought of themselves as Anglicans, but history was not to be made by them but by men who constituted the labelled movements in the Church of England.

Changes, reforms and concessions — the growth of Dissent in the cities, the Act of 1832 which gave the franchise to many Dissenters, Catholic emancipation — produced shifting alliances and varying responses among the differing groups of churchmen, though extremists always distrusted the ambitions of their opponents within the church. By 1833 many young High Churchmen at Oxford viewed the future fearfully, and when John Keble, an Oxford professor, preached, and later published, a sermon entitled 'National Apostasy considered', High Churchmen girded their loins and prepared for the fight.

Keble saw the Church of England, long the repository of ancient truths, being treated by the state as just one sect among many. To Keble, the state's task was to support the Church of England, not the churches of England. Others — J.H. Newman, E.B. Pusey — joined

Keble in letter-writing, meetings, and interminable discussions. Within two years of Keble's sermon, the prodigious productivity of these men — like many Victorians — included 66 *Tracts for the Times* which gave the movement one of its names: Tractarianism. (Another name was Puseyism, after E.B. Pusey who became a dominant figure; a third was the 'Oxford Movement' as the leaders all studied at and spread their influence from the university.) The tracts defended doctrines and practices and drew lines for the intra-church battles to come.

By 1840 criticisms of these High Churchmen, soon joined by numerous clergy, came from many corners, and to numerous Anglicans and Dissenters, Tractarians strongly resembled Roman Catholics. Confirming these suspicions, the Tractarians put to press in 1841 *Tract 90*, written by John Henry Newman, reconciling the basis of Anglican belief, the Thirty-Nine Articles, with Roman Catholic doctrine. Four years later Newman joined the Roman Catholic Church, becoming a cardinal in 1879. Newman's apostasy — or conversion — began a trickle of Tractarians into the Roman Church and painted those remaining within the Anglican fold with the Roman brush. Any proposal emanating from or even supported by High Churchmen aroused suspicion and hostility from many English Christians, Anglican or no, who saw the proposal as 'Popish'. The divorce debate, with divorce fiercely opposed by High Churchmen, had such an aspect.

The river of the religious life of the nation, after 1840, widened to cover disputes all over the world and narrowed to make a gorge between the cliffs of church and state. High Churchmen, constantly harping about the lack of state support for the Anglican truths whenever aid or relief was given to Dissenters or Roman Catholics, trapped themselves into seeking a separation of their church from the state in order to maintain their church's purity in the face of an increasingly unsympathetic Parliament.

Nothing was too distant to excite passions in those tense years. In 1841 the King of Prussia suggested the establishment of a bishopric at Jerusalem to serve the numerous English and Germans visiting the holy shrines. In politics the issue excited Anglo–German rivalries in commerce and foreign affairs, and in religion all the Anglican groups took positions, some applauding international religious co-operation, others castigating the contamination of the pure Anglican church with the descendants of Luther and Calvin. Education proposals in 1843 foundered on the rock of the respective roles of Dissent and Anglicanism, a rock still wrecking proposals in the twentieth century. Bills in Parliament to permit Jews to sit as members provoked outbursts in 1848 and

1849; this would introduce non-Christians into the body responsible for governance of the church.

To High Churchmen, the informal separation of church and state, begun in the 1820s, became a judicial separation in 1849 after a lawsuit about the beliefs of the Reverend G.C. Gorham. Presented to a parish living near Exeter, Gorham was refused the parish by the High Church Bishop of Exeter, Henry Phillpotts, on the grounds that Gorham's beliefs about baptism were heretical. Inasmuch as many Evangelical Anglicans shared Gorham's views, the dispute split the church and soon entered the law courts. Gorham lost in the Court of Arches but appealed to the Judicial Committee of the Privy Council, the supreme court in the ecclesiastical judicial system. In March 1850, the Judicial Committee, consisting of two laymen, two archbishops and a bishop, divided three to two in favour of Gorham with one archbishop and one layman taking the High Church position. Evangelicals and Broad Churchmen rejoiced while High Churchmen feared for a church with, as they saw it, an impure faith, a faith often determined by laymen. The Gorham decision prompted another exodus of Anglicans across the desert to Roman Catholicism, the most notable being Henry Manning, later a cardinal.

The decade of the 1850s then continued with minor squabbles but no major fracas. The church survived a Presbyterian Prime Minister, Lord Aberdeen. Convocation, a meeting of the entire church comparable to Parliament, met for the first time in nearly a century and a half in 1852. Dissenters gained more opportunities at Oxford and Cambridge Universities. A Dissenting proposal to permit marriage with a deceased wife's sister — it reappeared so often the rest of the century that Gilbert and Sullivan labelled it 'the annual blister' — failed of Parliamentary approval as High Churchmen convinced MPs that such marriages violated Levitical laws of consanguinity. After the judicial separation of church and state by the Gorham judgment, a cooling-off period permitted the parties to consider the advantages of the union, but forces outside the church then conspired to bring forth the Divorce Bill.[5]

The starting-point for the arguments about divorce, the Bible, confused many. The passages discussed in the debate included one from the Old Testament, Deuteronomy and several from the New Testament:

Deuteronomy ch. 24
1   When a man hath taken a wife and married her, and it come to passe that shee find no favour in his eyes, because hee hath found

some uncleanness in her, then let him write her a bill of divorcement, and give it in her hand, and send her out of his house.

2   And when shee is departed out of his house, she may goe and be another man's wife.

3   And if the latter husband hate her, and write her a bill of divorcement, and giveth it in her hand, and sendeth her out of his house; Or if the latter husband die, which tooke her to be his wife,

4   Her former husband which sent her away, may not take her againe to be his wife, after that she is defiled; for that is abomination before the Lord, and thou shalt not cause the land to sinne, which the Lord thy God giveth thee for an inheritance.

St Matthew, ch. 5

31   It hath been said, Whosoever shall put away his wife, let him give her a writing of divorcement.

32   But I say unto you, that whosoever shall put away his wife, saving for the cause of fornication, causeth her to commit adultery; and whosoever shall marie her that is divorced, committeth adulterie.

St Matthew, ch. 19

3   The Pharisees also came unto him, tempting him, and saying unto him, Is it lawfull for a man to put away his wife for every cause?

4   And hee answered, and said unto them, Have ye not read, that he which made them at the beginning, made them male and female?

5   And said, For this cause shall a man leave father and mother, and shall cleave to his wife; and they twaine shalbe one flesh?

6   Wherefore they are no more twaine, but one flesh. What therefore God hath joyned together, let not man put asunder.

7   They say unto him, Why did Moses then command to give a writing of divorcement, and to put her away?

8   Hee saith unto them, Moses, because of the hardness of your hearts, suffered you to put away your wives; but from the beginning it was not so.

9   And I say unto you, Whosoever shall put away his wife, except it be for fornication, and shall marry another, committeth adultery; and whoso marrieth her which is put away, doth commit adultery.

10   His disciples say unto him, If the case of the man be so with his wife, it is not good to marrie.

11   But hee said unto them, All men cannot receive this saying, save they to whom it is given.

12   For there are some eunuches, which were so borne from their mothers wombe; and there are some eunuches, which were made eunuches of men; and there be eunuches, which have made themselves eunuches for the kingdome of heaven's sake. He that is able to receive it, let him receive it.

St Mark, ch. 10
2   And the Pharisees came to him, and asked him, Is it lawful for a man to put away his wife? tempting him.
3   And he answered, and saide unto them, What did Moses command you?
4   And they said, Moses suffered to write a bill of divorcement, and to put her away.
5   And Jesus answered, and said unto them, For the hardness of your heart, he wrote you this precept.
6   But from the beginning of the creation, God made them male, and female.
7   For this cause shall a man leave his father and mother, and cleave to his wife;
8   And they twaine shalbe one flesh; so then they are no more twaine, but one flesh.
9   What therefore God hath joyned together, let not man put asunder.
10   And in the house his disciples asked him again of the same matter.
11   And he saith unto them, Whosoever shall put away his wife, and marry another, committeth adultery against her.
12   And if a woman shall put away her husband, and bee married to another, she committeth adulterie.

St Luke, ch. 16
18   Whosoever putteth away his wife, and marrieth another, committeth adultery; and whosoever marrieth her that is put away from her husband, committeth adultery.

Romans, ch. 7
2   For the woman which hath an husband, is bound by the law to her husband, so long as he liveth; but if the husband be dead, she is loosed from the law of the husband.
3   So then if while her husband liveth, shee be married to another man, shee shalbe called an adulteress; but if her husband be dead, shee is free from that law, so that she is no adulteress, though she be married to another man.

1 Corinthians, ch. 7

10   And unto the married, I command, yet not I, but the Lord, Let not the wife depart from her husband.

11   But and if shee depart, let her remain unmarried, or be reconciled to her husband; and let not the husband put away his wife.

12   But to the rest speake I, not the Lord, If any brother hath a wife that beleevth not, and shee bee pleased to dwell with him, let him not put her away.

13   And the woman which hath an husband that beleevth not, and if hee be pleased to dwell with her, let her not leave him . . .

15   But if the unbeleeving depart, let him depart. A brother or a sister is not under bondage in such cases; but God hath called us to peace . . .

39   The wife is bound by the Lawe as long as her husband liveth but if her husband bee dead, shee is at liberty to bee married to whom she will, only in the Lord.

The immediate conclusion drawn by interested participants was that the Old Testament permitted divorce whereas the New Testament pointed both ways on the matter. In particular, St Matthew permitted divorce for the wife's adultery whereas the other writers all prohibited divorce. What to do?

W.E. Gladstone, the future Prime Minister and the leading opponent in the House of Commons of divorce reform in 1857, and Christopher Wordsworth, then Canon of Westminster and later Bishop of Lincoln, both took up the task of reconciling the conflicting passages. Their technique involved a very close examination of the texts and a study of what assumptions might be contained in the questions and answers. While Gladstone and Wordsworth, and others, produced arguments diverging in certain particulars, all appealed to the authority of Scripture and, to a much lesser extent, the authority of the Church Fathers. Gladstone's efforts, published in the *Quarterly Review* in July 1857, ran to over 35 pages, while Wordsworth's sermon explaining his argument contained 20 pages when printed. The reasoning of both men became too intricate and subtle to be widely understood or remembered. Gladstone's article was of such complexity that his opponents quoted it against him in efforts to prove that the passages could not be reconciled. These works concluded that, while divorce was permitted, neither party could remarry during the lifetime of the other. To most people this meant the same as no divorce, a position taken publicly only by Lord Redesdale, and corresponded to the long-standing practice of the ecclesiastical courts of granting divorce *a mensa et thoro* but not *a vinculo matrimonii*.[6]

This position coincided with that of the Roman Catholics, something which greatly hindered Gladstone and others. Hostile attitudes to Catholics reappeared constantly in the debate and the apparent identity of doctrines severely handicapped the High Church party in its appeals to the laity, especially in Parliament. So Protestant was Parliament that the Duke of Norfolk, the leading Catholic peer, found himself forced to argue as though he were a Protestant. The series of conversions to Catholicism by members of the Oxford Movement over the previous decade caused many laymen to suspect the 'Romanising' tendencies of the clergy. The prejudice against Catholics — centuries-old but reinforced as recently as the 'papal aggression' of 1850 — combined with this suspicion to permit men to reject arguments for divorce that appeared too 'Catholic'. This same combination precluded any effective appeal to the authority of history of the church itself because such appeal had to rely on Church Fathers, themselves, of course, too 'Catholic'. Protestants relied solely on the Bible and, when it proved unclear, confusion reigned.

Tools to solve the problem of the conflicting Scriptural passages lay surprisingly close at hand, though few Englishmen knew of them. Scholars in Germany had, for nearly half a century, analysed the Bible in new ways. Their work tolerated inconsistencies in Holy Writ — something few Englishmen were prepared to accept — and sought historical explanations. If the explanation of the world's origin in Genesis clashed with modern geology, these critics argued that Genesis approximated the understanding of people thousands of years ago; anyway, the creation, being not directly relevant to moral life, was not crucial to Christianity. Biblical scholarship then (and today) disposed of the problem of Matthew's permission for divorce by suggesting that the exception about adultery is a later addition to Jesus' words, not part of the original. Few Englishmen, however, knew much about German scholarship — learning German did not constitute part of English education — and even fewer accepted the German techniques anyway. In 1846 Marian Evans, known to us by her later *nom de plume* of George Eliot, translated a German study, D.F. Strauss's *Leben Jesu*, but the work attracted only a small English readership. In contrast with Germany, English biblical studies remained stunted and many theological works, including those of J.H. Newman, the best thinker of the day, contained cheap debating tricks resembling undergraduate disputes, rather than serious scholarship.[7]

With English biblical scholarship labouring so hard to bring forth so little about divorce, the position of High Churchmen was further compromised by the church's attitude to divorce in the past. For over a century and a half, Parliament had passed divorce Acts and bishops had not protested. The first divorce, that of Lord Roos, had produced an episcopal debate in the House of Lords, and a pamphlet recapitulating the arguments appeared, but the bishops had voted on both sides when the Bill was passed. The first divorce petition by a commoner, in 1701, had been referred to a committee of the Upper House, chaired by the Bishop of Salisbury. In 1820 the bishops, under great political pressure, voted in favour of the Bill of Pains and Penalties which contained a clause divorcing Caroline from George IV. Moreover, that clause had been debated, not silently slipped into the Bill. Most damningly, clergymen had, in the past, obtained divorces. As early as 1763, William Hazeland persuaded Parliament to pass a divorce Act for him, and over the next century at least 13 clergymen had had Bills enacted for their relief:

> John Green married Elizabeth Hooke in 1756 in Norwich. He later took a living in Lincolnshire and, as befit an eighteenth-century clergyman, was important in his area. He even obtained a Parliamentary Act as part of the enclosure of his parish, so much did he resemble the landed gentry. Elizabeth, however, ran off with one Goddard and was divorced in 1773.[8]

> The Honourable and Reverend Thomas James Twisleton's wife, after two children, decided to become an actress. In 1794 they signed a separation deed as he objected to such a life for his wife. After discovering her adultery in 1796, he sought a Parliamentary divorce in 1798 (as did his brother-in-law the next year — a divorcing family). The only dispute to entertain the House of Lords revolved around support (and presumably paternity) of one of the children.[9]

Four of the clergy divorces had been obtained in six years at the end of the eighteenth century — during the divorce epidemic. Then followed a lull until 1835 when India, travels on the Continent, and residing at the English seaside had produced clergy divorces similar to the others of the day:

> The Reverend Frederick Grueber Lugard, a curate in Leicestershire, married Grace Price Morgan in 1834. Seeking to improve

his prospects, Frederick became a chaplain in the service of the East India Company in 1838. Grace returned to England in 1843 because of her health, and, still at English seaside resorts recovering in 1846, she became pregnant by James Kelson. Frederick, still in Madras, conducted his divorce in 1848 through his brother-in-law, the Reverend John Travers Robinson. Grace and James, now living in Paris, did not contest the proceedings, James consenting to an award of £1,000 in the crim. con. suit. Even the clergy in India lost wives, but all was not lost as Frederick married again (twice) and later fathered the future Lord Lugard, the great colonial administrator of the twentieth century.[10]

Lugard's divorce, one of six clergy divorces in the decade and a half before 1850, had been finalised in the second great wave of clergy divorces. The Evangelical revival affected the attitudes of clergy, and their wives, to end the first surge in 1800; High Church attitudes brought an end to the second in 1850. To be fair, not all of these men may have remarried — thereby observing the strict interpretation of the Bible – though Lugard did. Nevertheless, their examples of Parliamentary divorce undermined the High Churchmen's arguments against divorce.

The leadership of the High Church opposition to divorce reform in 1857 in Parliament fell to the Bishop of Oxford in the Upper House and W.E. Gladstone in the Lower; neither was a fortunate choice in so far as divorce was concerned. Samuel Wilberforce, Bishop of Oxford and the son of William Wilberforce who had organised the Society for the Reformation of Manners and led the successful fight to abolish the slave trade in 1807, took to religious politics naturally. While he came to do good, he also did well. Though not the highest of High Churchmen, for 23 years he presided over the Oxford diocese which included the university, the hotbed of religious agitation by High Churchmen. He worked hard in his diocese and many tipped him — and he half-expected — to become the Archbishop of Canterbury in 1868. Nevertheless, despite his obvious talent, he aroused suspicions by his ambition and seeking of applause. Known as 'Soapy Sam', Wilberforce explained that the nickname came from the fact that he often got into hot water but always came out clean; less charitably, his opponents said he was too slippery to get ahold of. In 1860, Wilberforce was invited to Oxford University to 'smash Darwinism' (*The Origin of the Species* had been published in 1857), joked and wondered which side of Darwin's family contained the ape ancestor. T.H. Huxley, a supporter of

Darwin's ideas and an atheist, rose from the audience to declare it better to be descended from an ape than from such a talented and influential man who could use only ridicule in a serious discussion. Wilberforce's political approach to religious problems and his lack of the holy intensity of a Newman or a Keble offended many of his own supporters who saw him as shallow. Moreover, his two brothers and his daughter became Roman Catholics, so he was tainted with that problem, as were so many High Churchmen.

Wilberforce and his fellow High Church bishops opposed the divorce reform in 1857, though he had voted for such a Bill in a previous Parliamentary session. Furthermore, the bishops maintained, taking a very exalted view of Parliament, that England had no divorce in the past as each Parliamentary divorce represented merely a special dispensation from the laws of the land, not of God. These actions and arguments persuaded few about the bishops' consistency. When outright opposition failed in 1857, Wilberforce fell back to seeking a clause in the Bill which would prevent the remarriage of the divorced. This would have had the effect of making a divorce merely a judicial separation and, though a man could have been free of a wife who shamed him, this proposal would have vitiated the reform as far as most were concerned.

In the House of Commons W.E. Gladstone led the opposition to divorce, though he too was compromised in his integrity. In 1857 Gladstone had been active in Parliament for over two decades and was still only one-third of the way through a political life that reached nearly into the twentieth century. Though prominent already in the 1840s, in 1857 he was still a decade away from his first spell as Prime Minister. In his personal life, Gladstone, happily married, gathered prostitutes from the London streets and offered them aid in leaving their life of shame, a task so difficult and tempting that he scourged himself regularly. In 1838 he had published *The State in its Relations with the Church*, a book considered difficult to read then and virtually unintelligible today. For Gladstone the state, which had a moral conscience, had a responsibility to shape individual character through controls of conduct; the church should aim at conduct by influencing that character. However, by 1851 he had confessed that his book contained out-of-date doctrine and that he had, after its publication, found himself 'the last man on a sinking ship'.[11] Thereafter a leading Parliamentary supporter of the Church of England, he never undertook any reforms of that institution. He opposed many changes — the Privy Council's judicial supervision of the church, divorce reform — and eventually concluded that the church's connection with the state harmed, not helped, the former. His speeches in 1857 betray no clear ideas about the relationship of the state to a national church, though elsewhere he maintained the state should do nothing to hurt the church.

Gladstone's past proved an impediment to him in other ways. He had been in the Cabinet in 1854 which introduced a divorce reform Bill. In 1850 his testimony in the House of Lords had been the chief evidence in the divorce of his friend, the Earl of Lincoln, testimony which came from a trip to Italy to find the eloped Countess. And he, too, had a Roman Catholic in the family, a sister who 'went over' in the 1840s. In 1857 when the Divorce Bill appeared certain of passage, he abandoned his direct opposition to the Bill and attempted to delay it by long speeches and stirring up the problem of equality of grounds for wives. Gladstone's religious fervour resembled that of a Newman or a Keble but his deep political nature made his actions difficult for contemporaries to decipher. One wag observed that if Gladstone had found the ace of trumps up his sleeve during a card game, he would have believed God put it there. Such a man could not stop the drive to divorce in 1857.

All of this High Church opposition to the Divorce Bill in 1857 produced one concrete result — a 'clergy conscience' clause. The final Act contained provisions which permitted an Anglican priest to refuse to officiate at the remarriage of a divorced person. This item resulted from the petitions circulated among the clergy in the early summer of 1857 which garnered over 6,000 signatures. The government gave way to the pressure and allowed the exemption. However, divorce supporters, to rub the clergy's noses in the mess, inserted another provision which allowed divorced persons to use their parish church if they could find another clergyman to officiate. To intrude another clergyman into a parish church would have given great offence to any clergyman though, as most divorced people took their second marriage vows in the Registry office, the event possibly never occurred.

Besides High Churchmen, other Anglicans took varying positions on divorce, with many coming out in support. They relied on the passages in St Matthew permitting divorce for adultery or, more rarely, denied that any of the biblical texts should govern the practice of the state. Appeals to the practices of other Protestant countries occurred also but, overall, the first Evangelist sufficed. The religious policy of Palmerston's government lay in the hands of the secular Prime Minister himself and in those of his stepdaughter's husband, the Earl of Shaftesbury. Descended from the great Whig leader of the seventeenth century as well as the eighteenth-century philosopher, Shaftesbury had strong Evangelical beliefs. A philanthropist, he devoted his life to social problems and is remembered today for his legislative efforts to improve factory conditions. Shaftesbury, usually present in the House of Lords during the debates of 1857, never spoke on divorce; however, along with several bishops not of the High Church party — such as A.C. Tait, Bishop of London and future Archbishop of Canterbury — he voted for the Divorce Bill.

The leading theologian of the church, F.D. Maurice, also added little to the divorce debate. Maurice led a life of concern for the English working man, becoming in the 1840s a Christian Socialist — two words few Englishmen fitted together successfully. In 1857 Maurice preached a series of sermons at Lincoln's Inn Chapel, an ideal forum to discuss divorce when many saw divorce reform as merely a legal reform. However, the Divorce Act received the royal assent in August and it was November before Maurice broached the topic in his sermons. Often murky in his writings and speeches, Maurice exceeded himself on the occasion of divorce. He clearly approved the transfer of divorce proceedings to a secular court and probably sanctioned the 'clergy conscience' clause; as to the grounds of divorce or the problem of remarriage, by contrast, he was so obscure that no hearer could have left with a clear idea of Maurice's beliefs.[12]

Most Englishmen, after glancing at the biblical texts and discovering their contradictions, adopted the position of the section of the church they supported. Church parties, so well developed, meant individual examination of the problem was not common. High Churchmen were not out-debated in Parliament or proved wrong in their theology by such as Maurice; that they lost the battle over divorce meant their numbers, even in Parliament where they were overrepresented, were few.

The general drift — or the result of the three decades of conflict before 1857 — produced growth in most religious bodies, with concomitant growth of opportunities and rights, especially for non-Anglicans. To eliminate irritants, the state assumed responsibilities for areas — marriage, probate, education — long part of the Church of England. Marriage itself, regulated by the state for over a century, had ceased to be a sacrament but failed to become a contract; for many, since the state controlled marriage at the beginning, it could also control the end. On such issues, debate revealed a vacuum in English religious life — a vacuum of authority; where did answers lie? Many High Churchmen — they came to be called 'Anglo-Catholics' — turned to the traditions of the Western church, and several turned into Roman Catholics. Others, such as John Keble, the man whose sermons started the Oxford Movement, increasingly sought to withdraw the Church of England from, to his eyes, the incompetent and impure meddlings of politicians. Keble, though reserved, intellectually arrogant and humourless, was the most influential parish priest in Anglican history. But he lived in a world far removed from that of most English Christians: his Hampshire parish, Hursley, was owned by a neighbouring squire who never accepted Dissenters or atheists as tenants.[13] Keble, therefore, never faced nineteenth-century issues close to home. Keble's fellow-clergy came to emphasise Christ's presence in the church, the sacraments, a holy life. That all of this turned the Church of England into 'the Tory Party at prayer' and elevated the position and authority of the clergy themselves were unplanned consequences. The outcome of the divorce debates was to strengthen greatly the clergy's control over the church, as divorce clearly took people out of the fold.

Dissenters, long seeking freedom from religious oppression, wanted the state to take a neutral posture, helping Christianity, not individual Christian churches. Concerns with individual salvation, reaching non-believers, and personal behaviour led, after 1857, to efforts to use the state for moral purposes such as observance of the Sabbath, temperance, and control of obscenity. Divorce, with its avowed purpose of deterring and punishing adultery, harmonised well with this thrust.

Broad Churchmen alone sought to maintain the direct connection of church and state, but religious controversies in the 1860s and the governments of Gladstone and Disraeli combined to destroy Broad Church influence. Maurice, however, had sapped the intellectual vitality of the Broad Church efforts at maintaining the connection in his Lincoln's Inn sermons. As both the state and the church were divinely ordained, divorce could be a matter for either. Basing his religious beliefs on a foundation of the family — his analysis of the Old Testament led him to believe that the family preceded the state and the church — he thought adultery fundamentally violated that institution. Hence, divorce became incidental — the family was destroyed by the adultery, not the divorce. In Maurice's theology some things of this world, such as the Divorce Bill, were simply irrelevant.[14]

While the various branches of English Christianity failed to achieve unanimity of doctrine about divorce, religion influenced divorce nevertheless. Adultery was banned — the Seventh Commandment brooked no exceptions — and all Christians agreed on that. The great confusion over divorce did not obscure the badness of adultery. Adultery, long illegal but rarely punished, was now to be prosecuted by the private means of the outraged spouse. Separating themselves from the irreligious hordes, Anglicans, Dissenters and Roman Catholics followed Anglican clergy to a new status — Respectability. Rarely has an ideal been so neatly turned into a basis of power, the power of the Respectable. Dissipation, sneakiness, unfaithfulness — not particularly Christian sins, but certainly Respectable sins — also fit into the new structure. As Respectables were usually religious, all this flowed together to make divorce the ultimate unRespectable act. Religion, not the churches, did have a role. Divorce itself would threaten a person's Christian posture, but the Divorce Act hurt only the Church of England.

English Christians failed to agree about divorce, and many other things. Even the bishops in the House of Lords rarely acted unanimously and Convocation, meeting again only in the 1850s, had not dealt with divorce. As Christians failed to present a united front, politicians worried less about the religious implications of divorce. Nevertheless, Christians all contributed, inadvertently, as they convinced politicians that the Divorce Bill steered a middle course between the extremes of secularist proposals of easy divorce and the desires of Roman Catholics, with their fellow-travellers, the High Churchmen, for a prohibition of divorce. To Victorians a middle course, a *via media,* corresponded to the best in English character and religious history. Moving the English state into a new era of religious neutrality as among Christians, the Divorce Bill, to politicians, merely separated church and state. Broad Churchmen hoped to open religious life to new influences and new ideas and they believed a universal moral sense still governed English life, informing both the church, in its broadest, Christian sense, and the state — the union of church and state could be maintained. With, however, the two most militant elements in English Christianity — High Church clergy and Dissenters — seeking their own goals, the irreconcilable differences converted the political separation of the church and state into a religious divorce.

Notes

1. Horton Davies, *Worship and Theology in England* (Princeton University Press, Princeton, 1961–1970), 5 vols; Norman Sykes, *Church and State in the Eighteenth Century* (Cambridge University Press, Cambridge, 1934). See also note 4. Recent general histories of Dissent do not exist.

2. K. S. Inglis, 'Patterns of Religious Worship in 1851,' *Journal of Ecclesiastical History,* 11 (1960) 74–81; David M. Thompson, 'The 1851 Religious Census: Problems and Possibilities,' *Victorian Studies,* xi (1967) 87–97; W. S. F. Pickering, 'The 1851 Religious Census — A Useless Experiment', *British Journal of Sociology,* 18 (1967) 382–407.

3. *The Nonconformist,* 10th June, 19th August, 11th November, 2nd December, 1857; *Monthly Repository,* new series, vii (1833) 136 et seq.

4. John Bossy, *The English Catholic Community 1570–1850* (Darton, Longman & Todd, London, 1975); Eamon Duffy (ed.), *Challoner and His Church* (Darton, Longman & Todd, London, 1981).

5. M. A. Crowther, *Church Embattled* (Archon, Hamden, Conn., 1970).

6. *Quarterly Review,* 102 (1857) 251–88; *DNB*, Redesdale; John Morley, *The Life of William Ewart Gladstone* (Macmillan, London, 1903) vol. 1, p.179.

7. Crowther, *Church Embattled,* Ch. 2.

8. *Lords Journal,* vol. xxx, p.580.

9. Ibid., vol. xli, p.541.

10. Ibid., vol. lxxx, pp.149–55.

11. See note 6. Richard Shannon, *Gladstone* (University of North Carolina Press, Chapel Hill, 1984) pp.343–4, 113, 140, 170, 269.

12. F. D. Maurice, *Kingdom of Christ* (Rivington, London, 1842) 2nd edn; W. M. Davies, *An Introduction to F. D. Maurice's Theology* (SPCK, London, 1964); F. M. McClain, *Maurice* (SPCK, London, 1972); Frederick Maurice, *Life of Frederick Denison Maurice,* (Macmillan, London, 1884) pp.128–32; F. D. Maurice, *Sermons Preached in Lincoln's Inn Chapel* (Macmillan, London, 1891–2) vol. 2, pp.301–21.

13. Frances Awdry, *A Country Gentleman of the Nineteenth Century* (Warren & Son, Winchester, 1906) p.96.

14. See note 12.

4   The Reformers: Lawyers and Politicians

Victorians rightfully saw law reform as one of their great successes. Commencing already at the end of the eighteenth century, reformers began to rationalise the laws and courts which had been growing since the early Middle Ages, and their efforts trickled through the Parliamentary maze to the statute books. While Whigs and Liberals most often pushed reforms, even the Tories joined in occasionally and Robert Peel, a future Prime Minister, made his reputation in the 1820s with law reforms. That the absurdity of the three-step system of divorce (*a mensa et thoro* in a church court, crim. con. in a common law court, and private Bill in Parliament) survived to 1857 is striking testimony to the number of more serious problems that existed in English law before mid-century.

The laws of England needed reforming, having grown for centuries, nearly a millennium, without any systematic attention being paid by anyone to the whole, rather than the parts. By the beginning of the nineteenth century the accumulation of the bits and pieces produced not an ordered work or even a 'seamless web', but a jungle. The common law, the 'glory of England', originally determined disputes between feudal knights in the Middle Ages and then slowly metamorphosed into litigation involving land and crime. Eighteenth-century judges clumsily grafted commercial law on to the tree and Parliament made spasmodic alterations, usually by introducing new categories of crimes. The result was confusion. By 1800 to pick a pocket could bring the death sentence, while stealing a child offended no law at all. Laws overlapped and contradicted each other: one law made wilful destruction of trees a capital offence, another declared it an offence warranting seven years' transportation, and a third imposed a fine of £20. Benefit of clergy, originally a one-time exemption for medieval clerics from the death penalty, became a complicated set of rules moderating the extreme harshness of the criminal law; after 1705, the ability to read — the original test of clerical status — was not even necessary, and the whole mess disappeared only in 1827.[1]

The courts, though centred at Westminster with the judges riding Assize circuits twice a year, covered the countryside unevenly. Local courts survived or died due to a variety of causes and by 1800 were irregularly scattered over the kingdom. Debtors and creditors in and around Bristol, a thriving port with a long history, litigated in Bristol's

Tolzey Court, the Court of Conscience, the Court of the Honour of Gloucester, the Hundred Courts of Barton Regis and other neighbouring hundreds, while inhabitants of Manchester, one of the new and growing cities of the Industrial Revolution, made do with a manorial court, a remnant of the Middle Ages when knights possessed manors. Subjects of both areas could go to London for justice but expenses mounted quickly in the capital, and for the legal profession London remained, as always, the promised land. While a local attorney could make a nice living out of conveyancing, debt collection and estate supervision, London offered the big rewards and access to the levers of power. These many branches of the common law lacked symmetry or order, though Edmund Burke admired and praised the conglomeration as distinctly fitting the English personality, like a tree on a cliff face adapting itself to the cracks, gathering moisture and soil wherever it can.

The beautiful, or gnarled, tree of the common law stood alongside the now blasted tree of the church courts. In the Middle Ages, while rulers of England and the rest of Europe fumbled for procedures and ideas to cope with the incessant violence of feudal anarchy, the way was illuminated by churchmen, led by the Pope, who devised courts and doctrines subsequently copied and extended by kings. Medieval church courts, with a wide competence, dealt with heresy and behaviour of the clergy as well as the behaviour of all the king's subjects in areas such as defamation, incontinence, swearing, usury, tithes, perjury and church non-attendance. Occasional conflicts — Thomas à Becket's death at the hands of Henry II's knights — suggested that the church's courts could not be entirely separate from the king's courts, but the two jogged along together for centuries. The Reformation stripped the church courts of much work — monasteries disappeared and their lands, 25 per cent of England's acreage, fell into secular hands — and more work slowly disappeared as the common law courts gobbled up jurisdictions over slander and tithes and people ceased to litigate over church non-attendance and incontinence. The shrivelling tree had a few new growths, such as litigation over pew ownership, but by the nineteenth century probate constituted the major branch with surviving twigs, such as church rates. A contentious jurisdiction, though one with few suits, involved the clergy's beliefs; this area provided the heat and light of the nineteenth century in matters of baptismal regeneration, the nature of eternity, and the literal truth of the Bible. Divorce, though existent, was so small as to be a leaf, not a twig, on the tree of the church courts.

Church courts also covered the countryside unevenly, though the entire system was more rational than that of common law courts as a fairly clear hierarchy existed. Notwithstanding the fact that London's various church courts received the bulk of the business, diocesan courts throughout the realm remained active. As with the common law, London attracted the best talent and so unremunerative were many of the other courts that bishops pressed unqualified men into service. In testimony before a royal commission in 1830, one man admitted that he held four distinct offices under the Archbishop of York; the Reverend Matthew Marsh, Chancellor of the Diocese of Salisbury, after stating he had no ecclesiastical law education, claimed, 'as soon as I was appointed, I read Oughton; and have since read, with great attention and satisfaction the printed Reports of Haggard, Dr Phillimore, and Dr Adams; many of the judgments several times over'. The four proctors practising before the Reverend Marsh's court actually made their livings as common law attorneys, their qualifications as proctors being quite few. Evidence in church courts was taken by deposition, not testimony before the court where a witness's behaviour might betray perjury. The procedures, the law, and the personnel, being outside the experience of most Englishmen, provoked one reformer to exasperation: 'A more perfect system of hocus-pocus, anything more like a duel with hatchets in a dark cellar, can hardly be imagined.'[2]

The two court systems had different personnel, although the solicitors and proctors tended to be the same men outside London. The great names of English law — Bracton, Coke — were common lawyers, and church court practitioners remain unmentioned in histories. The lawyers for both systems, the common lawyers and the civilians, further divided into barristers and solicitors, advocates and proctors; barristers and advocates addressed the courts, and solicitors and proctors dealt with clients, prepared briefs, wrote deeds and wills, and the like. Wealth, power and fame flowed to a few barristers every generation and the judges of all the courts, except church courts outside London, came only from the ranks of the barristers and advocates. Young men going into law chose one area — common or church law — and one division; few ever later crossed the line within the professions. Lord Chancellor Hardwicke began as a solicitor but later rose to eminence as a barrister; Stephen Lushington acquitted himself well as a common lawyer before becoming a civilian and one of the greatest Victorian judges. But these were exceptional men.

Though Charles Dickens, enlivening his works with descriptions of legal institutions and portrayals of their characters, painted pictures requiring urgent attention, changes came slowly. While *Great Expectations, A Tale of Two Cities, David Copperfield, The Pickwick*

Papers, and *Bleak House* all contain marvellous, sometimes exaggerated, vignettes of London's legal life, Dickens's pictures still depicted the reality after 1850 in many instances. By 1800 such reformers as Samuel Romilly and Patrick Colquhoun had nibbled away at the inequities and inanities of the criminal law. In the 1820s Robert Peel, future Prime Minister, pruned many of the death penalties from the ancient tree and introduced professionalism into enforcement with his policemen, nicknamed 'Bobbies' or 'Peelers' after their creator. The tide rose rapidly after a six-hour speech in the House of Commons by Henry Brougham in 1828. Brougham, born and educated in Scotland, had long been a Whig interested in reforming law and education. A man of tremendous energy, he aroused suspicions everywhere he went, even among his friends, as his ambition frequently led him into dubious political manoeuvres. Lord Chancellor for four years after 1830, Brougham assiduously tackled the backlog of causes in Chancery, the court of *Jaryndice v. Jaryndice* in *Bleak House,* and he founded the Law Amendment Society in 1844 which thereafter provided a focus for legal reformers. His speech in 1828 ranged over diverse matters, including judicial qualifications (limit political influences in appointments), wills (make requirements uniform throughout England) and legal fictions (John Doe and Richard Row still lived), though not divorce. His sustained interest in law reform suggests genuine commitment, and, as to divorce, he was counsel to Queen Caroline in 1820 and lived to support the Divorce Bill in 1857.

Brougham's criticisms strike us as so obvious that it is a matter of some wonder that so few made them earlier and so little notice had been taken. Nevertheless, Brougham's speech accelerated the pace of reform and it brought to the Houses of Parliament views long advocated by a group of men labelled 'Utilitarians'. Eighteenth-century philosophers, strongly given to rational approaches to questions, developed a doctrine of utility, a doctrine taken up by Jeremy Bentham and made his own. Applying the test of 'the greatest happiness for the greatest number', Bentham found many English institutions lacking, none more so than the law. 'What's the utility? What's the use?' became hard to answer when asked of a franchise excluding the vast majority of men and all women despite their contributions to English economic life after the Industrial Revolution. Similarly, church livings, greatly unequal in wealth, or laws, with their confusions, inconsistencies and waste, could not withstand Utilitarian scrutiny. Bentham devoted much time and effort to legal reforms and, though too radical and systematic for most Englishmen, his ideas, slightly watered down, provided the blueprint and techniques for reformers during the rest of the nineteenth century.

Utilitarians, unlike many philosophers, descended to the scramble of politics to achieve concrete results; by mid-century, Utilitarianism had so spread throughout educated society that it was impossible to ignore the criticisms. By 1850 the mantle of Bentham had fallen on John Stuart Mill, the prodigy son of a Utilitarian father, though Mill's dominance as a thinker came only in the 1860s following publication of his *On Liberty* (1859), *Representative Government* (1861) and *Utilitarianism* (1863). As Mill's political and moral standards conformed, in many ways, to those of his contemporaries, his articulation of various aspects of Utilitarian ideology only confirmed what many already thought. There was general acceptance of Mill's idea, best expressed in *On Liberty* (begun in 1854), that the individual was free to do anything which did not affect others.

As to divorce, however, Utilitarians failed to provide clear answers, partly because divorce was not a major issue before the 1850s. Bentham saw marriage as a contract which should be dissoluble at will, though under some government supervision. John Stuart Mill's intellectual position, on the other hand, remained unknown, largely because of his personal position. In the early 1830s Mill, stunted emotionally by his childhood education, had fallen in love with Harriet Taylor, wife of John Taylor, a drysalter and wholesale druggist. Whatever the nature of their relationship, platonic or no, they could not marry until Harriet's husband died. While Mill in *On the Subjection of Women* (1869) supported divorce, he had first thought on the matter as early as 1832, shortly after meeting Mrs Taylor, and concluded, with Bentham, that marriage should be a contract, easily dissolved.[3] However, he published nothing on the matter until over three decades later.

Mill's approach and his general ideas, seeping through society, helped law reformers over one obstacle: the effect of divorce. The question arose, in Utilitarian terms, as to whether divorce contributed to the general happiness of people by releasing two people from an unhappy union or whether it reduced that happiness by sending people to law courts rather than encouraging compromises on marital difficulties? An answer might have come from historical experience but England had insufficient experience with divorce to look to history. Scotland, on the other hand, had 300 years of experience with laws providing divorce more readily than those proposed for England in the 1850s. Without discussing cultural differences between the two parts of the British island, everyone agreed that the Scots character had not been harmed by the divorce practice, and from Brougham on, men with experience of Scottish practice supported reform in England. Thus reformers concluded that divorce affected the husband and wife only, not the society. Only if divorce became too common would society be endangered and that could be avoided by maintaining the strong prejudice in public opinion against divorce and by keeping its cost high enough to preclude the masses, perhaps unresponsive to the pressures of opinion, from obtaining divorces. Finally, reformers concluded that divorce itself was not an evil as most men, including J. S. Mill, had trouble accepting the notion that the individual's freedom included doing evil. Divorce would, they believed, serve only a few isolated cases where the marriage had already broken down — the evil was the marital breakdown, not the divorce, and no one expected divorce to rise much above the handful of Parliamentary cases heard yearly. The Utilitarian concept of the individual's freedom to pursue his own happiness, therefore, combined with the belief that divorce did not affect others and was not an evil in itself; permitting divorce raised no serious philosophical problems for Victorian Utilitarians.

Despite the reforming atmosphere of the 1830s and even though Robert Phillimore, a civilian and a member of the House of Commons, sought a royal commisison in 1830 to study divorce, two decades elapsed before such a commission was appointed. The Divorce Bill became law only in 1857 after other, more pressing reforms had been enacted. After 1830 the reform of the law continued, though mainly by tinkering, not wholesale changes. Parliament enacted laws making settled land easier to sell, giving trustees more powers, enhancing the safety of bills of sale, regulating pawnbrokers, and on and on. The 1840s witnessed the commencement of the attacks on the poor state of training afforded to young men aiming for the law. Their education, or lack of it, before 1840 scandalised reformers, though a few bright and dedicated young men came through very well. In 1843 reformers introduced entrance examinations for the profession. A royal commission in 1854 made wide-ranging recommendation, and the universities began giving law degrees, but progress was slow and intermittent. No school of law, though proposed, ever emerged and the distinctions between barristers and solicitors survived abolitionist efforts. For divorce, the consequences of this impetus to reform legal education came when reformers resisted establishing, or empowering existing, local courts to deal with divorce. Local availability would have greatly reduced divorce costs but reformers believed that legal talent, already stretched by the growth of cities outside London, would be spread too thin if divorce courts dotted the landscape. Fears of the ethical temptations of divorce — collusion especially — led reformers to keep divorce, and divorce lawyers, in London and under the watchful eyes of the leaders of the legal profession. The only concession to the pressures for local courts came in clauses of the Divorce Act protecting women's property. A woman, earning a living or acquiring property after desertion by her husband, could, after 1857, obtain locally a court order protecting her property from the absconding husband.

Attacks on the church courts increased after the report in 1853 of the Royal Commission on the Laws of Divorce, and continued until the great success of 1857 when both probate and divorce were removed from church court jurisdiction. Most of the reformers' interest during this period focused on the probate administration, where the multiplicity of jurisdictions — one for each diocese and other historical relics, called 'peculiars' — and the uncertainty created when a deceased owned property in several jurisdictions. The lack of judicial expertise offended critics, and probate, the most lucrative part of church court jurisdiction, appealed to greedy common lawyers. The ecclesiastical nature of the proceedings offended Dissenters. Testamentary and matrimonial matters 'are purely questions of Civil right between individuals in their lay character, and are neither Spiritual nor affecting the Church Establishment,' said one reformer.[4] After two and a half decades of criticism, reformers easily moved the Probate and Letters of Administration Bill through both Houses of Parliament in 1857. So uncontentious was the reform that the principle of the Bill — the second reading — was accepted in both Houses without a division.

Like probate reform, divorce reform resulted from a quarter of a century of criticism and agitation, led by Henry Brougham but joined by many others. Brougham introduced divorce reform Bills in the 1840s, brought private petitions to the attention of the House of Lords constantly, and obtained a report in 1844 on the 200 matrimonial lawsuits throughout the country in the previous four years. But Brougham had companions in his crusade. Stephen Lushington, a Whig MP in the 1820s and 1830s, who joined Brougham in Queen Caroline's defence in 1820, was one of the few lawyers of the day trained in both the common and the ecclesiastical law. Lushington, a member of the Royal Commission on Ecclesiastical Courts, continued to address the issue of divorce, even after his appointment as a church court judge in 1838. Lord Lyndhurst, a sometime Lord Chancellor in Tory governments and son of the American expatriate painter John Singleton Copley, became quite a reformer in the 1850s, seeking greater equality for women in divorce; he took over Lord Cranworth's Bill in the House of Lords in 1856 and, in committee, produced the Bill which formed the basis of the Act of 1857. Lord St Leonards, another Tory Lord Chancellor, served on the Royal Commission on the Laws of Divorce in 1850 and supported the Bill in the House of Lords. Lord Campbell, a future Lord Chancellor, took much credit, not all of it due, for the final Bill which he believed derived directly from the royal commission of which he was the chairman. Howard Elphinstone, an MP in the 1830s and 1840s and member of the Law Association, fought hard and often in the House of Commons for divorce reform, even forcing a division on the issue in 1843. The Law Association itself kept the issue before its members with three articles in its reports between 1845 and 1855. And, as discussed earlier, the life and writings of Caroline Norton, a legal reformer though not working from the same background as the lawyers, contributed to the result.

Outside the doors of Parliament the public's imagination was stirred by two trials of the mid-1840s which highlighted the absurdities and unfairness of the three-step system:

Herbert William and Jane Evans married in April, 1842, at the ages of 21 and 19, respectively. In November 1842, Henry Elliot, a friend of both, visited the couple at their home near Beaumaris in Wales. Herbert became suspicious when he 'detected his wife and Mr Elliott exchanging glances and making signs to each other'. Later when Herbert and Henry went hunting, Henry feigned illness and returned to the house. Shortly afterwards, Herbert also returned to the house and, taking a maidservant with him, surprised Jane and Henry in bed. In 1843 Herbert gained a verdict with £500 damages in his crim. con. suit.

However, he failed to obtain a divorce *a mensa et thoro* in the Arches Court in London because, as he could not testify, only the maid could prove the adultery; the ecclesiastical law, unlike the common law, required two witnesses and Herbert, therefore, failed to prove the adultery! This suit confirmed dramatically that two separate systems of law existed, and no appeal could harmonize the result.[5]

In 1845 Justice William Maule sentenced Thomas Hall, a convicted bigamist, at the Warwick Assizes. Maule, noted for his irony, lectured Hall (and the nation, as *The Times* reported the speech) that his crime was the failure to divorce his first wife before he took his second. No matter that Hall's first wife was given to dissipation and drunkenness; no matter that she deserted him and left him with small children. Had he merely taken a concubine, the law would not have bothered him. 'But your crime consists in having — to use your own language — preferred to make an honest woman of her. Another of your irrational excuses is that your wife had committed adultery, and so you thought you were relieved from treating her with any further consideration — but you were mistaken. The law in its wisdom points out a means by which you might rid yourself from further association with a woman who had dishonoured you; but you did not think proper to adopt it. I will tell you what that process is.

'You have acted wrongly. You ought to have brought an action for criminal conversation; that action would have been tried before one of Her Majesty's judges at the assizes; you would probably have recovered damages; and then you should have instituted a suit in the Ecclesiastical Court for a divorce *a mensa et thoro*. Having got that divorce, you should have petitioned the House of Lords for a divorce *a vinculo*, and should have appeared by counsel at the bar of their Lordships' house. Then, if the Bill passed, it would have gone down to the House of Commons; the same evidence would possibly be repeated there; and if the Royal assent had been given after that you might have married again. The whole proceeding would not have cost you more than a £1000'.

'Ah, my lord, I never was worth more than 1000 pence in all my life.'

'That is the law, and you must submit to it.'[6]

Maule's emphasis on the costs of divorce represented one of the strongest lines of attacks of Utilitarian reformers, but the silliness of the entire system offended most who thought at all about divorce.

These efforts failed to produce reforms before 1857 because a vested interest — the civilians — fought long and hard to maintain their livelihood. Removing divorce from the church courts appealed to reformers, but dissension broke out when the choice of a different court was debated. As not many divorces occurred, few thought a separate court necessary or worth while. The Privy Council was suggested but its expertise was doubtful and it was busy with other matters. Giving the practice to Chancery, the initial proposal of Lord Cranworth in 1856, brought howls from the reformers as that court's inefficiency and expense remained notorious. Civilians exploited this problem and with every proposal, up jumped a speaker in Parliament wanting to know what was to become of the advocates and proctors. The solution of this matter in 1857 came when civilians agreed to accept government annuities for up to half of their lost income. The expensive results of that compromise appeared in 1862 when a report containing the annuities was published (see Table 4.1 on the following page).

Doctors' Commons, the inn of court for civilians, was abolished in 1857 and, though advocates continued their practice before the new divorce court after 1857, the civilians — advocates as well as proctors — disappeared with time. The church courts, stripped of probate and matrimonial suits, continued but barely, with the occasional theological dispute to enliven a nearly dead institution.

The two decades of reforming agitation had, nevertheless, not produced a single change in the laws and procedures governing divorce. All had not been wasted, however, as the reformers had drawn attention to the absurdities of the system and, by their constant speeches, writings, and reports, created the impression that divorce was a bigger matter than the four Parliamentary divorces per year warranted. Also, a view of English history had been created which met the objection that English law did not recognise divorce, that Parliamentary dispensation from the law by private Act meant no divorce existed. Best expressed by Lord Cranworth, the Lord Chancellor, and Sir Richard Bethell, the Attorney General, the argument sustained the Divorce Bill in 1857 and constructed an authority which justified the final Act. True, the argument went, the common law of the courts did not recognise divorce — it only treated the crim. con. — but the 'common law of all England' did. The legal reformers synthesised the proceedings of the previous 150 years into a tradition of divorce — the law of England, taken as a whole, had been granting divorces. This approach also meant that the grounds of divorce were established and need not, therefore, be debated. Given this view, Utilitarians and Englishmen imbued with Utilitarian ideas proceeded with what they did best, reforming institutions and attacking the privileges of the old order. Divorce reform became merely procedural reform and could be seen as an extension of other minor legal reforms of the courts of the common law and Chancery.

Divorce reform, after 1853, the year of the report of the Royal Commission on the Laws of Divorce, repeatedly came before the Parliamentary, if not the public, eye as Lord Chancellors of the various governments introduced Bill after Bill. Bill after Bill disappeared into

Table 4.1: Annuities to Civilians. Compensations and retiring allowances, exceeding £150 per annum, payable to proctors and officers of the late ecclesiastical and prerogative courts, on the 31st December, 1860 (selected individuals).

Name	Office	Rate per annum		
		£	s.	d.
Rev. E. S. Bathurst	Registrar, Consistory Court of Norwich	547	14	10
Henry Allen Bathurst	Proctor, Prerogative Court of Canterbury	354	6	0
	Registrar of the Court of the Commissary of the Archdeaconry of Norwich	65	0	0
William Fell	Proctor, Consistory Court, Lichfield	527	13	11
Rev. George B. Moore	Clerk of the Seat, Prerogative Court of Canterbury	341	16	0
Rev. Robert Moore	Registrar, Prerogative Court of Canterbury	7,990	2	5
William Price Moore	Proctor, Prerogative Court of Canterbury	453	5	1
Henry Raikes	Registrar, Consistory Court Chester	3,498	8	4
Edward Steward	Proctor, Consistory Court, Norwich	27	16	5
	Registrar, Royal Peculiar of Great Cressingham, Norwich		16	6
	Registrar, Court of the Peculiar Jurisdiction of Castle Rising etc., Norwich	3	5	5
	Deputy Registrar, Court of the Commissary of the Archdeaconry of Norwich	97	12	2
	Deputy Registrar, Court of the Official of the Archdeaconry of Norwich	109	16	2
Charles Toller	Examiner, Prerogative Court of Canterbury	200	2	9
	Proctor, Prerogative Court of Canterbury	523	4	9
Edward Toller	Proctor, Prerogative Court of Canterbury	784	17	2
	Seal Keeper, Consistory Court of London	14	1	5
Edward William Toller	Proctor, Prerogative Court of Canterbury	261	12	4

Note: These are selected names from a list of 160 names. The total of the annuities was over £100,000

Source: *House of Commons Parliamentary Papers,* 1862, (100), clxxiv.

the morass of Parliamentary committees and fell to the demands of time for other Parliamentary business. Foreign affairs — the Crimean war with the terrible winter and the fruitless charge of the Light Brigade, the incident of the ship *Arrow* when Britain shamelessly forced China to accept foreign trade, a war in Persia — alternated with the abolition of transportation for crimes and efforts to obtain stricter observance of the Sabbath in London to keep divorce reform at bay. Credit for breaking this pattern in 1857 falls to the Prime Minister, Palmerston. Himself not above reproach in sexual matters — he had been a Regency dandy and was to be cited as a co-respondent in the divorce court in 1863 — Henry Temple, Viscount Palmerston, had been an MP since 1807. (He might have been Prime Minister sooner had he not been caught in the bedroom of a lady-in-waiting to the queen; Victoria never forgave him that escapade.) First achieving the highest rung, the office of Prime Minister, in 1855, he had promptly been toppled by English actions in China. Palmerston 'went to the people' and won a large Parliamentary majority in the election of March 1857. He then set out to demonstrate his strength, to friends and foes, by pushing the Divorce Bill through a House of Commons containing an impressive opposition of Gladstone, Disraeli and Lord John Manners. In the Lower House, he met delaying tactics, which foreshadowed tactics employed by Irish MPs in the 1880s, by a calm declaration that the House could sit until September, if necessary, to pass the Bill. In fact, the House of Commons argued the Bill in committee during the middle of a very sultry August 'when men would almost give up Magna Charta itself to avoid another sitting.'[7]

Divorce reform appealed to Palmerston as the type of minor reform he, not particularly interested in domestic matters, could support. His tenacity in 1857 was partly due to a desire to support his Lord Chancellor, Cranworth, whose previous effort had been called an 'abortion' against the cutting tongue of Attorney General Bethell. Palmerston also kept the Houses sitting as little other legislation had passed during the short three-month session which had been disrupted by the news of the Indian Mutiny. Palmerston's Parliamentary strength made his government careless about explaining their position and refuting their opponents, but as *The Times* said, 'The Divorce Bill offers one of those occasional instances in which a large majority furnishes the best answer to ingenious and plausible arguments.'[8]

The Divorce Bill was passed in 1857 because, the year before, Parliament had settled several issues relating to women. Although Brougham and his fellow law-reformers kept the idea of divorce reform alive, they were not the only people in the field skirmishing for changes in the marital relationship. Barbara Leigh Smith, the founder of English feminism, had published *A Brief Summary, in Plain Language, of the Most Important Laws Concerning Women Together with a Few Observations Thereon* in 1854. Shortly thereafter, she formed a committee to work for reform of all laws affecting women. This committee campaigned hard not for divorce, but for changes in laws governing married women's property, publicising the injustices done to women by their avaricious, selfish and cruel husbands. In 1856 a petition seeking redress of the laws and signed by, among others, Elizabeth Barrett Browning, Mrs Gaskell and Harriet Martineau was presented to Parliament. Bills, supported by Leigh Smith's committee, appeared in 1856, exciting opposition from those who called the proposal breaches of the marital relationship, 'mischiefs', and 'vicious'. The Divorce Act included provisions, carried over from the 1856 Bill, protecting the property and earnings of divorced and judicially separated women, though not married women generally, and effectively killed further efforts by Leigh Smith and her committee.

The second matter which Parliament took up in 1856 touched the grounds of divorce for women. The recommendations of the Royal Commission on the Laws of Divorce had, in essence, been that divorce was for husbands, as that had been Parliamentary practice for over a century and a half. However, many law reformers, including those in the Law Association, believed public opinion would support divorce by a wife when the husband's adultery was 'flagrant and perservering'. In 1856, after Lord Chancellor Cranworth introduced his Divorce Bill in the House of Lords, a select committee of the Upper House scrutinised the Bill and effected several compromises. The committee was dominated by Lord Lyndhurst who sought to give wives additional grounds, such as adultery combined with cruelty, incest, bigamy, rape, desertion, transportation, four years' penal servitude, and a mistress in the 'common residence' of the pair. The opposition, led by former Lord Chancellor St Leonards, whittled down these proposals and the compromise produced a final Bill later that year. It recognised only incest, bigamy, and adultery with cruelty or four years' desertion as legitimate reasons for a wife's divorce petition. Wives had gained some grounds — cruelty and desertion — over the prior Parliamentary practice and that compromise remained part of the Act in 1857.[9]

The Divorce Act of 1857, as it finally emerged from Parliament, conformed to the beliefs of many that its changes were merely procedural:

The Divorce Act, 'An Act to amend the Law relating to Divorce and Matrimonial Causes in England', received the royal assent on 28th August, 1857. The Act established 'The Court for Divorce and Matrimonial Causes' to handle divorce and abolished the church courts' jurisdiction over nullity of marriage, restitution of conjugal rights, and jactitation of marriage; these rare situations would henceforth fall within the cognisance of the divorce court (§ § 2,6). Judges of Assize could deal with judicial separations, a power removed a year later (§ 16). The legal profession, uniting advocates, proctors, barristers, attorneys, and solicitors, would handle the court's business though any proctor whose income suffered could get compensation for one-half of his loss from the Treasury (§ § 15,64). Divorce could be granted to a husband for his wife's adultery and to a wife for her husband's adultery when combined with incest, bigamy, rape, sodomy, bestiality, cruelty, or desertion for two years (§ 27). Various bars to a petition included connivance, condonation, mutual guilt, and collusion (§ § 29,30,31). Though crim. con. was abolished, a husband could still claim damages as well as costs from his wife's lover (§ § 33,54). Powers to deal with child custody, use a jury, examine witnesses orally, and order maintenance and alimony were given the court (§ § 32,35,36,46). Deserted and judicially separated wives had future earnings and property protected — the meagre results of feminist efforts (§ § 21,25,26).[10]

Lord Campbell, a future Lord Chancellor and the chairman of the royal commission in 1850, confided in his diary that the Divorce Act was 'framed almost exactly according to the recommendations of the commission over which I had the honour to preside — preserving the law as it has practically subsisted for 200 years.'[11] Campbell overlooked the protections for women's property, won by the budding feminist movement, represented by Barbara Leigh Smith's committee, and the expanded grounds for wives which Lord Lyndhurst manoeuvred into the law. Though various bars to divorce — collusion, connivance and condonation — were retained and the divorce court judge was instructed to follow old law as much as possible, the Divorce Act did represent change, resulting from the politicians' views as to the art of the possible. The presence of feminists wanting greater protections helped convince Campbell and others that they walked a middle road, one of mainly procedural reforms. Even the old system, in its death throes, worked to the advantage of the reformers by producing an example of all that was wrong:

The Evans married in 1850 and lived at Cheltenham and London. Mr Evans was a magistrate and a Deputy Lieutenant in Gloucestershire, but Mrs Evans began seeing a lot of Mr Robinson while her husband was absent from the London house in 1853 and 1854. Mr Evans hired a private detective who, after much work and lots of talk with servants, gathered enough evidence for Mr Evans to proceed. The first crim. con. suit went against Mr Evans but the judge set the jury's verdict aside and a second trial produced a victory for Mr Evans with £400 damages. However, after a trial on 9th June, 1857, in the Court of Arches in London, Mr Evans was denied a divorce *a mensa et thoro*, largely because the judge believed the detective 'got up' too much of the evidence. Mr Evans then had Mr Robinson indicted for perjury for his testimony in the Court of Arches but the jury could not agree on a verdict. As the *Gloucester Journal* said, reporting the suit because it involved people living at nearby Cheltenham, under the old system of divorce 'strange things occur'. (Mr Evans obtained a divorce in 1859 under the new law, when *The Times* referred to the case as 'of dirty notoriety'.)[12]

Law reformers, working to eliminate the old absurdities, enshrined Respectable marriage in the Divorce Act. As divorce would be difficult — adultery was uncommon, at least among Respectables — and not cheap — the new procedures still cost several hundred pounds — marriages would be, for most ,'till death do us part'. Yet, the merest possibility of divorce meant marriage was a game worth playing, and the high cost of a divorce reflected the high value of marriage. All Respectables could afford divorce, though tremendous financial sacrifices would be necessary in the lower rungs of the economic ladder. Retaining adultery as the only grounds to dissolve a marriage retained the idea, common to the law and Christianity, that marriage was a union of two bodies into one; what cohabitaton united, only adultery could destroy. Moreover, adultery, with its notion of fault, reinforced Respectable attitudes to individual responsibility and the consequences of fecklessness.

Respectables agreed with Thackeray's 'Damages, Two Hundred Pounds' in believing a wife did not commit adultery without provocation by her husband. And everyone knew marriages broke down in many cases long before any adultery occurred. A logical consequence of these beliefs would have been to grant a divorce when the parties agreed that the marriage was dead, rather than wait for the all-but-inevitable adultery. This, however, would 'open the floodgates' of divorce, violating the legal traditions, and smacking of the practices of French Revolutionaries. Moreover, one partner, abandoning Respectability, could be found guilty; the other, in theory if not in practice, remained untainted and, more important, Respectable. Appearances still counted; indeed, they counted for more than in the past.

Nowhere was the bedevilment of appearances more apparent than in the various bars to a divorce, especially collusion and mutual guilt. Following the legal tradition, reformers maintained in the Act that if both parties committed adultery — both had 'unclean hands' — no divorce could be granted. Two wrongs not only did not make a right, they destroyed the right to a divorce. The consequences of the mutual guilt bar and the knowledge that marriages broke down before adulteries appeared created the problem of collusion. That an adulterous spouse, badly wanting out of a marriage, might not point out the sins of the mate had been a problem for judges since the eighteenth century. The divorce court judge, aided after 1860 by the Queen's Proctor who investigated suspicious circumstances, was directed to deny divorces in cases of mutual guilt, and he did so. Divorce established the guilt of one party, who then ceased to be Respectable. Divorce was to be an adversary process — joy to the lawyers — and the bars of collusion and mutual guilt attempted to ensure that. Not a criminal law, the Divorce Act imposed severe sanctions by means of community pressures; hence, guilt and innocence had to be maintained. Nevertheless, notions of guilt, of innocent and guilty parties, caused great trouble to the divorce court in years to come.

Respectables sought to improve the moral tone of society by reducing the frequency of adultery. If keeping wives from straying had been the only goal, then legislation permitting judicial separations — cutting off the guilty wife's financial support and freeing the husband from living with her — would have sufficed. Similarly, a divorce which precluded the guilty pair, the lovers, later marrying would have been consistent with that goal. To Respectables, however, a guilty wife would then face the choice of living with her lover unmarried or becoming a prostitute — still more adultery. UnRespectables, who had little apparent Parliamentary strength in the passage of the Divorce Act, wanted divorce, not separation, as they sought remarriage; few doubted that unRespectables would concern themselves overmuch about adultery. Divorce which permitted remarriage was, therefore, the best means of reducing adultery in English society.

The lives of women such as Ann Dawson (discussed in Chapter 2) were not lived in vain as the Divorce Act, while not giving wives equality in law, remedied some abuses of the past. The many women whose husbands had deserted them for the wilds of Australia and the United States, or the wiles of other women, could seek relief. Judicial separations were cheaper than before and, if the desertion was combined with adultery, divorce was available. As most believed any man who would strike a women would also be adulterous — he must have found another women in order to treat his wife so abysmally — cruelty of the kind suffered by Ann Dawson provided grounds for divorce.

Yet the double standard lived on. Or did it? Here the history of divorce had great weight — to legal reformers the Act did not change past practices, so the double standard must be maintained. Women's forgiving natures, 'spurious issue', separate 'proclivities' of the sexes — all reinforced the historical argument. Male self-interest — after all, Parliament comprised only men — played its part. Nevertheless, the additions of cruelty and desertion gave Respectable wives considerable equality. Could any Respectable husband, committing the unRespectable sin of adultery, not fall prey to other unRespectable faults of cruelty or desertion as well? Some believed the grounds essentially equal, as husbands with their 'public' responsibilities — competing in the world of trade — could be held to a lower standard in keeping their mates happy; wives, after all, had only their family to attend to. For Respectables, the standards of behaviour were not as separate — though not equal — as the double standard enshrined in the Divorce Act implied. For unRespectables, the double standard in the Act was very real; but the Divorce Act was not passed for the benefit of unRespectables.

What defects in prior divorce practice could not be remedied the Divorce Act tried to turn into supports for the Respectable marriage. Under the old system the expenses were nearly unlimited. Written depositions with the cost calculated by the word, court hearings on every issue, innumerable appeals to the Court of Arches and the Privy Council — all had been valuable weapons in the hands of recalcitrant wives. The 'power vested in the hands of a vicious woman, whose guilt is manifest' to drag the case on and on was ended. Under the old system a man's wife could 'torture him' and 'make him pay the costs of his own rack and thumbscrews'.[13] The problem of expense, not eliminated merely reduced, meant couples would forgive transgressions and seek to repair their marriages, rather than repair to divorce court. The costs of a divorce would well plummet both parties into financial circumstances where Respectability would be difficult to maintain — a significant deterrent. By making divorce within reach of all Respectables, its use as a deterrent was greatly increased. The new system, with only one court and limited possibility of appeals, not merely reduced the costs, it also made certainty of result more likely. The effectiveness of divorce as a threat was enhanced far more than the figures for uncontested divorces suggest; the possibility of extensive litigation with attendant bankruptcy was gone.

Publicity, the other great problem of divorce, was similarly to be used to support Respectability. That newspapers would continue to report divorces was agreed but, with more divorces and therefore divorce less of an event, the attention overall should be less. Nevertheless, publicity would destroy any hope the couple might have of maintaining Respectability. With the appearance of a national press, any behaviour not acceptable to Respectables could be shown to a national audience. No longer would divorces be reported only when of interest locally — the Gloucester paper covered only suits arising in the neighbourhood — and national standards of Respectability would emerge.

The Divorce Act tackled the problem exposed by Caroline Norton as two clauses gave legal protection to the earnings of separated women. Despite these provisions, feminism was not part of Respectability and the Divorce Act effectively quieted that movement for a decade. Though Norton continued her efforts to obtain further relief for herself and others, she never received the publicity she had attracted in 1838 or the 1850s. Her life and works, nevertheless, did more than prick the consciences of Respectable society and show the inequities of the system. Knowing no shame in conventional terms, she was barely socially acceptable. Even Melbourne would not introduce her to Victoria until after the queen's marriage. Lady Holland, a staunch Whig in a staunchly Whig family, thought Norton unRespectable despite her family connections; and Lady Holland was in a position to know, being herself divorced and excluded from many circles. Yet, with her crusader's interests and her flair for publicity, Caroline Norton was a new type of woman. In her, Respectables, male and female, saw the future and did not like it. The Divorce Act of 1857 attempted to avert that future.

The Divorce Act, symbol and reality of Respectable power, would, of course, permit unRespectables to divorce. Even they, however, had to conform to Respectable standards inasmuch as mutual guilt or actions giving encouragement to, conducing to, adultery could bar a divorce. Habit might even lead to conviction, some hoped. Though not Respectable, those who denied Respectable values still had to conduct their lives in accordance with Respectable standards, at least if they ever wanted a divorce. Though unRespectables might divorce, the Divorce Act was not for them. The Divorce Act, unlike divorce itself, was for Respectables. Politicians and lawyers, not always a holy alliance, combined to bring about the Matrimonial Causes Act of 1857, the Divorce Act, and holy matrimony has never been the same since.

Notes

1. Leo Radzinowicz, *A History of English Criminal Law and its Administration, from 1750* (Macmillan, New York, 1948) vol. 1, p.22; 5 Anne c. 6.

2. *House of Commons Parliamentary Papers*, 1843, xix, 485, 480; *Westminster Review*, 65, (1st April, 1856) 341.

3. F.R. Hayek, *John Stuart Mill and Harriet Taylor* (Routledge & Kegan Paul, London, 1951) pp.61–74.

4. *House of Commons Parliamentary Papers*, 1831–2 (199), xxiv, 13.

5. *English Reports*, 163, p.1000 (1844).

6. *Punch*, 5th July, 1856, p.2; *The Times*, 3rd April, 1845; *Hansard*, vol. 147, col. 1833.

7. *The Examiner*, 29th August, 1857.

8. *The Times*, 4th August, 1857.

9. Dorothy M. Stetson, *A Woman's Issue: The Politics of Family Law Reform in England* (Greenwood, Westport, Conn., 1982) Ch.2; House of Lords Record Office, House of Lords Committee Book, 1856. vol. 5.

10. 20 and 21 Victoria c. 85.

11. Mary S. Hardcastle (ed.), *Life of John Lord Campbell* (J. Murray, London, 1881) vol 2, p.421.

12. 27 *Law Journal*, 31, 57; *The Times,* 21st January, 1857; 9th December, 1858; *John Bull*, 13th June, 27th June, 1857; *The Examiner*, 13th June, 1857.

13. *Westminster Review*, 65 (1st April, 1856) 352; Edward Muscott, *The History and Power of Ecclesiastical Courts* (J. Snow, London, 1845) p.12.

5   After the Act: Victorian Divorce, Part II

In January 1858 the newly appointed judge, Sir Cresswell Cresswell, opened 'The Court for Divorce and Matrimonial Causes', and, within the first twelve months, 253 petitions seeking divorce and 87 seeking judicial separations were filed. The law reformers were aghast. Lord Cranworth, who as Lord Chancellor carried the Divorce Bill through the House of Lords, had, during the debates, predicted the numbers of divorces would rise from the four per year obtained by Parliamentary proceedings to perhaps 18 or 20 while Lord Brougham anticipated about 100. But 253! Cranworth, after 1858, mentioned that he had been 'once or twice twitted' about the volume of cases. Whereas Cranworth, an easygoing, sociable man, could dismiss his bad prediction, Lord Campbell, who earlier bragged in his diary about his great influence in passing the Divorce Act, cringed before what he saw as an epidemic. *The Times*, staunch supporter of the Divorce Bill in 1857, worried about the deluge and predicted the volume was merely the result of a backlog from the unreformed past. A report to the House of Commons bolstered this hope as the listed dates of adulteries complained of in divorce petitions ranged back to 1823 with nearly 80 per cent occurring before 1857. No one, violent opponents or eager supporters, had, according to *The Times*, 'the least idea of the quantity of matrimonial misery which was silent'.[1]

Unfortunately for these hopes of a rapid decline after the past was disposed of, the number of petitions remained in the hundreds — the tide refused to retreat — and slowly Victorians came to accept that 200 or 300 marriages would be dissolved yearly. Did easier divorce laws create or merely reveal 'matrimonial misery'? No one knew, or knows, the answer. Solace was taken, however, when the flood of divorces was shown to be a trickle compared with the number of marriages. A few hundred divorces nearly disappeared when placed alongside the 170,000 marriages yearly; reformers breathed a little easier.

Equal worry for reformers arose when they discovered that wives petitioned for divorce. Advocates of reform had long operated on the premiss that divorce would be for husbands, and *Punch*, even after the passage of the Act with grounds for wives included, had not expected wives to seek divorces. If the grounds for wives had remained what they were before 1857 — bigamy and incest — the predictions would have come true. The addition, however, of cruelty and desertion when coupled with adultery gave wives more opportunity. And they took it. In the first year of the new court wives filed 97 of the 253 petitions. Lord Campbell discovered that wives, rather than suing for a judicial separation after the husbands' adulteries, 'merely' added a charge of cruelty and sought a divorce instead — 'a most disastrous consequence', he wrote. Either wives feared the stigma of divorce court less than the cruelty of their husbands or there was more cruelty than expected. In any case, reformers had badly misjudged the women of England.[2]

'The flood of corruption' which was being poured over the land' — Lord John Manners's words describing the newspaper reports of divorce trials — summarised the views of many. Queen Victoria, writing to Lord Campbell about censoring the reports, was not amused. The cases, she penned, 'are of so scandalous a character that it makes it almost impossible for a paper to be trusted in the hands of a young lady or boy. None of the worst French novels from which careful parents would try to protect their children can be as bad'.[3] Besides corrupting youth, the reports, some thought, were worse than the pornography previously purveyed in London's Holywell Street, attacked by the Obscene Materials Act of 1857:

> Mrs Woodward, daughter of a Worcester clergyman, sought a divorce in 1859. Mr Woodward, a solicitor in Pershore, married her in 1847, but she discovered, after twelve years of marriage, that he led a double life. He continued an affair with the woman who kept his house before his marriage, setting her up with a house in Gloucester. In scenes resembling 'French novels', he there passed weeks or even months at a time, posing as a commercial traveller, and fathering three children. Divorce granted.[4]

> Naomi Vicars sought a divorce from James for his incestuous adultery. In 1831 James, a cotton spinner and son of a mill owner, had an illegitimate daughter, christened Mary Ann Vicars. He and Naomi, a widow, married six years later but he left her in 1852. Naomi soon found James living with Mary Ann, now 21, who was 'frequently seen in her father's bedroom in her nightdress'. Mary Ann had three children by James. Divorce granted.[5]

Sir Cresswell ordered women and children out of the court during one trial and heard another, involving 'unnatural practices', *in camera*. Not surprisingly, some thought these reports 'ten times more scandal' than those of the crim. con. suits before 1857. When a minor amendment to the Divorce Act — and there were several in the first decade — came before the House of Commons, MPs exploded, venting their rage and disgust on the entire divorce system. Nevertheless, divorce court proceedings became such a popular spectator sport that people had difficulty obtaining seats. Commons speakers believed that couples, wishing to end their marriages, attended court in order to learn the grounds, procedures and any relevant tricks — the court was a 'School of Divorce'.[6]

These alarms were sounded, more loudly, because Respectables predominated in the initial years of the divorce court. The reasons for this are not hard to find but contemporaries found them only small solace. People who had rebuilt their lives after an adultery and a broken home came to the court to free themselves of a mate who transgressed years earlier, back three and a half decades in one instance. Here, indeed, was a backlog of 'matrimonial misery' being worked through.

Mary Isabella Brookes married William in 1823 but, after two children were born, he deserted her in 1833. Although employed as a bootmaker, he never contributed to her living expenses; he did make an offer in 1850 to live together again but she refused.[7]

Dr Beale, an MD in Paddington, married in 1852. Discovering his wife's adultery with a man they met at a tea party, he 'immediately sent her to her mother's house' in 1855. Before 1857 he successfully sued the lover, a clerk in the railway booking office, in an action of crim. con., winning £100. He sought, in 1859, to terminate completely his connection with his wife with a divorce, something beyond his means before 1857.[8]

A government report, released in 1862, compiled the dates of the adulteries involved in divorces (see Table 5.1). While reassuring the nervous that a backlog existed, the report emphasised that many people welcomed the cheaper procedures.[9]

After the floodtide of Respectables ebbed out of the court, the flotsam of unRespectability was presented to the judge, the press and the kingdom. The lawsuits reported in the newspapers in the decade after 1857 were not, as detractors proclaimed, a 'School of Divorce'. Rather, Respectables found the divorce court a 'School of Marriage'. People seeking Respectability had long had the problem of ignorance as to the essentials of the condition, a problem always confronting status categories — a problem rarely solved, though the flow of etiquette books has always provided one solution. Some media, such as *The Times*, focused on externals: clothing ('he wears a brown greatcoat'), behaviour ('reads a serious newspaper daily'), or residence (Belgravia, not Stepney). Historians, even one of the most sensitive, G.M. Young, can do little better — 'to attend a place of worship, to abstain from spirits, to read a serious newspaper and put money into the savings bank', a Respectable man is one 'whose ways bear looking into, who need not slink or hide'. Whatever other qualities it involved, in 1860 Respectability clearly meant marriage. But what was the proper relationship between husband and wife? The Victorian family has often been portrayed as an authoritarian husband dominating a submissive, though angelic, wife, with lots of obedient and silent children, all sitting

Table 5.1: Divorces and Dates of Adultery. Summary showing the number of petitions for dissolution of marriage arising out of alleged acts of adultery, committed previous to the passing of the Divorce and Matrimonial Causes Act; and the number of petitions arising out of alleged acts of adultery committed subsequent to the passing of the Act, distinguishing the number in each year

Year in which alleged adultery occurred	Number of petitions	Year in which alleged adultery occurred		Number of petitions
1823	1	1851		34
1832	2	1852		28
1833	3	1853		40
1834	2	1854		4
1836	1	1855		41
1837	1	1856		72
1838	2	1857, up to 28 Aug.	43*	
1839	2	subsequent		
1840	5	1857 to 28 Aug.	51	94
1841	8	1858		106
1842	2	1859		89
1843	3	1860		75
1844	10	1861		23
1845	8			
1846	11	Total Number of Petitions for		
1847	19	Disolution of Marriage filed since the		
1848	16	passing of the Act, 11 Jan. 1858 to		
1849	8	30 July 1861, the date of the		
1850	29	Return		781

* Act passed 28 August 1857.
Source: *House of Commons Command Papers*, 1862 (99), xliv 503.

stiffly in a room stuffed with bric-à-brac. The range of possibilities, however, gives the lie to most efforts to generalise because some fit the image, such as the Gladstones and the Gaskells, while others do not — the Disraelis and the Jacob Brights. These examples, from the literary and political elite, were not easily duplicated in the thousands of houses where the father went daily to work in a trade or profession while the mother ran the house with the help, not of a myriad servants, but one or two. Who managed the family's finances, controlled the children's education, decided about birth control — these may have varied immensely; but, as to the Respectable family, one thing was required of spouses — faithfulness.[10]

The close attention Respectables paid to reports of divorce court proceedings had a hand in the clearer demarcation of Respectable behaviour. While the Divorce Bill had been passed to punish transgressors against the marital bond — something all Respectables agreed upon — the divorce court also came to educate Respectables about such things as cruelty, desertion, and condonation. Physical violence between spouses clearly violated Respectable standards but other acts might constitute cruelty so the divorce court patiently worked out acceptable behaviour, often by deciding what was unacceptable:

Mrs Reeves, a wealthy widow, fell in love with Mr Reeves, a private in the Royal Artillery. In 1860 she purchased his discharge and they married. They cohabited one night at Shrewsbury, and he then sent her to London to get more of her money. Two weeks later, when next they met, he kicked her as she would not give him the money. The judge, granting the divorce, ruled that one act of violence sufficed if it produced a reasonable apprehension of more to follow.[11]

Mathias Brown, son of a crêpe manufacturer, married in 1854. As befit the upper middle class of the day, the Browns lived at various addresses in England and on the Continent. He drank, a lot. Rejecting Mrs Brown's efforts to separate herself from her drunken husband, the judge said, if cruelty included drunkenness, it 'would have a wide application'. However, if his behaviour made her ill, it was cruelty. While drunkenness never became a ground for divorce, illness caused by a husband's actions became a refrain.[12]

Frances Henrietta Curtis sought a judicial separation from John George Cockburn Curtis. Married in 1846 despite her parents' objection that 'his station in life was beneath hers', the couple had five children and had, by 1858, lived at several addresses in London as well as in New York City. Their life was a trial. He refused to allow their first child to be baptised as he believed infant baptism wrong and, when the child died, he would not give Frances tea as they were then praying. Perhaps he spat in her face once (the witnesses disagreed). He accused her of infidelity — no evidence — and she taunted him that 'perchance' the children each had a different father; he boxed her ears in return. In 1850 he had brain fever for a period during which time he physically assualted her and threatened to murder her. They went to New York as his career as an engineer was failing. He would not let their children play with others, told the children 'Mamma was naughty' after an argument, tore up her *Harper's Magazine*, and insisted on opening the curtains to the hot tropical sun of summer in New York City. She wrote to her father who went to New York and had John confined in a lunatic asylum; the rest of the family went back to England. John, out of the asylum, took a job in Spain, only to return to England to hunt her out despite her assumed name. The judge, granting the separation, said cruelty must be bodily injury or a reasonable apprehension of it. Mr Curtis's brain fever, in this instance, did not excuse his threats. The judge also said much of the trouble arose from the attitude and interference of her father, F. Solly Flood, a barrister. The judge refrained from any comments about the husband's religion which obviously caused him to view his wife as the source of evil and made him extremely rigid in his attitudes.[13]

Cruelty, if alleged by the wife, had to be proved but, by English law, spouses could not testify on such matters. As a wife was often the only witness about threatening words or physical violence, the sense of fairness pervading the law required that her testimony be made availble, and it was duly done in 1859 when Parliament made the first of a series of technical adjustments to the Divorce Act. Despite the horror about the number of wives seeking divorces, reformers did not go back on the decision of 1857, and women continued to represent about 40 per cent of petitioners for divorce throughout the rest of Victoria's reign.

Forgiveness of the erring spouse was to be encouraged — at least if many of the speakers of 1857 are to be believed — by making divorce an ordeal to be feared and certain to mete out punishment. In legal terms forgiveness meant 'condonation' and the eyes of the nation watched in 1858 when the head of Fortnum and Mason came to the Divorce court:

Frederick Keats, a widower of 46 with three children, married Esther Elizabeth Marett, aged 30 with no fortune, in 1854. They lived at his country house, Braziers in Oxfordshire, and Gloucester Gardens in London. Frederick was sheriff of London and Middlesex in 1856 and, following the expiration of his term of office, they toured the Continent before settling in Brighton in September 1857. Frederick travelled up to London frequently in connection with the affairs of Fortnum and Mason and with obtaining his 'quietus' from his year as sheriff. Esther, during the absences, developed an acquaintance with Don Pedro de Montezuma, a Spaniard of 'great musical talents'. Frederick becoming suspicious, 'high words passed on several occasions'. A separation, giving her £500 a year, was nearly agreed upon when, in January 1858, Esther ran off with Don Pedro. They were found living first at the Lord Warden Hotel in Dover and then at Dublin where they passed as brother and sister-in-law under the names of Don Juan de Monteblanco and Miss Marsh. (Whether they deliberately chose aliases with sexual innuendo never was discussed.) Don Pedro then disappeared abroad. Before the trial in December 1858, Esther and her relations worked on Frederick's pride and fear of scandal to attempt a reconciliation. A series of meetings and letters produced ambiguous meanings: did Frederick forgive Esther her adultery or did he accept her new situation without rancour? After re-examining all the letters and conversations and casting an occasional aspersion on Frederick's wisdom, Sir Cresswell Cresswell decided, in granting the divorce, that, though Frederick forgave Esther, as no 'conjugal cohabitation' followed, condonation had not occurred.[14]

The result of this suit meant a spouse might, as a good Christian, forgive the sin and still be able to shed the sinner who brought disrepute on the family. Moreover, guilty spouses, once forgiven and taken back to the marital bed could rest easy there as no divorce could be threatened. Sir Cresswell found a rule which corresponded to Respectable patterns and, with its emphasis on actions, not thoughts, made life easier for Respectables.

Respectables understood that a sinning spouse who was living with a lover was guilty of desertion but, especially outside the upper classes, many less clear situations could occur:

In *Keats v. Keats and Montezuma*, Sir Cresswell laid to rest the fears of upper-middle-class men that their frequent absences from home might provide their wives excuses for waywardness. 'It cannot be imputed to a man, who is immersed in business, that he is neglecting his wife, and has not a proper affection for her because he attends to that business.' What would become of MPs who remain at Westminster until all hours of the morning? What about barristers who go on circuit for over a month twice a year? This cannot mean they give their wives 'almost a licence to receive attentions from other men'.[15]

Rose Jane Lacey married Henry in 1851. He was a commercial traveller and she a milliner; both businesses failed. In 1853 he left her without making any arrangements for her support and wrote a year later that he would never communicate with her again. As Mr Lacey kept his whereabouts secret, Mrs Lacey placed a notice in *The Times* of her intentions to seek a judicial separation. After the judge approved service of process on the husband's father, Mrs Lacey proceeded. The case settled the problem of dealing with a deserting spouse who could not be located.[16]

The Smiths, 'in very humble circumstances', married in 1848. He was a man of such 'dissipated habits and bad temper, that he treated his wife with great cruelty'. He sold their furniture for drink and spent the £80 she inherited from her father. No divorce granted as Mrs Smith had not objected to this gem of a man leaving her![17]

The culmination of the 'School of Marriage' came in 1865. In one lawsuit Respectables saw everything that was not Respectable:

The Christmas season of 1864 was enlivened for gossips by the fighting Chetwynds. Blanche, the daughter of the Reverend and Honourable Arthur Chetwynd Talbot, the brother of the third Earl Talbot and eighteenth Earl of Shrewsbury, married William Henry Chetwynd in 1854 when she was 18, he 42. Living at Longden Hall, Staffordshire, the couple had two children before, in 1864, she sought a divorce because of his adultery and cruelty. So far, nothing but a country society divorce.

Before the trial began, Blanche was threatened by 'a gentleman of high position in the county of Stafford' that if she did not withdraw her petition, he would publish 'the whole truth'. After being fined £300 for his contempt, the 'gentleman' agreed not to meddle further.

Blanche's case against William revealed him to be a coarse, filthy and disgusting farmer. During an argument he threw a plate at her 'with the meat he was eating upon it'. He picked up their daughter and made her spit on Blanche. The son he made kick Blanche and 'spell the word w—— in my face letter by letter'. One witness mentioned 'some other language which [William] had used to [Blanche] too disgusting for repetition'. He beat her dog. He beat her with a doormat. William kept only female servants and, to verify his adultery with them, Blanche and other servants sprinkled flour outside William's room to track the comings and goings during the night. His letters to a former servant the judge described as 'incredible obscenity'. Evidence hinted William fought the divorce because of the money she brought to the marriage. William's first solicitor quit in disgust at his efforts to stop the divorce; his second solicitor, more pliant, 'created' evidence by changing a hotel entry book.

William retaliated in an effort to show Blanche had been adulterous. Her too close associations with Henry Matthews, a barrister on the Oxford circuit, and with a theology student were dragged before the court; both men denied the allegations, Matthews returning from a commission in Vienna to testify. Blanche rode well — William said he had married her because she was always first in the hunt — and associated with horse dealers and jockeys (thoughts of 'Skittles' — see page 113 — an excellent horsewoman). She had smoked a pipe, not once but twice! She praised George Sand's *Lelia* and Byron's *Don Juan*, possessed two French novels, and made diary entries suggesting an overheated imagination or an affair with Matthews.

Other evidence adduced was of a mixed nature. She had refused to visit the Marquis of Anglesey (he was a co-respondent in a divorce suit in 1860 and his Staffordshire house the centre of a fast set), ran up a milliner's bill of £474, and converted to Roman Catholicism. (One rumour had it that priests were behind the divorce so as to get her fortune.) Moreover, she was pregnant when they married. (Gossips said that the father was her father. Her governess, who was her father's mistress, drugged her and got her father drunk so that the connection would silence Blanche, who knew too much.)

The final arguments and summing up heard Blanche described as 'not a person of great delicacy or refinement' and William as a 'man who had made his house a brothel, whose life was adultery, whose language was obscenity', not 'a man who was calculated to refine her'. The jury, out 30 minutes, gave her the divorce to the 'applause by the people at the back of the court'.

Three months later they reappeared in court, fighting over her legal costs, which had exceeded £500.

Four months further on a child custody fight saw both parents denied custody and the children given to Sir George Chetwynd, Baronet, William's brother, free of the control of either parent. Out of his income of £1,159 per year, William paid yearly £200 for the children and £250 to Blanche *dum casta et sola vixerit*. She died, never remarrying, 33 years later.[18]

Virtually everything this pair did, despite their aristocratic and religious connections, violated Respectability. Such a public airing scandalised, titillated and informed Respectables — knowing what not to do could be as useful as knowing what was required.

At the same time that the divorce court educated Respectables about marriage, it also deterred spouses, especially wives, from adultery by the fear of swift, sure exposure and punishment. So certain was the belief that the Divorce Act deterred adultery that the Registrar of the Divorce Court, in reporting the dates of the 'matrimonial offences' (see Table 5.1, p.88) specified in divorce petitions, divided the year 1857 at 28th August, the date of the royal assent. Presumably adultery declined late in that steamy August as news of the new law spread throughout the land.

The first divorce court judge, Sir Cresswell Cresswell, did his part to make the Act effective, disposing within a year of 24 of the 50 suits brought in the first three months after 1st January, 1858 — a remarkable feat in English law, long noted for its dilatoriness. Cresswell maintained his pace, bringing down criticism on himself for his haste, but soon was overwhelmed by the volume. Minor amendments to the Divorce Act in the 1860s so succeeded in balancing speed and volume against fairness that complaints of delay did not occur throughout the remainder of the century. Moreover, appeals from decisions in divorce court were astonishingly rare — only one in the first decade.

Deterrence depended upon spouses responding rationally to the threat posed by the divorce court but insanity soon raised its ugly head, especially among wives in divorce court, who, often idle, often expected to be 'sensitive', often crossed the line between fact and fantasy:

Mr Robinson, a civil engineer, wanted a divorce from his wife of 15 years. He named as co-respondent Dr Lane who had a hydropathic establishment at Moor Park, Surrey. (Hydropathic treatments —

water cures — were frequented by Victorian ladies with miscellaneous ailments.) Testimony elicited that Dr Lane 'paid great attention to all the ladies', walking in the grounds with them and visiting them in the morning in their rooms. The chief evidence of the adulteries came from Mrs Robinson's diary.

> I leaned back against some firm dry heather bushes, and laughed and remarked as I rarely did in that presence. All at once just as I was joking my companion on his want of memory, he leaned over me, and exclaimed — 'If you say that again, I will kiss you.' You may believe I made no opposition, for had I not dreamed of him and of this full many a time before? What followed I hardly remember — passionate kisses, whispered words, confessions of the past. Oh, God! I never hoped to see this hour, or to have my part of my love returned. Yet so it was. He was nervous, and confused, and eager as myself. At last we roused ourselves and walked on happy, fearful, almost silent.
>
> Oct. 10. I entreated [Dr Lane] to believe that since my marriage I had never before once in the smallest degree transgressed. He consoled me for what I had now done, and conjured me to forgive myself. He said he had always liked me, and had thought with pity of my being thrown away, as my husband was evidently unsuited to me, and was, as he could plainly see, violent tempered and unamiable. Then we spoke of his early age, thirty-one, his marriage, the sweet, unsuspicious character of his wife, rather than pain whom he would cut off his right hand, and were just discussing my own bitter misery and wish for death, my former life and fortune, when we were met by Lady Drysdale [Dr Lane's mother-in-law].'

Dr Lane, flabbergasted by the charge of adultery and the diary, sought to prove Mrs Robinson insane. Medical testimony of other doctors said she suffered from 'congestion of the uterus' which produced a morbid condition of the mind. Also erotomania. All would be aggravated by 'a woman taking measures to prevent conception'. Chronic congestion produces 'delusions on sexual objects' or increased sexual desire. Other evidence suggested Mrs Robinson's 'impatience of celibacy had twice hurried her into rash and ill-advised marriages'. Another witness, with no suggestion of adultery, compared his memory of a conversation with Mrs Robinson with what she later wrote in her diary and said she exaggerated everything and gave it a romantic interpretation. Divorce denied.[19]

John George Lambton, third Earl of Durham, married Ethel Milner, a granddaughter of the Archbishop of Armagh and 'one of the beauties of the day' in 1882. During their very brief courtship, she was very shy, rarely saying more than 'yes' or 'no' but the Earl, blindly in love, attributed her strangeness to her affection. After the marriage she became even quieter and in 1885 he sought a nullity of the marriage on the grounds of her insanity at the time of the marriage. Ethel attempted suicide in 1883 and her mother died a suicide in 1884. Hordes of the Earl's family connections trooped into court to describe her behaviour as strange at all times, while Ethel's family all said she had got worse since marriage. Medical evidence was heard behind closed doors. Everyone agreed she was insane in 1885. Other evidence included Ethel's lack of a response when the Earl confessed a premarital affair and that she had never written a cheque on her bank account since marriage — clearly insane. Apparently Ethel remained in love with a suitor, probably Lord Burghersh, from before her marriage who had been too poor to marry her and brooding on this led to 'sexual insanity'. (There is a slight suggestion of misbehaviour which produced great feelings of guilt — 'I've done a great wrong,' she said several times.) The judge, Sir James Hanner, quoting Milton on shyness, denied the suit for nullity. the Earl died without children in 1928 and was succeeded in the earldom by his twin brother. Ethel died in 1893.[20]

Habit and the economic realities for Victorian women explained the actions of other women who behaved unRespectably:

John Coulthart, aged 21, married Bridget White in 1853, knowing her to be a prostitute (she was 'a resident in a house of ill fame at Liverpool'). A few weeks later, because John made little money as a draper's assistant, they moved in with his parents. Bridget 'exhibited bad temper and was very troublesome' so they moved out again and ten days later John went to New York. During his four years in New York John sent Bridget 5s. and a pound of tea, along with information that his parents would supply her money and clothes. Bridget was soon back in the house of ill fame. John's petition for divorce was denied as he conduced to her adultery when he left her without subsistence.[21]

When insanity, habit or economics failed to supply a rationale for behaviour, bafflement overwhelmed observers of divorce court:

The Hon. Elinor Sophia Diana Cavendish, aged 30, ran off with the Hon. Cecil James Gordon, aged 60. She, the daughter of the Earl of Clare, left behind husband Francis William Henry Cavendish and their three children. Gordon, wed to Elinor's half-sister, left nine children behind. The two families had been very close until, without warning, the pair eloped to Nice in 1865. *The Times*, applauding the jury's award of £10,000 against Gordon as the co-respondent, castigated him because, being married, he could not even redeem their actions by marrying Elinor. Gordon's embarrassed financial circumstances and Elinor's recent inheritance of Clare money could not explain the blackness of the pair's behaviour. Also, the age difference — 30 and 60 — rankled. Why would she 'abandon her character, her position, and her prospects' to take up with a man twice her age? 'There seems a sheer propensity to guilt.'[22]

These occasional awkward situations aside and despite the publicity surrounding a few cases, such as the Chetwynds or Mrs Robinson, Respectables accepted divorce court and its trimmings. Certainly to some, the Divorce Act had 'shaken the morality of the courts, diminished the sacredness of marriage, set all husbands and wives athinking how to get rid of one another, filled the Court with collusion and subordination, and corrupted the youth of the metropolis'. To Respectables, however, the lessons learned from divorce proceedings reassured them about their own Respectability — 'I'd never do that' — and helped set the limits of Respectable behaviour. Few disagreed with *The Times*, when, on the tenth anniversary of the Divorce Act, its editorial opined that 'the establishment of the Divorce Court has been one of the greatest social revolutions of our time'.[23]

The Divorce Act worked — it accomplished most of the things its proponents hoped and its opponents feared. Once reconciled to the volume of divorces, Respectables ceased worrying about the widsom of divorce court as a social institution. For the remainder of the Victorian era, Respectables whose spouses 'fell' found relief in divorce court:

The Reverend Christopher Newman Hall sought a divorce in 1873 but, as he lacked evidence of his wife's adultery, his petition was dismissed. Six years later he reapplied and was successful — the adultery of 1873 being proved that time.[24]

In 1886 Evelyn Isabel Goldsmid, with £8,000 a year, married

Charles Congleton Bethune, with nothing. He kept a mistress, Mme de Mer, in St John's Wood, pushed Evelyn to the ground once, demanded separate bedrooms, used violent language, and neglected her generally. As this caused her 'mental anguish and injured her health', they were divorced.[25]

Robert Hall, manager of a hosiery shop in London's Oxford Street, married Ada, one of his assistants, in 1890. They separated one month later when he noticed she prayed longer after hearing the Seventh Commandment read at Church. He then learned, by her confession, she had slept with five men before marriage and another since. And that she herself was illegitimate. Her confession that 'I duped you into marriage' 'woefully deceiving' you, 'a Christian young man' overcame the judge's suspicion that this was a put-up case to satisfy Robert's family, who disapproved of the marriage.[26]

The Freegards married in 1849 and had six children before 1873 when they separated after she pawned £40 of items to support her habit of drink. John, a managing clerk for a group of solicitors, paid her an allowance for three years but she then disappeared. In 1880 he, his son, his daughter and a friend all identified a drowned woman found in Hackney Marshes as his wife. He remarried only to have his first wife turn up again in 1882. He immediately ceased living with his second wife and obtained a divorce from his first.[27]

While Respectability came harder to those below the middle class, divorce court records reveal many workers making great efforts:

James Endean, a Cornish miner, married Jane Cudlipp in 1840. After six children, Jane committed adultery with a brushmaker, Samuel Chambers, in 1851 and later married (bigamously) a labourer, John Batten, in 1860. In 1864 James filed a long affidavit about his problems finding enough money to pursue the divorce.[28]

William James Ellson, a Lambeth bricklayer, married Sarah in 1853, but, after one child, she moved in with John Hyman in 1858 and had three children by him. When William sought his divorce in 1866, he explained the delay by his need to save enough money.[29]

Giving relief to these Respectables and others was one side of the Divorce Act; deterring adultery was the other. And the dreaded publicity of a divorce trial kept Respectable couples out of court. The head of Fortnum and Mason, writing to his separated wife, lamented that 'the exposure must be great and withering to all parties'.[30] Efforts to reduce the newspaper coverage of trials — due to their salaciousness — were opposed, even by opponents of divorce, such as Richard Malins, because secret or unreported trials would remove 'that check upon the violation of the marriage vows which the fear of publicity now supplied'.[31] With such a rationale, the press freely published the exotic, and erotic, details, claiming it all as a public service (even as they also enhanced sales). A flutter of complaints about press coverage occurred in the late 1880s with a memorial seeking restrictions presented to the Lord Chancellor bearing hundreds of signatures, including those of W.E. Gladstone, T.H. Huxley and Cardinal Manning. Claiming adultery could be deterred without all the detail of intrigue and deception, the petition got nowhere with the Lord Chancellor or the Home Secretary, though some self-imposed restraint occurred in the press itself.

Improvement of marital morality did seem to result from the Divorce Act. With the costs of divorce reduced in 1857, husbands could use the threat of divorce and its publicity to deter potentially wandering wives. Hippolyte Taine, a French writer touring England in the 1860s, was told he could visit drawing rooms for 18 months without ever meeting an adulteress.[32] But did it deter the husbands themselves? Taine was only told he would not meet an adulteress, not an adulterer. A speaker in the House of Commons had, in an unguarded moment in 1857, suggested nearly the entire House had committed adultery at least once. The loophole, of course, was the double standard, written into divorce law, whereby the husband's adultery when not compounded by cruelty or desertion gave the wife no cause for divorce (though she could get a judicial separation). The double standard had long meant that an occasional adultery, as opposed to a sustained attachment, brought less opprobrium down on the husband:

Emma Bowles Milford, married in 1855, wanted a divorce in 1866. Husband Alfred admitted his adulteries but denied any cruelty. Alfred's adulteries began in 1858 when he 'became very intimate with a lady' at Budleigh Salterton. Against his wife's wishes, he christened their second child after his lady friend and hung a picture of the friend in the house. By 1862 he was consorting with 'Miss B.', asking Emma whether she thought Miss B. pretty. Unfortunately for Emma, the acts of cruelty never put her, in the judge's mind, in any reasonable fear of danger — the legal definition of cruelty. No divorce, only a judicial separation.[33]

The Dickinsons married in 1866. When Mr Dickinson brought his mistress to the family home, Mrs Dickinson told him one of them must leave. He responded that she could do as she liked but his mistress was staying. Mrs Dickinson left and obtained a divorce as the judge believed the husband's conduct forced her to leave; the judge called this, in legal terms, the husband's desertion.[34]

The Kochs lived happily from their marriage in 1872 to 1883 when Mrs Koch discovered her husband 'had formed a liaison with a servant named Mary Mooney'. He refused to stop the adultery or discharge Mary. Mrs Koch left. Justice Gorell Barnes decided this was the husband's desertion as by moral, if not physical, force he drove her from the house.[35]

Ellen Millicent Ashburneu married Walter Sickert, an artist, in 1885. By 1895 she found him unfaithful. After a separation and her forgiveness, he wrote 'it was no use further concealing the fact that he had never been faithful to her and never could be'. She left him and sought a divorce for his adultery and desertion. The judge, again Gorell Barnes, granted the divorce, holding that Walter's conduct obliged his wife to leave him so it was the husband's desertion.[36]

After 40 years the double standard was evened only a little by denying husbands the legal right to persistent adulteries. Curiously, the judges had worked themselves into the position of saying that the wife's departure was the husband's desertion. An easier route would have been to call persistent adultery 'cruelty', but this definition had been settled decades earlier to require illness or fear of violence — late Victorian wives of strong mettle therefore could not claim cruelty.

Wives could obtain judicial separations when their husbands committed adultery but did not desert or become cruel. Although this gave the wife a separate income (if the husband could afford to maintain two households) and freedom to live separately, it also left her, even if totally innocent, with some stigma — at the highest levels separated individuals would not be invited to the royal court:

The Cudlipps married in 1832 and Mr Cudlipp, an attorney, kept moving his practice from Birmingham to Birkenhead and back. After their furniture was sold at a court-ordered sale, Mrs Cudlipp supported herself as a governess. Separation granted, as without a house, she had nowhere to live; her husband deserted her.[37]

After John and Mary Cargill married in 1848, John practised as a physician in Newcastle-upon-Tyne. In 1850, John sent Mary back to her father and went to Australia. When he returned in 1858, he offered to resume cohabitation, but the judge ruled this did not ruin her claim to a separation for his desertion.[38]

Mrs Thompson, the daughter of a publican in Leeds, secretly married Mr Thompson, an engraver, in 1838. His work failed in 1842 and he went to London seeking employment. His letters to his wife went unanswered as Mrs Thompson's father, who opposed the marriage all along, forced her to break all communications. The letters reveal a man first puzzled and then hurt by his wife's silence; eventually he gave up writing altogether as he concluded she wanted to having nothing further to do with him. The husband's actions did not constitute desertion and no separation was granted.[39]

For the half century after 1857 divorces outnumbered separations four to one and wives sought separations ten times more often than husbands — one effect of the double standard. Judicial separations did not offer a satisfactory solution to Respectables and certainly did not to unRespectables, who wanted to be free to marry again.

This problem led to the fear that a husband would 'accept' a charge of adultery in order to escape a marriage — a fear which pervaded thinking for the rest of the century after 1857. Collusion between spouses, usually to suppress evidence of mutual guilt (which quashed a divorce), was thought common, and certainly the bulk of divorce petitions were unopposed in any real sense. One reason, of course, arose from the facts of divorce; adultery was a provable fact and usually indefensible. Numerous couples, once the facts were known, came to an arrangement, perhaps after much acrimony, before the suit commenced so opposition did not appear. The spectre, and the reality, of collusion produced an amendment to the Divorce Act in 1860 which gave the Attorney-General, acting through a divorce court official called the Queen's Proctor, the power to intervene in suits to prove collusion. To give the Queen's Proctor time to prove his case, a waiting period of three months (lengthened to six months in 1866) was established between the end of the trial (when the judge pronounced a decree *nisi*) and the date the divorce became effective (decree absolute):

> Mr Hechler proved his wife's adultery with Mr Bennett in a trial in 1888. The Queen's Proctor, finding evidence of Mr Hechler's adultery and the couple's collusion to cover it up, intervened. The judge rescinded the decree *nisi*, dismissed the petition for divorce, and put the costs of the entire suit, including those of Mr Bennett and the Queen's Proctor, on the husband.[40]

> In 1885 the Butlers sued one another for divorce. At the trial, Mrs Butler testified about her husband's adultery with 'Miss W.' and his cruelty. Because Mr Butler did not proceed against his wife, despite his petition, the judge grew suspicious and sought the Queen's Proctor's intervention. An agreement to suppress evidence was found: 'Petitioner (Mrs Butler) to give evidence of cruelty to the satisfaction of Court, and of the respondent's adultery with Miss W., and if the Court was satisfied on that evidence the decree for dissolution was to go. The petitioner accepted her husband's denial as to adultery with Mrs J., and being satisfied that the witnesses who deposed to adultery with Miss S. and Miss —— were mistaken as to identity, withdrew the charge. The husband's petiton should be withdrawn, and he should pay a lump sum to his wife in lieu of alimony, and the costs of the suit.' Divorce denied for collusion.[41]

Throughout the remainder of the century the Queen's Proctor received notice of suspicion, usually from the divorce court judge, and investigated the couple's conduct. Stopping divorces in about 5 per cent of the suits, this official was a fearsome shadow looking over all proceedings. Because of him, couples whose marriages were breaking up could not throw caution to the winds. Restraint, the appearance of Respectability even, had to be maintained, although the divorce itself would destroy their Respectability.

Any notions that divorce might be romantic — leaving a cold husband to marry a sympathetic lover — were soon dispelled by the suits themselves. Wives' petitions, needing to allege cruelty or desertion, meant up to 40 per cent — the proportion of wives' petitions — of the proceedings produced evidence of physical violence or callous feelings:

> Jane and Thomas Scott married in 1840 and she immediately took to drink. She hit him with a poker, threatened him with a knife, and

threw a glass at him. So much for submissive wives![42]

The Astropes were united in 1847 but separated in 1854. In 1856 he was arrested for embezzlement, was twice imprisoned for debt, and was living with his mistress.[43]

Frederick William Dickens, the novelist's brother, was sued for non-payment of maintenance in 1861. The couple, judicially separated in 1859, disagreed regularly. He did not pay her £60 per year maintenance and was declared bankrupt in 1862, which wiped out his arrears. The couple repeatedly appeared in court to fight over money.[44]

Men carried their notions of authority to such levels as denying wives access to children within their own homes, enforcing periods of silence, forcing wives into prostitution, and engaging in physical violence. Drunkenness represented much of the problem, but the judge repeatedly refused to permit habitual drunkenness to be sufficient grounds for divorce; it would 'have a wide application', the judge declared.[45] Artists faithfully reflected this view of adultery as fundamentally unhappy. Respectability triumphed again, and Tennyson, as usual, mirrored society's beliefs with his *Idylls of the King*, which paints adultery in very unromantic colours. Similarly, William Morris's portrayal of Queen Guenevere succeeded in 1858 in further staining the happy myth about England's past.

Satisfaction with the divorce court remained high and even the cost of divorce brought little criticism before the 1890s. The early reports reveal many people in such occupations as service, bootmaking, and dressmaking. In 1871 — the only year for which a systematic study of occupations exists — slightly under 20 per cent of petitions came from the working classes, while gentry and professionals accounted for over 40 per cent. In 1881 *The Times*, stretching the truth a bit, wrote, 'The Divorce Court was avowedly established for the benefit of the poor' and the divorce court judge described most of the parties as poor. However, both these statements were connected with, as some saw it, an epidemic of aristocratic divorces and were made to defuse criticisms of the court and that high-born group. By the 1890s *Reynolds' News*, a working-class newspaper, discussed *in forma pauperis* procedures, but the costs, when uncontested divorces still could exceed £30, and when the yearly income of skilled artisans — 'the aristocracy of the working class' — might be £100, put divorce out of the reach of many. Divorce, like Respectability, divided society on lines other than class as workers separated into Respectable and Low, rich into Respectable and Fast, and the middle class into Respectable and Rest. Until Respectability was claimed by large numbers of workers, criticisms of the divorce court based on its expensiveness had little impact on those who mattered — judges, MPs and the press.[46]

Like the poor, children attracted little attention in divorce. In 1871, 40 per cent of the suits involved childless couples, a marked contrast with the rest of Victorian society.[47] Moreover, the structure of divorces meant children had been disposed of before the proceeding — wives who eloped with lovers and husbands who deserted mates had left their children also. Adding to this, the presence of servants to help care for children and strong legal presumptions about who got custody at what age meant fights between parents rarely involved the divorce court in the matter of the children.

Whenever the custody of children was involved, the decision of the judge rested partly on what would be beneficial for the children as well as what would further the purposes of the Divorce Act:

Mrs Hyde sought a judicial separation from Mr Hyde in 1859 as well as the custody of their son, aged 13. As Mr Hyde, a publican in Gravesend, was living with another woman, Mrs Hyde was given custody so the boy might not see his father's evil example and Mrs Hyde could avoid visiting the house of her husband's mistress.[48]

The D'Altons married in 1867, while Roman Catholics, and had two sons. Mr D'Alton became a Protestant, however, and the strains led to a break up of the marriage. A judicial separation was decreed in 1877 (as a Roman Catholic, Mrs D'Alton did not seek a divorce although she had the necessary evidence) and then the child custody fight broke out. He had put the boys in a Protestant school but, during early negotiations over the judicial separation, had promised they could be raised as Roman Catholics. The judge was clearly in a dilemma as husbands normally had the right to control their children's religion but this husband had promised otherwise. The resolution left the boys at the Protestant school but their overall custody went to a third party.[49]

The Chetwynds had also lost custody of their children and the divorce court developed no clear pattern in this area.

Not only did the various aspects of divorce work satisfactorily, at least for Respectables, but the various groups involved in the great debates of the 1850s found nothing to encourage a resurrection of the issue. The Divorce Act silenced feminists. The inclusion of provisions protecting the earnings of deserted wives 'took the wind out' of feminist sails. Only in 1870 could minor changes in this area be obtained from Parliament and it was 1884 before the protections widened to include married women's property generally. The committee founded by Barbara Leigh Smith in 1855 to fight for such laws passed out of existence, and a new generation of women needed to form a new committee in the 1860s. Feminists often fought, in the decade after 1857, not so much to obtain more rights and responsibilities, as to prevent inroads into existing ones. For nearly two decades the battles over the regulation of prostitution, dominated feminist minds.

Since the 1830s, divorce, as a social issue, had been a risky topic for writers, a situation feminists knew. In the early 1860s *Englishwoman's Domestic Magazine,* a feminist organ founded in the late 1850s, carried a review of Caroline Norton's novel *Lost and Saved.* The latter half of the review, a long quote from John Milton, turned out to be the final paragraph of his *The Doctrine and Discipline of Divorce.* Milton's passage did not mention divorce explicitly, and the entire review never used the word 'divorce' because 'whoever deals with it does so with a halter on, under Locrian law'. (Under the constitution of Locri, an ancient Greek city-state, anyone proposing a change in the laws did so with a hangman's noose around his neck. If the proposal failed, he was hanged.) Feminists, whatever their opinions, avoided divorce as a topic.[50]

Feminism, never very Respectable because of its contacts with radicals, artists, and writers, was further damaged by the brush of one of its members with the divorce court:

Admiral Codrington sued Helen Jane Codrington for a divorce in 1864, and she countered claiming rape and cruelty. His evidence proved her adulteries, especially in Malta, with army officers. Helen's evidence was to be that he attempted to rape Emily Faithfull. Emily, a feminist and founder of an all-female printing business, was a childhood friend of Helen's. Originally, Emily's story was that, when Emily and Helen were sleeping in the same bed, the Admiral attempted to rape Emily. But, by the trial, the Admiral had intimidated her (how is unclear) and she denied the attempted rape, saying she was asleep all the time. Helen's lawyer then said Emily had told him the rape succeeded. The Admiral got his divorce and remarried, and Helen disappeared from sight. Emily, though badly damaged by the entire mess, remained active in feminist causes until her death in 1895.[51]

And the active feminist, Emily Ashurst Venturi, editor of *The Shield*, was divorced but her work was unimpeded. Feminism and divorce did not intertwine; the law of 1857 saw to that.

Law reformers rested satisfied with their work in 1857, and law reform stalled as it husbanded its strength to tackle the remaining major problem, the division of equity and common law, in the 1870s. Very minor amendments to the Divorce Act in 1858, 1859 and 1860 were followed by later, occasional changes, but no substantial alteration occurred in grounds, procedures, costs, or results. Opponents, too, abandoned the issue. While W.E. Gladstone, vociferous opponent in 1857, as late as 1889 could still write an article in the *North American Review* opposing divorce, few actively attempted to abolish divorce, even when given the opportunity of a technical amendment to the Divorce Act before Parliament.

The Church of England, on whose behalf Gladstone waged the battles of 1857, lurched into murkier water as the divorce of church and state of 1857 widened into a divorce between religion and educated thought in the 1860s. *Essays and Reviews*, published in 1860, put the case for biblical criticism in English life; two of its writers were convicted of heresy. J.W. Colenso, Bishop of Natal, was excommunicated for publishing a book, responding to Zulu questions, attacking the literal truth of the Bible. The Privy Council, in both instances, undid the church's judgment but, though the Broad Churchmen won the battles to make the criticisms, they lost the war of knowledge as clergy retreated further into High Church positions. Liturgy and ritual superseded the search for knowledge, and the divorce of church and state proceeded, each ignoring the other.

Educated thought, bothered by the pettiness of church matters, received another challenge in the form of Charles Darwin's *Origin of the Species*, published in 1859. Ideas about evolution had been floating around for years — even poets had been discussing them since the 1830s — and Darwin's work only completed what had long been started: the rejection of the Bible as conflicting with knowledge of science and history.

Ironically, the church's inability to grasp the new challenge of biblical criticism and religious doubt cost it the divorce battle. By the 1860s thoughtful churchmen believed Jesus had specifically forbade divorce;

any words to the contrary in the New Testament were later interpolations. If this belief had been presented in 1857, divorce could not have passed as the House of Commons would not have contradicted Jesus' words. The church, however, did not take any firm position until 1888 when a world-wide conference of Anglican bishops reaffirmed opposition to the remarriage of the guilty party. Even then, the church accepted divorce for adultery, so badly digested was the biblical criticism, and by the time the church might seek to abolish divorce, educated thought and the House of Commons were no longer listening to church voices.

Dissent, despite a new awakening and mass conversions in 1859, lost vigour and began a long, slow slide in popularity and influence. Nevertheless, in 1870 the battles over religion and education showed plenty of muscle in the Dissenting arm and Charles Stewart Parnell, the politician hounded from political influence by a divorce suit in 1889, offered ample testimony to the strength of the 'Noncomformist Conscience' — a term coined during his disgrace. As Respectability meant no divorce, the issue of divorce rarely raised itself in practical terms. Though the clergy of the Church of England agitated in the 1890s for further relief from the ability of divorced people to use parish churches to remarry, the matter arose more from internal church manoeuvrings than from any glut of remarriage applications. More importantly for Dissent, and to a slightly lesser extent for the Church of England too, religious belief and membership usually meant Respectability. Respectability meant no divorce so the various bodies never dealt with the matter at first hand.

Many thoughtful people, ceasing to believe in religion, at least traditional Christianity, turned to applying the techniques of science to society. Lord Brougham, in addition to his efforts for a new divorce law in 1857, helped found the National Association for the Promotion of Social Science. Including leading thinkers and politicians — Lord Shaftesbury, John Stuart Mill, Charles Kingsley, John Ruskin, Edwin Chadwick — this organisation sought to uncover the 'moral laws of the universe'. While a paper entitled 'The Law of Marriage and Divorce as at Present Existing in England, Ireland, and Scotland' appeared in 1861, the association turned to other areas — education, prisons and public health. The family, a favourite topic of twentieth-century social science, was ignored, largely because Victorians were so unanimous that studies would be superfluous. The few investigators, be they social scientists like Henry Maine (*Ancient Laws*) or churchmen like F.D. Maurice, found in the family the basis of society. No surprises there!

So secure were the Victorians about their divorce law that press reports concerning divorce in other countries always contained an unstated assumption that all would do well to conform to English standards. Like the Empire! The various states of the United States provided much copy as the statistics flowed in from 'the land of the free'. Figures revealing that Connecticut and Ohio produced one divorce for every eleven marriages served to emphasise the unRespectability of the Great Republic. An American, who, after his former wife remarried, discovered he still loved her, committed suicide in her Parisian hotel after she rejected him — such were the consequences of easy American divorce.[52] All was confirmed in 1889 when the United States Department of Labor published a report on divorce which suggested divorce had become a threat to the social order. The various states of the American republic permitted more divorce than all of Europe combined!

Countries lacking a divorce law, on the other hand, appeared backward to English Victorians. Canada still had legislative divorce until the 1890s and Australia's Divorce Bill in 1890 underwent opposition similar to that in England in 1857 as the churches opposed the Bill and the Anglican church refused to remarry the divorced. Still harsher criticism was reserved for European countries dominated by the Roman Catholic Church. *The Times* followed developments in France and the newly unified Italy as well as the papal *curia*, and satisfaction with England's solution beamed from the pages.

England, centre of commerce and one of Europe's easier places to obtain a divorce, attracted Continental couples — though so long as the United States provided easy divorces, England never became a divorce haven:

The Duchess de Santo Teodora sought a divorce in 1876 from the Duke, a Neapolitan nobleman. The Duchess, granddaughter of Admiral Tollemache and an English heiress with £120,000, married in 1854 only after agreements had been signed that the couple would reside annually in England for six months and on the Continent six months. In 1860, after a fight, the Duke threatened to put her in a convent, which by Neapolitan law he had the power to do. Mobilising her connections, the Duchess got Prime Minister Palmerston to cast his blanket of protection of a British subject over her, and, after the British Legation at Naples withstood the local gendarmes, the couple resumed cohabitation. However, the Duke soon took up with 'an opera singer' and refused to spend six months a year in England.[53]

In 1866 the DeBarros, Portuguese subjects and cousins aged 14 and 16, came to London to be married. The wife, daughter of a failing Portuguese businessman, was induced to marry her cousin in order to save some of the property of her soon bankrupt father, who subsequently went insane. A decade later the couple sought to nullify the marriage as, being cousins, it was not valid in Portugal and the entire undertaking had been a sham as they never intended to reside in England and never consummated the marriage.[54]

The success of the Divorce Act came from its close connection with Respectability. Many qualities made up a Respectable: rational (unless a woman), emotional (unless a man), responsible (not frivolous), public spirited (not selfish), thrifty and temperate (not dissipated), religious (or at least moral), and so on. But uniting all was 'seriousness', a seriousness about life. While this need not mean no laughing, it could. The Earl of Shaftesbury, eminently Respectable and seriously engaged with reform legislation all his life, received letters and sermons arguing that smiling was not a sin, though he remained unconvinced, and dour, to his death. To Respectables life was not funny but people could be ridiculous. Anyone could feel superior — and feeling superior was one consequence (and unintentional purpose?) of Respectability — to those who involved themselves in ridiculous situations:

Louis Clovis Bonaparte, son of Prince Louis Lucien Bonaparte, sought to nullify his marriage to Rosalie on the grounds of bigamy. Rosalie married Norfolk Bernard Megone in 1884; Megone sought to divorce her in 1885 but his petition was dismissed for collusion. Bonaparte and the Megones then went to Scotland where Mr Megone, a tea merchant, established a (sham) office for his business in Edinburgh and thereby claimed Scottish domicile. (Bonaparte paid for all of this.) Megone obtained his divorce, and Bonaparte married Rosalie at the Isle of Man. In 1891 Bonaparte and a solicitor defrauded Rosalie of her jewels, worth £20,000, which Bonaparte then gave to Laura Scott to induce her to marry him (he was still married to Rosalie). Rosalie sought a divorce for Bonaparte's bigamy but failed to allege his adultery (apparently the marriage with Laura went unconsummated). Next Bonaparte sought the nullity on the grounds that the Scottish divorce was a fraud on the Scottish court.[55]

Nothing exhibited people in ridiculous situations more often than the divorce court, and Respectable society was amused.

After the shock about the flood of petitions in the first years after 1857 wore off, divorce passed from the limelight and the occasional references — and lack of effort to change the law — suggesting Respectables were satisfied with the law and its effects. The number of petitions, growing from around 200 in 1860 to over 550 in 1900 outstripped the increase in the marital population, and divorce was twice as common in 1900 as it had been in 1860. But no one noticed. In 1900, for every 20,000 married couples in England and Wales, fewer than three sought divorce in any year. (By contrast, of such 20,000 couples in 1980, over 240 would seek a divorce in that year.)

The world, thought Respectables, would do well to imitate the English model — the *via media* between American licence and Roman Catholic backwardness. When the French approached a divorce law in the years after 1875, the English watched, with relish. After the fears induced by various French revolutions, the annoyance of the 1830s over French ideas about the place of women, and the disgust with French novels at mid-century, the English took great pleasure in observing the struggles of French liberals against Roman Catholic opposition. When success came in 1884, *The Times* congratulated the nation across the Channel and thought the effect of the new divorce law 'will be to make the French a much more serious people than they are today'.[56] If the English thought a divorce law could make the French Respectable, its success at home must have been indeed unlimited.

Notes

1. *The Times,* 23rd June, 1865; *Hansard,* vol. 151, col. 567; *The Times,* 12th January, 1859.
2. *Punch,* 5th September, 1857; *Hansard* vol. 151, col. 1386.
3. A.C. Benson and Viscount Esher (eds.), *Letters of Queen Victoria* (J. Murray, London, 1907) vol. 3, p.482.
4. *The Times,* 21st June, 1859.
5. *The Times,* 4th December, 1858.
6. 29 *Law Reports* 28; *Hansard,* vol. 151, col. 860, vol. 160, col. 1734.
7. *The Times,* 6th December, 1858.
8. *The Times,* 7th February, 1859.
9. *House of Commons Command Papers,* 1862 (99), xliv, 503.
10. G. M. Young, *Portrait of England,* annotated edition (Oxford University Press, London, 1977) pp.171, 42; Lee Holcombe, *Wives and Property* (University of Toronto Press, Toronto, 1983) pp.131, 120.
11. 32 *Law Reports* 178.
12. *The Times,* 6th December, 1865.
13. 27 *Law Reports* 16.
14. 28 *Law Reports* 64.
15. Ibid..
16. *The Times,* 17th December, 1859.
17. Ibid., 7th February, 1859.
18. Ibid., 11th January, 20th, 27th, 30th July, 4th November, 17th and 22nd, 23rd December, 1864, 13th, 16th, 19th, 21st January, 1865; 34 *Law Reports* 65, 130; 35 *Law Reports* 21; John Vincent (ed.), *Disraeli, Derby and the Conservative Party, Journals and Memoirs of Edward Henry, Lord Stanley 1849–1869* (Harper & Row, New York, 1978) pp.226, 371, 374 n.1; I thank Professor John Vincent and Nicola Vincent for calling additional details of the suit to my attention.
19. 27 *Law Reports* 57; 29 *Law Reports* 178.
20. *The Times,* February and March, 1885.
21. Ibid., 4th December, 1858.
22. Ibid., 3rd March, 1866.
23. *Hansard,* vol. 151, col. 1860; *The Times,* 28th May, 1867.
24. *The Times,* 14th May, 1879.
25. Ibid., 23rd June, 1890.
26. Ibid., 24th March, 1891.
27. 52 *Law Reports* 100; *The Times,* 6th June, 1883.
28. PRO, J77/17.
29. Ibid..
30. 28 *Law Reports* 64.
31. *Hansard,* vol. 160, col. 626.
32. Hippolyte Taine, *Notes on England* (Isbister, London, 1874) p.99.
33. 36 *Law Reports* 30.
34. 62 *Law Times* 330.
35. 67 *Law Reports* 90.
36. 68 *Law Reports* 114.
37. 27 *Law Reports* 64.
38. 27 *Law Reports* 69.
39. 27 *Law Reports* 65.
40. 58 *Law Reports* 27.
41. 59 *Law Reports* 11.
42. 29 *Law Reports* 64.
43. 29 *Law Reports* 27.

44. 28 *Law Reports* 94. *The Times,* 25th January, 18th April, 2nd June, 2nd, 16th, 23rd July, 1862.

45. 31 *Law Reports* 46; *The Times,* 6th December, 1865.

46. *The Times,* 21st April, 1882; *Reynolds' News,* 5th July, 1891, cited in Griselda Rowntree and Norman H. Carrier, 'The Resort to Divorce in England and Wales, 1858–1957', *Population Studies,* 11 (1958) p.198.

47. Rowntree and Carrier, 'The Resort to Divorce in England and Wales, 1858–1957', p.226.

48. 29 *Law Reports* 150.

49. 47 *Law Reports* 59.

50. *Englishwoman's Domestic Magazine,* 7 (1859) pp.140–2.

51. William Fredeman, 'Emily Faithfull and the Victoria Press', *The Library,* fifth series, xxix (1974) p.139: James Stone, 'More Light on Emily Faithfull and the Victoria Press,' *The Library,* fifth series, xxxiii (1978) p.63; *The Times,* 30th July, 1864.

52. *The Times,* 28th June, 1879, 2nd September, 1879, 26th February, 1874.

53. 49 *Law Reports* 20.

54. 49 *Law Reports* 1; 45 *Law Reports* 43.

55. *The Times,* 18th November, 1891, 13th January, 20th July, 2nd August, 1892; 63 *Law Reports* 1.

56. *The Times,* 11th August, 1884.

6 Victorian Hypocrisy

The Divorce Bill received the royal assent on 28th August, 1857. In that same year the three Dickens brothers, including the writer Charles, left their wives, and Marian Evans, known to us as George Eliot, moved in with G. H. Lewes, a married man. The wife of the writer and poet George Meredith went holidaying that hot summer in Wales with her lover, the painter Henry Wallis, and conceived a son. Though diaries and correspondence reveal remarkably little about discussions involving divorce, Victorians did take stock of marriage and their marriages. Few, however, followed these inhabitants of the literary world whose pasts or hoped-for futures precluded divorce, even under the less expensive proceedings. Though challenged repeatedly, Respectability reigned supreme for the rest of Victoria's reign, and into that of her unRespectable son. However, developments, sometimes paralleling the history of divorce discussed in Chapter 5 and more than occasionally involving the divorce court, led to the charge of hypocrisy so often levelled against Victorians.

Many groups, in addition to the literary crowd, found reasons to fear the divorce court in the half century after 1857, though the apprehensions, and silliness, of Charles Dickens, after his separation in 1857, led the way as he published a statement of his marital problems and reasons for his actions which convinced few. Another writer, George Meredith, always more realistic in his works than Dickens, dealt with the problems of marriage in *The Ordeal of Richard Feverel*, published in 1859. Meredith laid the groundwork of his novel by sketching out the consequences to the family when the mother elopes, in this case with a 'greasy' poet turned guitar-player who had been the best friend of the father at university. Here the result was traditional in that the lovers fell on hard financial times and the mother was totally eliminated from her son's life. Meredith, however, then went further and became more topical when he introduced a *demi-monde*. A new type of woman in the 1850s, best exemplified by Catherine Walters, popularly known as 'Skittles', these *demi-mondes* — the term came from a play by Alexandre Dumas *fils* in 1855 — fascinated men, and women. Nothing but high-priced prostitutes to Respectables, *demi-mondes* nevertheless set the pace in clothing, slang and behaviour. 'Skittles' herself had a long affair with Lord Hartington, a leading Liberal politician and future Duke of Devonshire, and Aubrey de Vere Beauclerk's fascination with her in 1862 was cited as only one example of his many adulteries during his wife's divorce proceedings in 1890. *Demi-mondes* were so common that some said Hyde Park was impassable when they and their admirers all turned out.

When George Meredith, in *The Ordeal of Richard Feverel,* included a *demi-monde* as the agent of ruin of a young married man, he did no more than paint a picture often feared by Respectable parents. Nevertheless, the scene was so torrid that it cost him sales to Mudie's library, the largest circulating library of the day, which was concerned about the Respectability of the work.[1] Meredith devoted one chapter to the kiss — such was the nature of the 'fall' — between his hero and the *demi-monde*, Mrs Mount (made acceptable to readers by being a lord's wife — the choice of surname apparently attracted no notice):

A white visage reappeared behind a spring of flame. Her black hair was scattered over her shoulders and fell half across her brows. She moved slowly, and came up to him, fastening weird eyes on him, pointing a finger at the region of witches. Sepulchral cadences accompanied the representation. He did not listen for he was thinking what a deadly charming and exquisitely horrid witch she was.

Was it the champagne? the music? or the poetry? Something of the two former, perhaps: but most the enchantress playing upon him. How many instruments cannot clever women play upon at the same moment!

'If I change — if I can change . . . Oh! if you could know what a net I'm in, Richard!'

Now at those words, as he looked down on her haggard loveliness, not divine sorrow but a devouring jealousy sprang like fire in his breast, and set him rocking with horrid pain. He bent closer to her pale beseeching face. Her eyes still drew him down.

'Bella! No! no! promise me! swear it!'

'Lost! Richard! lost for ever! give me up!'

He cried: 'I never will!' and strained her in his arms, and kissed her passionately on the lips.

She was not acting now as she sidled and slunk her half-averted head with a kind of maiden shame under his arm, sighing heavily, weeping, clinging to him. It was wicked truth.

Not a word of love between them!

Was ever hero in this fashion won?'

Meredith's use of contemporary material challenging marriage appeared tame by the 1860s. Already in 1857 Parliament, reacting to the pressure of the Society for the Suppression of Vice (usually known as the Vice Society), passed the Obscene Publications Act. Directed at the sale of pornography in London's Holywell Street, the Act constituted England's first legislative attack on such material but the police enforcement was occasional. Another market, not openly pornographic, sprang up when 'sensation novels' sought to exploit legitimate concerns about the marital bond as well as Respectable willingness to be titillated by the sins of others. Bigamy plots occupied many of the sensation novels (bigamy was romantic, divorce ruins a plot by solving the problems) and only Mrs Henry Wood, in *East Lynne,* succeeded in using divorce as a theme:[2]

> Archibald Carlyle, a very Respectable and prospering county solicitor, married, out of pity, Lady Isabel, daughter of the profligate, bankrupt, and soon dead Lord Mount Severn. Lady Isabel entered this inferior marriage, unloving, because she was penniless with no one to turn to. After excruciating pages of details about feelings, Lady Isabel, mistakenly believing Archibald loved another, ran off to France with Francis Levison. Archibald divorced her and, after hearing she was killed in a train crash, married another. (By delaying the remarriage until the first wife's death, the author avoided antagonising Anglicans.) In fact, Lady Isabel survived the wreck but was badly scarred. Levison abandons Lady Isabel when his uncle dies and a baronetcy passes to him — he, in his new position, could not marry a divorced woman. Lady Isabel returns to England in disguise and becomes the governess, unrecognised except by a maid, in Archibald's household so that she can be near her children. After watching her young son die, she dies of her suffering, revealing herself only at the end. In an elaborate sub-plot, Levison is found guilty of a murder many years earlier and transported. Justice for the adultery is complete!

Mrs Wood's rewards for this plot included sales of over half a million and a plagiarised melodrama which remained popular for the rest of the century. (Despite the stereotypical characters she portrayed, Mrs Wood herself supported Mr Wood for years by her writing — he was a failure in business. Such were the varieties of Victorian families.) On a different plane George Eliot, still safely in the arms of G.H. Lewes, created situations where near-adultery provided the tensions for readers not willing to view the scenes painted by Meredith and Wood. The fate of these authors' works did not go unnoticed by them and others, as Meredith, today seen as the most serious thinker of the three, had the least commercial success with his books and Mrs Wood, whose work is now ignored in literary studies, made a nice living from her sales.

Artists prided themselves on being different. William Morris, struck dumb by the beauty of Jane Burden, daughter of an Oxford stable-hand, married her, but the marriage was a disaster. Jane, a 'stunner' whose countenance graces so many Pre-Raphaelite paintings, became sickly and melancholy and by 1870 was having an affair with Dante Gabriel Rossetti. All remained friendly, the threesome living together for a few years, while Morris moved towards, but probably never had, an affair with Georgiana Burne-Jones, his best friend's wife. John Millais rescued Effie Gray from her terrible marriage to John Ruskin; she obtained an annulment on the ground of non-consummation after seven years of marriage. When artists turned from life to art, their success was not great, either. Augustus Egg's three-picture series, entitled *Past and Present*, exhibited at the Royal Academy in 1858, traced, in melodramatic scenes, the fall of the unfaithful wife from middle-class comfort and emotional security to abject poverty under London's Blackfriars Bridge. The scenes were so painful that no one would buy the series. Artists and writers learned, if they did not already know, that Respectables dominated the market and failure to meet their standards forfeited sales. Dickens was well justified to worry about the effects of his marital discord on his financial affairs.

Respectability never was accepted by all inhabitants of the British Isles and some unRespectables were quite prepared to use the divorce court to escape their marriages:

> Dame Frances Weller Gethin sued Sir Richard Gethin for a divorce in 1861. Sir Richard, in the early 1850s had been guilty of adultery but, under the Parliamentary system, she could not divorce him as no incest or bigamy was involved. In 1856 Sir Richard asked Dame Frances to commit an adultery so they could divorce. The judge had to rule on the issue of collusion — there was none, he decided, as both acted independently of the other — but the whole affair reveals no fear of divorce court in this couple.[3100]

> General Latour sued Une Cameron Barclay Latour for a divorce in 1861. They had married in 1826 and she eloped with George Miles in 1833. The General won a crim. con. suit for £1,500 in 1834 as

well as his suit in the Court of Arches in 1838. For the last 25 years he had been living with another woman. Divorce denied due to delay and mutual guilt.[4]

Many individual artistocrats had no desire to be thought Respectable but the aristocracy as a group, like artists and writers, came to fear the divorce court, though more slowly and for different reasons. Throughout the century a 'fast' set existed where marital fidelity was not highly valued. From the Pagets in 1800 divorces ran through their descendants and relations, eventually involving the Prince of Wales and his Marlborough House set (see Figure 6.1). Henry Bayly Paget, first Earl of Uxbridge, had two sons who figured in three divorces — Sir Arthur Paget married the divorced Augusta Vane (he was the co-respondent) and Henry Paget, the first Marquis of Anglesey, eloped with Charlotte, daughter of the divorced Earl of Cadogan and wife of Henry Wellesley who divorced her, causing a divorce from Caroline, daughter of the fourth Earl of Jersey. Two of the children of the first Marquis of Anglesey became involved in divorces, as did his great-grandson's wife. Two of his grandchildren married into the Chetwynd-Talbot families, which produced the fighting Chetwynds in 1865. The seventh Earl of Cardigan — of the charge of the Light Brigade — was the lover in a divorce in 1826, the defendant in a highly publicised crim. con. suit with Lord William Paget in 1842, and the owner of Deene Park which Respectables would not visit in the early 1860s. The Pagets married into and associated with families where divorces occurred, and the entire group was joined by the Prince of Wales for the last third of the century.

Another noble family, the Pellews, had marital problems from 1820 when the future Viscount Exmouth divorced Elizabeth Barlow (herself the daughter of Sir George Barlow who divorced in 1813). The Viscount's brother, Fleetwood, married Harriet Webster (whose mother was divorced in 1797 so she could marry Lord Holland) and their grandson eloped in 1849 with the Countess of Lincoln, whose husband promptly divorced her, Gladstone providing the evidence. Fleetwood's second marriage, after Harriet died, to Cecile, Countess de Melfort, ended in divorce in 1859 and she married the future Earl of Berkeley, himself the descendant of a family with more than its fair share of marital confusion (see Figure 6.2). Naughtiness among the aristocracy did not begin with the Prince of Wales or only in the 1880s; it had existed throughout the whole century. The Prince's involvement, however, made for more publicity and criticism.

The Prince of Wales certainly played his part in making Victorians look like hypocrites. That he survived to become king is a tribute to Respectable support of hierarchy and order as necessary pillars of English society. Edward, Prince of Wales, described by Walter Bagehot, an insightful writer of the 1860s, as 'an unemployed youth', was denied any significant royal duties by his mother, Queen Victoria, at least partially because he was so indiscreet. His intellectual powers impressed no one and his most serious reading included such works as *East Lynne,* though the moral lessons of that work had no obvious effect on his behaviour. At least as early as 1861 he was misbehaving and shortly afterwards he was nearly blackmailed for conduct with Giulia Barucci, a stunning courtesan in Paris. At about the same time he was beseeched by Lady Susan Vane Tempest, a daughter of the Duke of Newcastle (whose divorce in 1850 later caused Gladstone such embarrassment). Lady Susan, a widow, whose improvident marriage cost her the affection of her parents and her in-laws, was probably pregnant with the Prince's child. In 1870 the Prince was even in divorce court in connection with 'the Warwickshire scandal':[5]

Sir Charles Mordaunt, aged 32 and the MP for South Warwickshire, married Harriet Moncrieffe, aged 18 and only daughter of Sir Thomas Moncrieffe of that Ilk, seventh baronet, in 1866. Claiming she did not marry for love and believing adultery is 'what everybody does', she commenced a life, unknown to her husband, of casual adulteries with several men, including Lord Cole, Sir Frederick Johnstone, and Captain Farquhar. After two miscarriages, she conceived a child by Lord Cole while Sir Charles was on a fishing holiday in Norway. Subsequently, a casual conversation with her husband about Sir Frederick Johnstone — 'Why isn't he married?' 'The rumour is that he has a disease which can be conveyed to his children' — educated her about venereal disease. Too late. When the child was born, the combination of her adulterous past and fear of venereal disease caused Harriet great worry about the child's health, especially its eyes. When the three–day–old child's eyes began showing the anticipated problem, Harriet rapidly went insane. She confessed all. 'Charlie, you are not the father of that child. Lord Cole is the father of it, and I am the cause of its blindness.' After she told the vicar's wife 'I only did it two or three times in London,' the vicar refused to church her because of the scandal. (Also he owed the living to Sir Charles.) By the date of the trial, less than a year after the baby's birth, Harriet was completely insane. Now very plump, she was uncommunicative, sometimes relieved herself on the floor and

Figure 6.1: The Pagets, their Marriages and their Friends

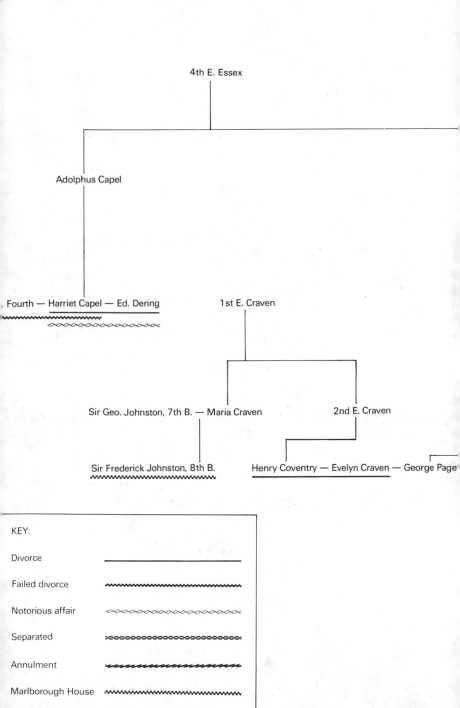

ohn Capel — Caroline Paget
Sir Charles Paget
6th E. Essex
Algernon Capel — Caroline Paget
2nd M. Anglesey — Ellen Burnard — James B
ouisa Heneage — George Paget
M. Hastings — Florence Paget — Sir George Chetwynd, 4th
3rd M. Anglesey
5th M. Anglesey — Lilian Chetwynd

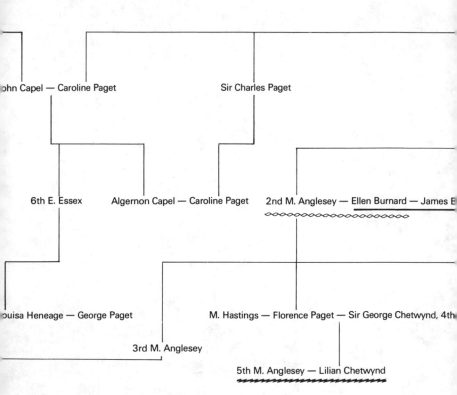

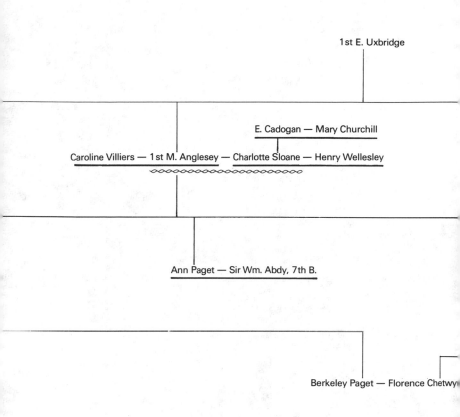

1st E. Uxbridge

E. Cadogan — Mary Churchill

Caroline Villiers — 1st M. Anglesey — Charlotte Sloane — Henry Wellesley

Ann Paget — Sir Wm. Abdy, 7th B.

Berkeley Paget — Florence Chetwy

Sir Geo. Chetwynd, 2nd B.
Wm. Paget — Francis Rottenbu
Blanche Talbot — Wm. Chetwynd
Sir. Geo. Chetwynd, 3rd B.
Sir. Geo. Chetwynd, 4th B.

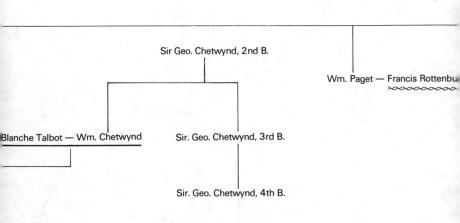

Alfred Paget
Richard Gardiner
Gerald Paget — Lucy Gardiner
Mina Gardiner — Ch. Beresford

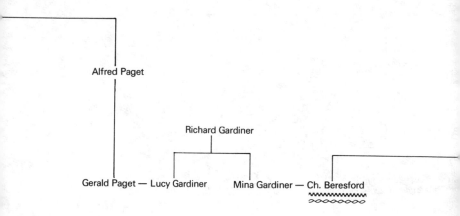

2nd M. Waterford
4th M. Waterford
arcus Beresford
5th M. Waterford — Florence Grosvenor — John Vivian

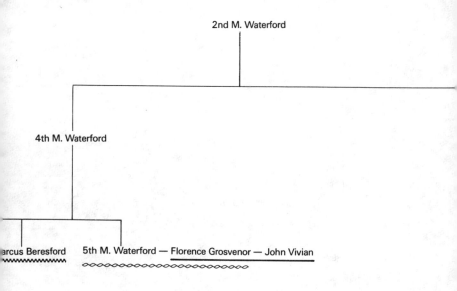

2nd E. Talbot
ara Beresford — 18th E. Shrewsbury
Arthur Talb
19th E. Shrewsbury
Wm. Chetwynd — Blanche Talb
0th E. Shrewsbury — Ellen Mundy

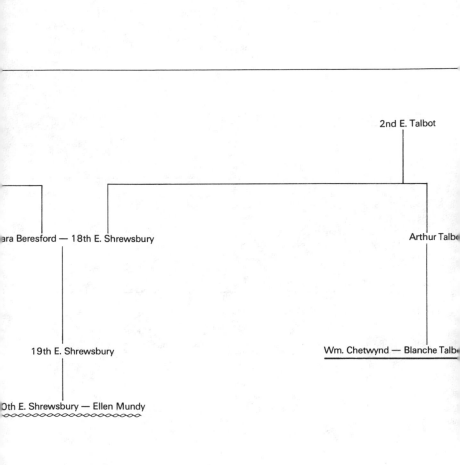

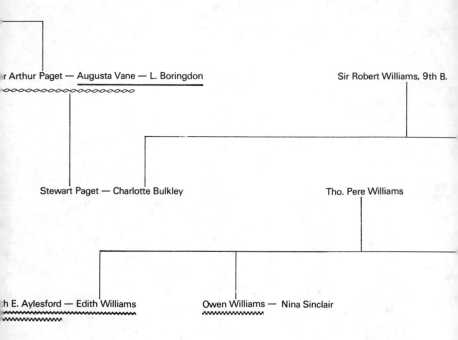

r Arthur Paget — Augusta Vane — L. Boringdon   Sir Robert Williams, 9th B.

Stewart Paget — Charlotte Bulkley   Tho. Pere Williams

h E. Aylesford — Edith Williams   Owen Williams — Nina Sinclair

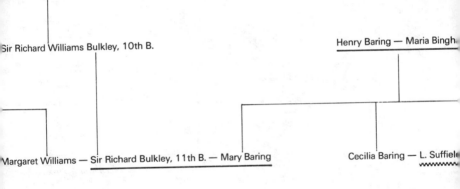

Sir Richard Williams Bulkley, 10th B.

Henry Baring — Maria Bingh.

Margaret Williams — Sir Richard Bulkley, 11th B. — Mary Baring

Cecilia Baring — L. Suffiel

6th E. Cardigan

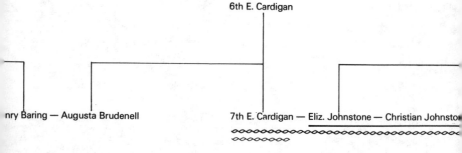

nry Baring — Augusta Brudenell   7th E. Cardigan — Eliz. Johnstone — Christian Johnsto

4th E. Dysart
Jane Tollemache
Admiral John Tollemache
7th E. Stair — Laura Tolleache
L. Tollemache
John Tollemache

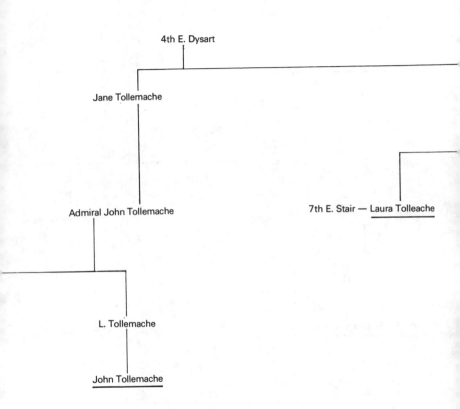

Ctess Dysart
Louisa Tollemache — 6th D. St. Albans
Charles Tollemache
h E. Coventry — Mary Beauclerk
1st M. Ailesbury — Maria Tollemache

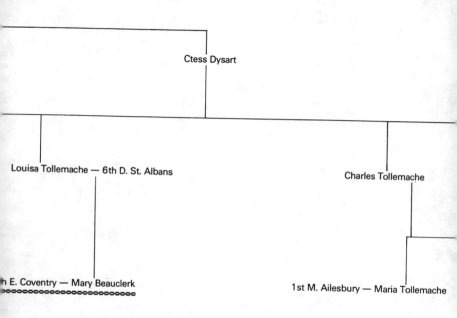

William Tollemache
Sir G. Sinclair, 2nd B. — Catherine Tollemache
8th E. Dysart — Maria Toone
Henry Bertie Tollemache — Emilia Sinclair
Sir John Sinclair, 3rd B. — Emma Standis
Owen Williams — Nina Sinclair

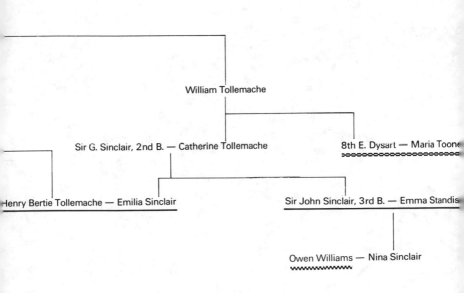

Figure 6.2: The Pellews

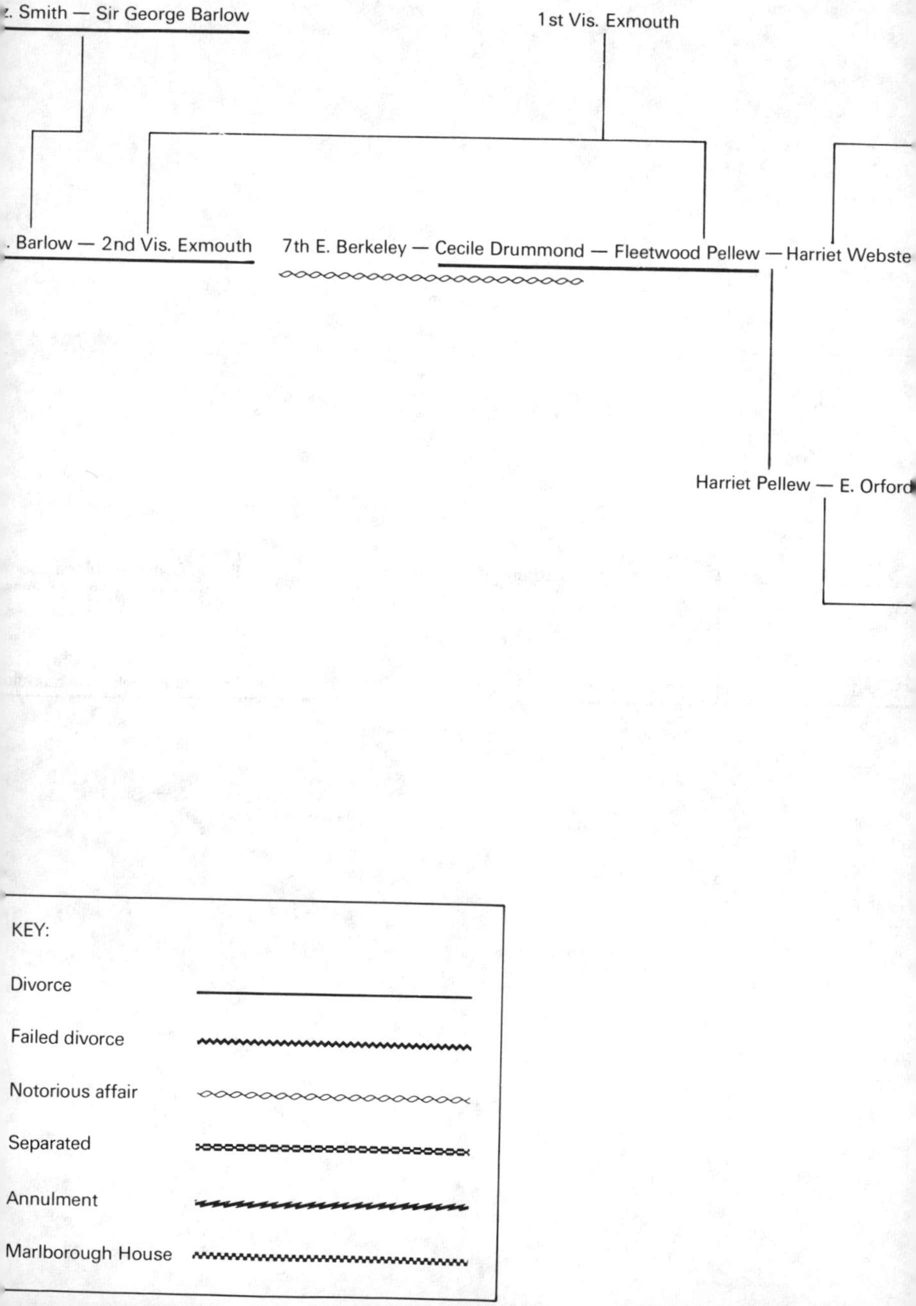

z. Smith — Sir George Barlow   1st Vis. Exmouth

. Barlow — 2nd Vis. Exmouth   7th E. Berkeley — Cecile Drummond — Fleetwood Pellew — Harriet Webste

Harriet Pellew — E. Orford

KEY:

Divorce	
Failed divorce	
Notorious affair	
Separated	
Annulment	
Marlborough House	

Sir Godfrey Webster — Eliz. Vassal — L. Holland
Sam. Budding
Henry Webster — Grace Budding
D. Newcastle
L. Walpole
Ctess Lincoln — E. Lincoln
Thomas Cli

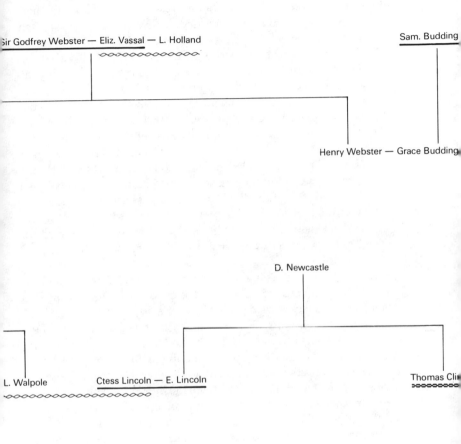

then besmeared herself with the excrement, ate coal and cinders, and ignored the baby when it was shown to her. The issue of the hearing was, not a divorce, but whether she was sane enough for the trial for divorce to proceed. Harriet's family resisted the divorce for her. After seven days of evidence, the jury, out five minutes, said she had been insane since before the proceedings began. Sir Charles, before Harriet became pregnant, had been told the Prince of Wales was making afternoon calls on his wife. He asked her to stop seeing the Prince as he had 'a bad character'. When Harriet confessed her adultery to Sir Charles, she named the Prince as one of her lovers but he was not named as a co–respondent (the evidence was too flimsy). The Prince was subpoenaed to testify in an effort to make the prospect of the trial so horrifying to the parties that a compromise might be reached. When that failed and after some letters from the Prince to Harriet appeared in the press, he was finally called to testify so that he could clear himself of any adultery. His appearance in the box was brief — too brief for gossips — and when asked if any criminal acts had occurred with Harriet he replied, in the words of *The Times*, '(in a very firm tone) — There has not.'

Edward, despite this initial brush with unRespectability, continued in his ways, justifying the opinion of the queen and others of his irresponsibility. The acknowledged leader of English 'society' after 1870 Edward conducted himself in most unRespectable ways. His affairs with Lillie Langtry, Sarah Bernhardt, Lady Brooke, Agnes Keyser, Mrs Keppel and others were the common gossip of London society, though not widely known to the populace at large. His conduct and that of those around him did much to create the hypocrisy which has since been attributed to all Victorians. Fear of divorce court was profound, and the Prince of Wales undertook extensive negotiations and made vile threats to keep people out of it, so concerned was he with the problem. The Princess of Wales never took up the adulterous life, though she did have a great admirer in Oliver Montagu, younger son of the Earl of Sandwich. His devotion, a chivalrous and pure one characteristic of a few followers of the courtly tradition, meant that he had eyes only for her and that they always danced once together — but it never gave rise to gossip. The Prince, though in court again over a gambling scandal, managed to stay clear of divorce court after his first appearance, but his friends did not.

Despite growing fears about political attacks on the aristocracy, these people could not give up their traditional fast life. While many of the aristocrats, including the Prince of Wales and his Marlborough House set, managed to keep their peccadillos quiet after the scandal of the Mordaunt divorce, the Prince continued his feckless life of flirtation and romantic intrigue. To vary the routine of his aimless life, the heir to the throne decided that a trip to exotic India — the jewel in the crown — would forestall boredom and involve him, at least marginally, in government affairs. He gathered an all-male troupe of his hangers-on — the trip included lots of hunting — and left England in the autumn of 1875. No sooner had the royal gang arrived in the subcontinent than a divorce scandal exploded back in England, with debris landing on His Royal Highness himself:

While the seventh Earl of Aylesford, 'Sporting Joe', hunted in India, his Countess, 'Goosey', eloped with the Marquis of Blandford (the heir to the Marlborough dukedom). The lovers wanted divorces — Blandford was 'wildly infatuated' — but family and friends wanted to keep it quiet. 'Aylesford is already so unsavoury that it will not do for him to appear in the divorce court.' The Prince was entreated to pressure Aylesford to stay out of court but, it turned out, the Countess had compromising letters from the Prince himself. The letters found their way into the hands of Blandford's brother, Lord Randolph Churchill (Winston's father). The threatening and posturing split the Prince and Lord Randolph for years. Aylesford failed to obtain a divorce in 1878 while Marlborough, always in money troubles, settled £10,000 on Lady Aylesford's child of whom he was the reputed father. 'Sporting Joe' subsequently moved to Texas where he died in 1885, at the age of 35.[6]

The lives of the nobility, once the Pandora's box was opened, appeared to be one long adultery. The 'other man' in the Aylesford case — the Marquis of Blandford — found his divorce suit entertaining the kingdom in 1883:

Blandford, eldest son of the seventh Duke of Marlborough, was the rebellious son of a man 'sober-sided and serious-minded, devout and chaste, devoted to the interests of the church'. In 1869 in Westminster Abbey he married Lady Albertha Hamilton, the sixth daughter of the Duke of Abercorn, a woman 'as good as she was beautiful', but, according to the family biographer, A.L. Rowse, 'really stupid'. After the Aylesford scandal, Lady Blandford sought a judicial separation and obtained a separation deed, but the couple reconciled in 1878. However, when Lady Aylesford had a baby in 1881, Lady Blandford sought and obtained a divorce in 1883. In 1892 she returned to divorce court on behalf of her 19-year-old son, trying to get him an allowance from his father, now the eighth Duke of Marlborough. The Duke, in very serious financial trouble, married a rich American widow who, after his death in 1892, married Lord William Beresford. Lady Albertha lived until 1932.[7]

The Blandfords disappeared from the gossip of the nation and immediately reappeared when the Marquis was back in divorce court, named as a co-respondent in Lord Colin Campbell's divorce petition in 1886:

Lord Colin, the fifth son of the Duke of Argyll, proposed to Gertrude Blood three days after their meeting. Her parents, apparently climbing the social ladder, pushed the marriage ahead in 1881 even though Lord Colin had a perineal fistula which prevented consummation for several months while he underwent a series of operations. Trouble broke out and in 1884 Lady Colin received a judicial separation and in 1884 both parties filed petitions for divorce. Her petition alleged Lord Colin's seduction of a maid who, upon medical evidence, was found to be *virgo intacta*. Lord Colin named as co-respondents the Duke of Marlborough (as Blandford had become), Colonel Sir William Butler (an old family friend of Lady Colin), Captain Shaw of the Metropolitan Fire Brigade (another family friend) and Doctor Bird (their family physician). Evidence revealed that Lady Colin and Marlborough — called 'this expert in the divorce court' — saw a lot of each other and that Lady Colin was a talented writer and singer who worked in soup-kitchens in Stepney two days a week. The jury, which visited the house in Cadogan Place to check a servant's story about seeing an adultery through a keyhole, found after 18 days of hearings and three and a half hours of deliberation that no adulteries had been proved.

Lady Colin edited *Etiquette of Good Society* in 1893; she also received £20,000 under Marlborough's will and was painted in the nude by Whistler.[8]

This spate of divorces coincided with other concerns about the aristocracy. The slowly spreading effects of the electoral franchise reform of 1867 and the secret ballot in 1872 reduced aristocratic political power, and the purchase of commissions in the army — the last bastion of the aristocracy — was abolished in 1871. These declines in function reflected themselves in many areas of life besides the casual adulteries of the Marlborough House set, and the confusions rampant in the minds of these aristocrats produced other behaviour baffling to many. Mrs Campbell, after her sensational divorce involving Sir Charles Dilke, converted to Roman Catholicism and became involved in Labour Party politics, dying only in 1948. Even those around the Prince of Wales were not immune to the problems of ennui, despite his feverish activity:

> Margaret Blunden, married to the heir of the earldom of Warwick at the age of 19, was, within five years, conducting a torrid affair with Lord Charles Beresford. A double divorce so the couple could marry was barely averted. When the affair ended badly, Margaret, now Lady Brooke, sought the Prince's intervention to pressure her former lover. The feud continued, the Prince taking Lady Brooke's side, and Lady Brooke soon became the Prince's mistress. A divorce was nearly attempted in 1892 by Lord Brooke when the Prince, Beresford and the Duke of Marlborough (naturally) would have been named as co-respondents. By the early 1890s Lady Brooke was supervising country house parties at Easton where the chief purpose was to find a lover for a few days. She became a good friend in 1892 of W. P. Stead, the newspaper moral crusader, and she later supported Joseph Arch, the organiser of the farm labourers' union; after 1895 she was moving towards Socialism, all the time conducting so many affairs that it might be said the Boer War was officered by her lovers.[9]

The Prince's use of naked power to keep his retinue from creating scandal, as well as in pursuing his own amorous desires, revealed this bankruptcy of principle in another form. Such lives as those of Lady Brooke, Mrs Campbell and the Prince raise complex problems about personalities — Sigmund Freud was studying these matters in Vienna — but also make charges of hypocrisy easy.

Simultaneously with the loss of many of the traditional aristocratic functions of politics and war, the 'New Domesday Book', a report of land ownership published between 1874 and 1876, revealed the concentration of 80 per cent of the land of the United Kingdom in the hands of 7,000 owners. Attention to the peccadillos of the titled came on the heels of Gladstone's Midlothian campaign cultivating a large electorate. John Morley, a Liberal politician attacking the aristocracy, said the House of Lords might need to be 'mended or ended'.[10] The new spirit might sweep out the old ruling class. Under these circumstances, many wanted to avoid giving reasons which might inspire the sweepers.

These fears among some aristocrats contributed to hypocrisy among the titled. Aristocratic names had always been seen in divorce reports — the Marquis of Anglesey nearly inaugurated the new court and the Chetwynds had relations throughout *Burke's Peerage, Baronetage, and Knightage* — but, with the Prince of Wales and the Duke of Marlborough in court, the publicity was much greater. When the wild life of a portion of the aristocracy inevitably produced a rash of divorce petitions, calls appeared, once again, to reduce the publicity surrounding the divorce court. Calls, once again, unsuccessful. The new ruling order of the 1880s, with a 'Nonconformist Conscience', maintained the horror of adultery and supported the stigma of divorce court. The 'Respectable society' was lower down the economic pyramid than its predecessor of the 1850s but its members were just as serious. Not envying the aristocracy their ways, these Respectables knew where power lay — the aristocratic manoeuvrings for secrecy and the fate of the politicians Dilke and Parnell evinced that. That such effort might be taken to avoid divorce court reinforced Respectables in their superior feelings and defeated efforts to reduce publicity. Perhaps Respectable distaste for aristocratic high jinks arose from other sources as well as the horror of the casual adulteries and nominal marriages exposed in divorce court. George Meredith, in *The Ordeal of Richard Feverel*, advanced the idea that 'the national love of a lord is less subservience than a form of self-love'.[11] When the idols have clay feet, Respectable worshippers feel betrayed. And nervous?

Professionals, as well as aristocrats, came to fear divorce court because the taint could destroy a professional practice. Husbands, and wives, would not trust a professional man, especially a physician, if it became known that he had once violated his trust. Dr Lane fought the allegation of his affair with Mrs Robinson because it would have destroyed his homeopathic clinic entirely. Publicity as well as guilt was the fear:

George Acland Ames of Cote House, Westbury-on-Trym, studied at the Dresden Conservatoire where he met Countess Henrietta Klara Poelzig of Poelzig Castle in the Duchy of Altenbury. She was a 'stunner' with 'a voluptuous figure'. They were married in Germany in 1854 when he was 27, she 18. In 1864 George went on a world trip 'for health reasons', leaving Henrietta at home, and in 1867 he discovered she had been unfaithful when he found a letter. She confessed all, naming several men, and attempted suicide; George sent her back to Germany and sought a divorce. The co-respondents named by George were a Captain Robinson (dead by the date of the divorce trial in 1869), one Heltenstein (a teacher who was insane by the trial), and Dr Gourlay, a physician at Weston-super-Mare, the coastal resort near Bristol. Evidence included Henrietta's confession as well as a maid's testimony that Henrietta told the doctor she would show him 'a German trick'. The adulteries appeared to be casual, not sustained, affairs, one being during the opening festivities for Brunel's Clifton suspension bridge. Dr Gourlay fought the accusations of adultery and the jury found no guilt on his part, though guilt with the dead and insane co-respondents. Dr Gourlay defended because his medical practice was at stake as the suit was reported in *The Times*, the *Bristol Gazette*, the *Clifton Chronicle and Directory*, the *Bristol Observer*, the *Daily Bristol Times and Mirror*, and the *Weston-Super-Mare Mercury*[12]

Surprisingly, politicians were the last group to have the effects of divorce demonstrated to them. The Earl of Lincoln, despite his divorce — in which no legal blame fell on him — continued active in governments after 1850.

In 1864 Timothy Joseph O'Kane, an Irish Radical journalist, sought a divorce from Margaret Matilda Augusta Morris O'Kane and named the Prime Minister, Lord Palmerston, as the co-respondent. Lady Palmerston thought the suit an extortion and certainly the lawyers acted in unusual ways to get the suit dismissed. The husband's comments at various times suggest money was the object — he sought £20,000 damages — and one of Palmerston's friends may have bought O'Kane off. Mrs O'Kane, 30 and attractive, had visited the 78-year-old Prime Minster but nothing more is known. People said that 'though the lady was certainly Kane, the question was, Was Palmerston Abel?'[13]

The fevered activity to quash the petition and the judge's strong words of support for Palmerston indicate all knew the situation to be potentially very damaging. Whether Sir Charles Mordaunt had any political future before the scandal of his wife cannot be known, but he had no political career after the trial involving her sanity. Only in 1886 did a politician have his career destroyed by a divorce case and he was probably innocent of the charges made:

In 1886 Sir Charles Dilke, a former Radical and a rising Liberal politician, was named as the 'other man' by Donald Campbell. At the trial Mrs Campbell admitted her adulteries, fleshing them out with stories of three-in-a-bed and Dilke's teaching of 'French vices' while Dilke, following legal advice, did not testify. Under the legal rules of the day, Mrs Campbell's uncorroborated confession did not prove Dilke guilty so he was dismissed from the suit but Mr Campbell obtained a divorce. 'She committed adultery with him but he did not with her,' ran the joke. Dilke's failure to testify was a disastrous political mistake and, realising this, he manoeuvred the Queen's Proctor into intervening. A second trial resulted, Dilke testified, Mrs Campbell elaborated her confession, the jury found no injustice occurred at the first trial, Mr Campbell kept his divorce, and Dilke was ruined.

Dilke's friends spent much time and money investigating the flaws in Mrs Campbell's story — it appears to have been a fabrication — and in the process uncovered a world of casual adultery among London professionals and their wives. To be fair, Dilke had led a fast life, carrying on a long affair with Mrs Mark Pattison — she and her husband were the models for Dorothea Brooke and Edward Casaubon in George Eliot's *Middlemarch* — before marrying her after her husband's death. Also Dilke had probably been a lover of Mrs Campbell's mother in years past![14]

Charles Stewart Parnell's sudden rise in the late 1870s to the leadership of the Irish party in Parliament thrust him into the London limelight. One of the observers of that stage was Katharine O'Shea, wife of Captain W.H. O'Shea. By 1880, the affair of Charles and Katharine was known to many, the Captain learning of it in 1881. After a duel was challenged but not fought, Charles and the Captain came to a settlement by which Charles promised to be discreet and, it appears, help the Captain if possible. At any rate, Charles found the Captain an Irish seat in Parliament a few years later. Katharine had a baby in 1882 (which died) and two daughters later; Charles was the father of all three. By 1882, members of the Liberal Cabinet knew of the affair and hints of it began appearing in the press in 1866. The O'Sheas did not divorce as all sought to get an inheritance from Katharine's aunt When the aunt died without leaving her money in a manner that the Captain could get his hands on it, he sought a divorce, naming Charles as the co-respondent. When the case came to trial in 1890, Charles did not have counsel and Katharine's held only a watching brief as both wanted the divorce to proceed so that they could marry. However, Katharine lost custody of all her children and, while the lovers married, Charles's political career died as Gladstone, with his Nonconformist political support, did not believe he could co-operate with a divorced man. Charles died within a year; Katharine lived well into the twentieth century.[15]

While various people — unRespectables, artists, aristocrats and professionals — rejected Respectability, they lived in fear of the divorce court, and engaged in hypocritical behaviour as a result. Additionally, divorce court continually revealed that not everyone accepted the same definition of Respectability. Nevertheless, these men and women were not those for whom the divorce court had been created in the first place. Ironically, several steps which Respectables took to strengthen Respectability and the divorce court created more hypocrisy.

Respectability, like all such notions governing people's lives, was hedged about by vagueness and inherent contradictions, problems which led, ultimately, to its destruction. Respectability had limits, for some, and those limits led people into activities which might bring them into divorce court, sometimes not unwillingly:

The Hawkins married in 1868 when her father discovered the couple was having intercourse. Mr Hawkins, hoping for an inheritance from his uncle and aunt, compelled Mrs Hawkins to keep the marriage a secret. He also paid her £2 a month. When Mr Hawkins sought a divorce in 1885 because of her adultery, the judge denied it, calling him a seducer who had conduced to his wife's fall.[16]

The Crommelins married in 1839, lived happily together for several years, and had six children. *The Times* reported the trial as follows:

In 1852 Mr C and a friend of his, Mr Hadyn, went to Australia upon a gold-digging adventure, and were accompanied by Mrs C and the children. In the same ship there was a young woman named Annie Carter, and a child, and it was remarked that great attention was paid to her by Mr C. Shortly before their arrival at Sydney Mrs C remonstrated with him on the subject, and he then said the best thing she could do was to return to England. They arrived at Sydney in January, and Mr C then repeated his proposal that his wife should go back in the ship by which she had gone out, and when she objected said, 'You must stop here and starve, or else go home'. He insisted on her returning and took a passage for her, gave her £50, and sent her back with three of the children, the other three remaining with him. He has since that time been living in the colony with Annie Carter as man and wife. It appeared he has since transmitted £600 to Mrs C; that she had an income of her own of about £20 a year; that she was in receipt of £93 a year, which had been left by a relation for the maintenance and education of the children; and that her friends had contributed to her support since her return to England. It was afterwards discovered that his adulterous intercourse with Annie Carter began in England, and that he was the father of the child which was with her on the outward voyage.

Mr Crommelin's counsel said that his client did not oppose the divorce but did wish 'merely to deny the imputation that he had acted unhandsomely towards his wife in regard to pecuniary matters'.

The judge said, 'it was very curious to observe what different opinions men had as to what constituted a good character. He never heard of more profligate, cruel, heartless, base conduct'.[17]

Mr Witt was divorced by his wife in 1888. After his former wife started living with another man, Mr Witt sought the custody of his children in 1891. A clergyman testified that Mr Witt was now Respectable — the taint was gone within three years.[18]

Mrs Bardon, after threats by her husband, earned their joint living by prostitution. Eight years after she left him, she sought a divorce and several witnesses testified she was Respectable.[19]

The divorce court itself had, built into its structure, elements which contributed to charges of hypocrisy. Collusion — the agreement of husband and wife not to fight in divorce court — challenged the whole foundation of the law of divorce. Divorce trials were, supposedly, adversary proceedings. However, throughout the history of English divorce the majority — the overwhelming majority — of couples came to an agreement, perhaps after much threatening and fighting, not to wash their dirty linen in public. This meant most divorces were unopposed and often counsel for the guilty party had little more than a watching brief with no cross–examination or procedural blocks being sought. This practice produced problems because divorce law denied a divorce to a petitioner who had also committed adultery (two wrongs did not make a right), had condoned the adultery, had connived at the adultery, or had conduced to the adultery. In default of a true adversary proceeding, the Queen's Proctor had the task of investigating these possibilities because few parties wanted to ruin the divorce by pointing out their spouses' sins. The Queen's Proctor usually acted because the divorce court judge 'smelled something fishy' about the evidence. Thus, thoughout the history of Victorian divorce, the 'floodgates' so feared by all never opened because the divorce court judge kept a lonely vigil on the implications of the behaviour detailed in divorce petitions and evidence. As late as 1895 the court refused to sanction an agreement between parties — England would not have divorce by consent:

> Florence Churchward was living with William John Holliday and wanted a divorce so they could marry. Her husband refused to file a petition until she, who had most of the income of the marriage, settled money on their only child. She finally settled such money and also put £100 in security for his costs of a divorce suit. When the petition came to a hearing, the counsel for the wife and the co–respondent offered no defence but the husband's counsel disclosed all. The judge decided that this was collusion because the guilty pair agreed to make no defence. Resistance might have proved mutual guilt, condonation, etc., and, as divorce law demanded adversaries, it was against public policy for parties to agree to forgo their opposition, the judge held.[20]

Informed estimates throughout the century were that nine out of ten divorces were based on at least a tacit agreement not to drag all the facts into court.

The law frequently works out its own internal logic and reaches results at variance with the original policy of the law, and divorce was no exception to this generalisation. The divorce court judges, addressing individual petitions, created rules which made hypocrisy more likely in other situations:

> In *Keats v. Keats and Montezuma,* the divorce involving the head of

Fortnum and Mason, the rule emerged that forgiveness must be evidenced by acts, not intentions.

When Mrs Bastock sought a judicial separation in 1858, the court was treated to an unseemly description of violence and cruelty, often witnessed by the couple's eight children. Mrs Bastock, however, frequently forgave Mr Bastock, but finally had had enough and sought the separation. Unfortunately for her, the judge found one remark in a letter she had written to her husband which he interpreted as forgiveness. Separation denied. One remark could thwart the petition, so any small slip had to be hushed up in future suits.[21]

Mr Bell sought a divorce in 1859 and named the Marquis of Anglesey as the co-respondent. The Marquis desired to marry Mrs Bell, so he put up no defence. However, the Bells' marriage settlement posed a problem as the divorce would deprive Mr Bell of income under that settlement and the divorce court judge had no authority to alter that settlement. The Marquis's counsel, therefore, told the jury that his client had no objection to a decision that the Marquis should pay £10,000 to Mr Bell for the adultery; this would place Mr Bell in the same position as he would have had under the marriage settlement. When the jury so found, the whole mess looked uncomfortably close to buying a wife.[22]

Table 6.1: Divorces after 1857

Period	Number of petitions filed for divorce or nullity (annual average)	Petitions per 10,000 married women, aged 15–49
1861–65	226	0.83
1866–70	248	0.86
1871–75	346	1.14
1876–80	460	1.42
1881–85	462	1.44
1886–90	556	1.55
1891–95	565	1.44
1896–1900	675	1.59

Source: Griselda Rowntree and Norman H. Carrier, 'The Resort to Divorce in England and Wales, 1858–1957', *Population Studies*, 11 (1958) p.201.

After 1865 Respectables, worrying about other matters, paid little

attention to the overall situation concerning divorce, and, as a consequence, they missed noticing a significant increase in the number of
couples divorcing. From 1858 to 1870 and again from 1875 to 1900,
divorces remained about constant as a proportion of the married
population of England; but between the years 1870 and 1875 the
petitions increased 75 per cent faster than the population (see
Table 6.1).[23] A symptom of this increase was the appearance
of the short-lived *The Newgate Calendar and the Divorce Court
Chronicle* in 1872, which printed divorce reports and historically
interesting trials. Otherwise, however, this dramatic increase went
largely unnoticed: the Contagious Diseases Acts and the Married
Women's Property Act occupied social reformers and feminists,
while law reformers reorganised the entire judicial system in 1873
and the Franco-Prussian War, the *Alabama* arbitration and Disraeli's
espousal of the Empire entertained those concerned with foreign
affairs.

This rise in divorce petitions came from a change in the law and, after
the divorce court appearance of the Prince of Wales, a greater
willingness by some to use the divorce court. The judge remained
the same — James Wilde, Lord Penzance, sat from 1863 to 1872
— and his decisions only slightly eased obstacles: alimony during
the proceedings was limited in some situations, which would encourage husbands; and behaviour leading to a health breakdown was defined as cruelty, which would lower wives' burdens.
The shortcomings of the Married Women's Property Act of
1870 pushed a few women into divorce as better protection for
their financial affairs could be had outside marriage. Publication
of *On the Subjection of Women* by John Stuart Mill stimu-
lated some into thought about servitude, but the percentage of
divorce petitions filed by wives actually fell in the five years after
1870.

A change in the law in 1869 permitted the parties to testify and
to be asked, though they were not required to answer, questions
about adultery.[24] A legislative effort to support Respectability, this
modification to the law was the major reason behind the rise in
divorces. This provision, enacted so that Respectables could deny
false allegations of adultery — an opportunity taken by the Prince of
Wales in 1870 — also gave parties wishing a divorce a new technique, however. The lover, put in the box, could stammer and turn red
before he refused to answer or the lawyer could comment adversely
on someone's refusal to testify; both situations would lead the jury

to believe the adultery had occurred and grant the divorce with less ado than all the lurid testimony of maids, hotel clerks, and the like. Also, the rise in numbers came from a greater willingness to accept the shame of appearing in divorce court, a shame now shared by the Prince of Wales.

The strict adherence of the divorce court judge to the rules of evidence of the other courts combined with the desires of some people to get a divorce at any price to produce situations where the evidence was 'got up' just for the benefit of the judge and jury:

> Thomas Allen, a military outfitter, married Harriet Ellen Allen in 1852, when she was still the mistress of another man. After three children, Thomas committed adultery in 1858, but Harriet forgave him. Thomas, in order to be rid of her, then concocted a scheme to get Harriet to commit adultery. With two friends, he introduced Robert D'Arcy to Harriet, had him to dinner often, allowed them to be alone and gave them many opportunities. Finally, when Harriet had to go to London on family matters, D'Arcy 'accidentally' joined her on the train and the hoped-for adultery occurred in a London hotel. At the trial it turned out D'Arcy was an alias (Did Thomas know his Jane Austen?) and the entire conspiracy came to light.[25]

> Mrs Bell sought a divorce in 1889, a divorce her husband did not oppose. The Queen's Proctor intervened in the suit and discovered that a clerk for Mrs Bell's solicitor had given Mr Bell money to visit a house of ill fame. The clerk had accompanied Mr Bell and witnessed the adultery.[26]

> When Mr Nicolas sought a divorce in 1899, the only evidence of the adultery was Mrs Nicolas's confession and a hotel register. This begins to resemble the 'hotel evidence' which became common in the 1920s as couples desiring a divorce arranged for the husband to register at a hotel and the evidence to be 'accidentally' sent to the wife, who then obtained a divorce.[27]

A natural consequence of years of divorces emerged by the 1890s as counsel and judges began to discriminate among various 'levels' of adultery. While the consequences of adultery remained divorce, the actions of respondents brought forth different condemnations from the judges. Army officers, especially in India, frequently committed 'mild' adulteries, while a man who committed adultery with a servant in the house had his actions described as 'a serious kind' of adultery. Sir Charles Dilke heard his activities called a 'ruthless adultery unredeemed by love or affection'. The reformers of 1857 would have been appalled.

All of these developments concerning the court paled, however, as the chief disadvantage of divorce, for many, came to be the expense and publicity — history repeated itself — as suits in the 1890s suggest that a paramount concern to some couples became the possibility of litigation financially ruining them as well as destroying their reputations:

Earl Russell, grandson of the Prime Minister Lord John Russell and son of Viscount and Viscountess Amberley (who were active in feminist affairs), married Mabel Edith Scott in February 1890 but they separated in June. (A friend said the Earl really loved his wife's mother.) In 1891 she unsuccessfully sought a judicial separation. During that trial hints of homosexuality against the Earl brought out that he had been sent down from Oxford for writing an 'improper letter to a man' and his grandmother advised the Countess to keep him away from his college friends. A family member, after 'the Oxford incident', had advised him to 'blow his brains out'. To counter this, the Earl admitted seducing a maidservant before his marriage. The Countess failed to prove cruelty and therefore lost her suit with costs going against her separate estate of £600 a year. She then sued the Earl in the Queen's Bench for £450 she had loaned him — the Earl was in the electrical engineering business. In 1895 the Countess filed a petition for restitution of conjugal rights, which the Earl claimed was nothing more than blackmail as it would bring out the matter of the 'unnatural offence' again. And again she lost — the jury agreed with the Earl — and both parties appealed on the matter of costs. Finally, in 1901, this battling couple divorced, though he went to Reno, Nevada, in the United States to accomplish it. Upon his return, and after his remarriage, he was prosecuted for bigamy — English courts did not recognise the Nevada divorce – and convicted. After serving a month's prison term, the Earl returned to the House of Lords as a divorce reformer, introducing Bills in 1902 and 1903. His second marriage ended in divorce in 1915 and his third wife left him when she 'discovered behaviour of a secret nature that made it impossible for a decent woman to stay'. The Earl died in 1931 without children and was succeeded in the earldom by his brother, Bertrand, the philosopher.[28]

And not merely countesses knew how to use the divorce procedures to their advantage:

> When Mr Clarke sought a divorce in 1890, he was ordered to pay alimony *pendente lite* of 8s. a week. When his wife successfully obtained an order for him to pay £135 into the Registry as security for costs in the suit, he, a joiner with three children at home, had to suspend his petition.[29]

> Mr Richardson, trying to find money to continue his case, though proceeding *in forma pauperis*, was denied damages against his wife's lover. Such damages, long justified as necessary to reimburse husbands for their loss, were denied as, in pauper cases, the money would go straight to the solicitor; this would unnecessarily encourage litigation and therefore was bad policy, the judge ruled. That it put one more obstacle in the path of the poor was not mentioned.[30]

By one estimate over three-quarters of petitions by the poor never made it to trial because the husband lacked funds to pay alimony during the trial as well as post-security to meet his wife's legal expenses if his suit failed. Only when the wife had substantial funds of her own might divorce be effective. In several cases after 1880 husbands with rich wives attempted to extort money from their spouses with promises to stay out of divorce court — this way lay equality, and collusion.

Respectables, seeking to strengthen the status and spread its values to others, directed sustained efforts at another area of sexuality — prostitution — and discovered the contradictions underlying their attitudes, especially those involving the double standard. After passage of the Divorce Act, prostitution occupied the attention of Victorians and their historians a great deal. William Acton's *Prostitution Considered in Its Moral, Social, and Sanitary Aspects*, and the efforts of the inhabitants of Marylebone in London to drive prostitutes from their neighbourhood, both events occurring in the same year as the Divorce Act, represented harbingers of the efforts of the 1860s to deal with the 'Social Evil'. The large number of women working the streets made prostitution an obvious issue. London especially, with its anonymity, its temptations, its poverty, swarmed with prostitutes, and estimates varied widely though the number 75,000 was commonly bandied about. But the size of an obstacle seldom deterred Victorians. Some, like W.E. Gladstone, the sometime Prime Minister, undertook a personal crusade whereby he talked with prostitutes about alternatives to their life. Organised efforts, such as those of the Marylebone residents, rarely lasted long and only moved prostitutes from haunts indoors to haunts outdoors or from one neighbourhood to another.

The first sustained thrust dealing with prostitution, the Contagious Diseases Acts of 1864, 1866 and 1869 (the 'C.D. Acts') arose from military concerns about enlisted men and the effects of venereal disease in towns near army garrisons and naval ports. Venereal disease had existed in England for centuries — and had infected enlisted men for centuries — but became a problem because statistics about its prevalence were gathered by those infected with the new attitude to social problems. The members of the National Association for the Promotion of the Social Sciences, Brougham's other interest in 1857, were in the forefront of this activity. William Acton, whose book of 1857 also analysed venereal disease, presented a paper to the Association and joined others from that group to clean up this aspect of the national health. The C.D. Acts enabled a policeman to name a woman as a 'common prostitute', which obligated her to undergo an internal examination for venereal disease every two weeks, with hospitalisation if found diseased. A woman who rejected the appellation or the examination faced a trial in which she had to prove her virtue, not the policeman her vice:

> Mrs Percy and her teenage daughter sang in Aldershot music halls for the entertainment of the troops stationed there. The special police for the C.D. Acts thought her life suggested prostitution and demanded she undergo a physical examination. She refused and, after her job ended (the manager probably was threatened with loss of his licence) fled. She returned to Aldershot, passing herself as having recently married (she had not), but, after further scrapes with the police, drowned herself in March 1875. A long series of investigations ended inconclusively but it became clear she thought she and her daughter were being unjustly persecuted.[31]

By the statistics then available, the C.D. Acts did reduce the incidence of venereal disease but opponents, led by Josephine Butler, believed working-class women, the Mrs Percys of England, were victimised, as police, often without sufficient justification, described them as prostitutes. Moreover, opponents thought male customers, as well as female prostitutes, shared the responsibility for the evils under attack — one of the few challenges of the day to the double standard. Regulation of prostitution, modelled on Continental practices, smacked of intrusion on traditional English liberties and new medical statistics challenged the efficacy of the C.D. Acts, anyway. Finally, many people disliked the state's apparent sanctioning of 'vice' implied in the C.D. Acts and, after a long campaign, including the outcry over the suicide of Mrs Percy, the C.D. Acts lapsed in 1886.

Respectables' attitudes to prostitution, venereal disease, and the C.D. Acts provided the backdrop for discussions of marriage and divorce. On one view, the C.D. Acts extended the thrust of the Divorce Act. Having regulated Respectable sexual activity through the Divorce Act, the law now regulated unRespectable sexual activity. (Soldiers, sailors, and prostitutes were unRespectable, without doubt.) By clearly defining the violators of the former — the adulteresses — and the practitioners of the latter — the prostitutes — and identifying them in court, sexual behaviour was delineated sharply. Unfortunately for such intentions, both divorce and prostitution revealed that both men and women shared in the sins of the world. As to Respectable women, prostitution, regulated or not, stood as the starkest of images of the fate of the fallen woman, and this accounts for much of its continued 'popularity' as a topic.

For three decades divorce court annually provided reports of a wife who, after discovery of her affair, became a prostitute, reinforcing the common, trite even, statements about the consequences of adultery:

Mr Hooke, a butcher near Tottenham Court Road in London, married Mrs Hooke in 1852. She left him in 1854 and led a life of prostitution in London. After a trial of only the briefest duration, he obtained a divorce in 1859.[32]

Mrs Bardon married in 1889 but her husband, 'a lazy, worthless fellow', forced her by threats to earn their joint living by prostitution. She left him in 1892 and had lived, in the judge's word, 'respectably' since. This included living from 1892 to 1895 with one man and from 1896 to 1898 with another, though the judge disbelieved any adulteries took place. Her background included a mother dying when she was five and, after her father remarried, a terrible home life, ending when she was turned out of the house at 20. She lived with her future husband and only with the help of their landlady could she force him to honour his promise to marry her. When she left her husband she found no refuge as her father was in an asylum and her stepmother on parish relief. By 1900 when the divorce action occurred, she had a protector, a Mr Dawson, who received much praise from the court.[33]

All was not terror and damnation as the repeated experience of women whose marriages failed led to a tolerance about prostitutes, for it became clear that in the economic situation of Victorian England many resorted to prostitution due to the lack of alternatives. Mrs Bardon's life proved that the 'fall' need not be permanent either.

Respectable men did not use prostitutes, though in their youth they might have, and, as men of the upper middle class did not, on average, marry until aged 30, their 'youth' was long. Frequenting prostitutes, these bachelors were less likely to attempt the virtue of Respectable women, married or no. In 1865 James Thompson's poem *Virtue and Vice* suggested a wife's 'freezing gloom' and disdain of 'carnal joys' increased the attractions of prostitutes; the topic of prostitution and the home could not be avoided completely. A few doctors, thinking chastity dangerous to a man's health, suggested prostitutes as a medical necessity for the young bachelors and the suffering husbands. Yet venereal disease, often a companion of prostitution, gained a man no sympathy, and evidence in divorce court that he had infected his wife brought forth condemnations of the harshest sort — 'vile', 'vicious', 'disgusting'. The overall result of the attention to the issues of prostitution was that Respectable husbands did not resort to prostitutes, though Respectable unmarried men might. The records of divorce court support this, as men were not commonly portrayed using prostitutes (though, to be fair, such evidence would be hard to come by). A necessary evil, prostitution, like divorce, supported virtue, and therefore Respectability. Was this hypocrisy?

The concerns of feminists with the problems of all women, including those of the working class, and the fecklessness of the aristocracy, which emphasised the class differences in the consequences of sexual misadventure, combined to call attention to the plight of people who lacked money to use the divorce court. In 1882 the divorce court judge, when talking of the number of 'poor' using the court, explained how to make the procedures available to more of them. *The Times* carried a letter in 1884 suggesting that the working class obtain divorces *in forma pauperis* with the assistance of a local clergyman or other substantial resident. A Bill in the House of Commons in 1885 to give divorce powers to the county courts, which would have eliminated the expense of taking a case and the witnesses to London, failed of passage. Nevertheless, in 1871 about a quarter of all petitions came from the working classes and perhaps one in ten of those was *in forma pauperis*. By the turn of the century between 5 per cent and 10 per cent of all petitions were *in forma pauperis*, but few of those petitions resulted in divorces as the costs became too great even by pauper proceedings.[34] As before 1857, those too poor for the legal system developed alternatives:

> The Whitworths married in 1872 and had five children, but Edmund Whitworth drank. Upon their parting in 1882, they both signed a (soon lost) paper which both believed freed them to remarry, which they did. In 1893 the divorce court regularised these new marriages by granting the Whitworths a divorce despite their mutual bigamies. Ignorance of the law was an excuse.[35]

> George Walton sought a divorce in 1859. The Waltons, married in Ireland in 1826, had twelve children. He had been a sergeant in the Rifle Brigade and she the daughter of a publican. After his discharge, the couple moved to Birmingham where he worked as a collector of rates for the borough. Mrs Walton took up with Francis Hibell, a wire-drawer with 15 children. George and Francis signed a separation deed which the Lord Chancellor, in denying the divorce for collusion, described as, in effect, an assignment of Mrs Walton to Francis.[36]

The only help for those who were not rich, beginning in 1878, came from a series of laws giving a woman the opportunity to live apart from her husband while he still remained obligated to support her, all to be ordered by a local court. As these separation orders were not 'permanent' — they lapsed if the couple reunited — they were not exact parallels of divorce. Because adultery was not at issue, moreover, Respectability could survive separation. By the end of the century, local courts were granting yearly over 8,000 separations and maintenance orders — 'the divorce of the poor'. The possibility of divorce on grounds other than adultery obtained a toehold here as some separation orders ran for years. Why not let such couples divorce, the marriage clearly being at an end?

Hypocrisy grew and changed in form after the passage of the Divorce Bill. The mere existence of the divorce court after 1857 produced fear in many who moulded their actions to the new reality. Writers, artists, aristocrats, politicians and professionals, as groups, were those most affected by the new sanctions, and, as some of the most visible of Victorians, they colour our view of the entire society. Moreover, as the leaders of that society, they might be considered to be the most representative, though predominant in all those groups, with the possible exception of the aristocrats, were the Respectables. Even the aristocracy could produce many examples of hardworking Respectables, from the Duke of Westminster, owner of London's West End, to even an occasional Paget. More troubling and more difficult to explain away is the Respectable attitude to prostitutes. Resisting arguments that prostitution might be connected with economic situations, or even that women accepted it as a means to the 'good life', Respectables took only a moral view. The C.D. Acts died as much from a belief that they encouraged immorality as they did from new attitudes to women or statistics. When the concerns over the issue of class appeared in the 1880s — with the new procedures for separation orders for the workers — Respectables were caught in a contradiction. If Respectability did not depend on money, and in theory it did not, why deny workers the opportunity to behave Respectably and divorce their wayward spouses?

'Immorality was the taint of the upper and the necessary disease of the lower classes.' The value of feeling superior to 'dissolute aristocrats' and 'over-tempted plebeians' pushed Respectables into tolerating hypocrisy.[37] Indeed, as that hypocrisy reinforced those feelings of superiority, Respectability gained by emphasising the hypocrisy. At the same time, those rejecting Respectability — the artists, writers, aristocrats, and miscellaneous other rebels — also enjoyed the satisfaction of thwarting the Podsnaps and Mrs Grundys.

Notes

1. Eric Trudgill, *Madonnas and Magdalens* (Holmes & Meier, London, 1976) pp.181, 226; Duncan Crow, *The Victorian Woman* (Allen & Unwin, London, 1971) pp.215-19; Lionel Stevenson, *The Ordeal of George Meredith* (Scribner, New York, 1953) p.72; George Meredith, *The Ordeal of Richard Feverel* (Constable, London, 1914) pp.452, 457, 458.

2. Margaret M. Maison, 'Adulteresses in Agony', *The Listener,* 19th January, 1961, pp.133-4; 'Sensation Novels', *Quarterly Review*, vol. 113 (1863) 481-514; Mrs Henry Wood, *East Lynne* (Dent, London, 1984); *East Lynne* (Dicks' Standard Plays, no. 333, 1883).

3. 31 *Law Reports* 43.

4. 31 *Law Reports* 64.

5. *The Times*, February 1870; 39 *Law Reports* 57; 41 *Law Reports* 42; 43 *Law Reports* 49; C. Hibbert, *Edward VII: A Portrait* (Allen Lane, London, 1976).

6. Randolph S. Churchill, *Winston Churchill* (Harper, New York, 1958) vol. 1, Companion, Part 1, Ch. 2.

7. A.L. Rowse, *The Churchills* (Harper, New York, 1958) pp.165, 195 et seq.; 52 *Law Reports* 17; 61 *Law Reports* 97; *The Times*, 12th February, 21st November, 12th December, 1883.

8. *The Times*, November and December, 1886.

9. Margaret Blunden, *The Countess of Warwick: A Biography* (Cassell, London, 1967).

10. Morley's line was part of a bigger concern by many people with the aristocracy in the early 1880s. See W.H. Burn, *The Age of Equipoise* (George Allen, London, 1964) p.328 et seq.

11. Meredith, *The Ordeal of Richard Feverel*, p.377.

12. Lance Tantum, *The Ames Family and the Divorce that Shocked Bristol* (privately printed, 1983). I wish to thank Mrs Anne Crawford for this reference.

13. *The Times*, 27th January, 3rd and 5th February, 1864; Jasper Ridley, *Lord Palmerston* (Constable, London, 1970) p.532.

14. *The Times*, 4th, 9th, 13th February, May, July, 1886; 55 *Law Reports* 42; R.H. Jenkins, *Sir Charles Dilke* (Collins, London, 1958).

15. F.S.L. Lyons, *The Fall of Parnell* (University of Toronto Press, Toronto, 1960); Sir Alfred Robbins, *Parnell* (Butterworth, London, 1926); 59 *Law Reports* 47.

16. 54 *Law Reports* 94.

17. *The Times*, 17th January, 1860.

18. 60 *Law Reports* 63.

19. 69 *Law Reports* 118.

20. *The Times*, 13th and 23rd November, 1894; 64 *Law Reports* 18.

21. 27 *Law Reports* 86.

22. 29 *Law Reports* 159.

23. Griselda Rowntree and Norman H. Carrier, 'The Resort to Divorce in England and Wales 1858–1957', *Population Studies*, 11 (1958) p.201.

24. 32 & 33 Victoria, Ch. 68. An Act for the further Ammendment of the Law of Evidence.

25. 30 *Law Reports* 2.

26. 58 *Law Reports* 54.

27. 68 *Law Reports* 66.

28. Duncan Crow, *The Edwardian Woman* (Allen & Unwin, London, 1978) pp.174–181. *The Times*, 20th February, 1892, 29th May, 13th November 1894, 5th April, 28th May, 1895; 64 *Law Reports* 105; 67 *Law Reports* passim.

29. 60 *Law Reports* 97.

30. 64 *Law Reports* 93.

31. J.R. Walkowitz, *Prostitution and Victorian Society* (Cambridge University Press, Cambridge, 1980).

32. *The Times*, 24th May, 1859; PRO J77/23/H17/24.

33. 69 *Law Reports* 118.

34. *The Times*, 26th April, 1882, 10th April, 1884; House of Commons Command Paper 6478, *Report of the Royal Commission on Divorce and Matrimonial Causes*, pp.44-6.

35. 62 *Law Reports* 71.

36. 28 *Law Reports* 97.

37. *The Times*, 12th December, 1859.

7   Divorce, Hypocrisy and Respectability

Hypocrisy — professing a thing while doing its opposite, living one life by day and another by night. That some Victorians were hypocrites is undoubted — all ages have them — but the level of hypocrisy was not constant throughout the latter half of the nineteenth century. Already in 1822 Sir Walter Scott, author of *Ivanhoe*, said people must pay 'a tax to appearances'. Many of the charges of hypocrisy grow out of the activities of people who did not consider themselves Respectable and did not accept Respectables' standards; these people, not the Respectables, are the hypocrites. Throughout the eighteenth century not everything occurred in the open and by 1830 the seriousness of Respectability forced more activities behind doors. Lady Holland, divorced in 1797, had married her lover, Lord Holland, and he was in the Whig Cabinets of the 1830s but not all hostesses welcomed them. By the 1850s the gap between appearances and reality, between ideals and actions, was small for Respectables. The high ideal of married life — and it was as high as it ever had been or was to be — comprised the core of Victorian life. Though never including everyone in any class, Respectable society started at the top of the economic scale and permeated all levels until it reached those with too little money to afford its necessary trappings. In the 1850s and 1860s, Hippolyte Taine was told that only one aristocrat was unfaithful, such was the standard of the day. (Taine's informant was wrong.)[1] No idea sweeps all before it and Respectability was no exception.

Divorce did not, contrary to plan, always destroy the lives of the divorced. Indeed, several people reappeared in divorce court:

George Augustus Hamilton Chichester married Lucy Virginia Elizabeth Mare in 1859 in Paris after her first husband divorced her. In 1863 George wanted to be rid of her and tried to prove she had married before her first divorce became final, which would invalidate the second marriage.[2]

Similarly, Mr Rogers sought, in 1864, to have his marriage to Mrs Halmshaw annulled as he claimed she rushed into the second marriage before time for the appeal of her first divorce had lapsed.[3]

These two examples confirmed what many believed: a fallen woman was not a good marital risk. A study by the Registrar-General in 1878 revealed that 696 marriages celebrated in the period from 1861 to 1876 involved at least one partner who had been in divorce court and in 13 of those marriages both parties were divorced. As over 4,000 divorces occurred in that period, the vast majority of those who were divorced never remarried, whether due to shame, memories, or death cannot be known.[4] The Registrar-General in annual reports about births, deaths and marriages displayed for all the number of divorced people who remarried (see Table 7.1).

Table 7.1: Marriages of Divorced Men and Women, 1861–1900

Year	Number	Year	Number
1861	10	1881	103
1862	29	1882	124
1863	20	1883	122
1864	22	1884	120
1865	48	1885	170
1866	23	1886	163
1867	33	1887	173
1868	40	1888	178
1869	47	1889	150
1870	34	1890	181
1871	50	1891	184
1872	58	1892	190
1873	62	1893	122
1874	61	1894	120
1875	69	1895	262
1876	90	1896	296
1877	82	1897	311
1878	107	1898	376
1879	115	1899	353
1880	117	1900	390

Source: *Annual Reports of the Register-General of the Births, Deaths and Marriages in England* (HMSO, London, 1878–1902).

The Times published the numbers in 1878 with an implication that few divorced people remarried — the numbers were about 20 per cent of the divorces — but the Registrar-General pointed out the next year the unreliability of the figures. The statistics were based on marriage register entries and individuals need not describe themselves as 'divorced' on that form; hence, the numbers were a minimum, as many others may have described themselves in ways the Registrar-General could not classify. Three other features of the remarriages emerge from the

Registrar-General's reports. In 1876, for example, over 40 per cent of the remarriages took place in London, with Marylebone and Kensington leading. These figures revealed London remained the centre of the divorce business as it had before the Divorce Act. The rise in the number of divorced people remarrying, as revealed in Table 7.1, came from either of two sources. These numbers rose faster than the numbers of divorces and could mean more divorced people remarried or more people were willing so to describe themselves on marriage registers. Either possibility indicates a decline in the stigma of divorce. The drop in numbers after 1892 probably relates to a controversy in the Church of England over marrying divorced people and many such individuals would not so describe themselves in order to avoid a confrontation with the clergyman or to protect him from the wrath of his fellows.

In a small way, silliness had its innings here too:

> Mr Goldsmid married Miss Fendall in 1866 before the British Consul at Calais. In 1870 she obtained a divorce for his adultery and cruelty. Deciding they could not live without each other, they remarried in 1872 in Aldgate. In 1877 she returned to divorce court for an annulment, claiming a technical mistake in the publication of the banns for their second marriage. They could not live with each other or without each other and fear of divorce court made no difference.[5]

Divorce did not dominate the life of the hypocrite. After 1857, hypocrisy raged in the area of religion as the educated classes lost faith in most of the dogmas of traditional Christianity but continued to maintain appearances, because, without religion, the masses might not be controllable. Similarly, the educated elite ceased believing adultery was forbidden — the Bible not governing their lives — and, as social scientists produced examples from around the globe, not universally abhorred. People began to think about adultery and, occasionally, to do it. Again, society rested on the pillar of the family and, if all caution was thrown to the wind, chaos would result.

All this doubt could not be resolved easily after the collapse of faith in the Bible. John Stuart Mill, the apostle of individualism, laid down guidelines for life, but on adultery and divorce he remained reticent, even after he regularised by marriage his relationship with Harriet Taylor. Carlyle, another prophet of the new worlds, came to believe that honest belief, even mistaken honest belief, was as important as truth, and the poet Arthur Hugh Clough suggested action itself brought belief, but neither thought divorce worth analysis. The old, the aristocratic, the privileged culture had been destroyed by the 1860s and a new spirit, a faith in science, legislation and progress, pointed intellectuals towards a brave, new world. Unfortunately for those who wished to conduct themselves in ways punished by the Divorce Act, no one devised an argument to support them. Who favoured adultery? Intellectuals lost faith in many Victorian certitudes but, their livelihoods depending on an audience, could not openly flaunt the code or even discuss changes in it. Divorce remained taboo; the 'Locrian halter' deterred even brave intellectuals. Nevertheless, change did occur.

As the individualism preached by John Stuart Mill filtered into the people from whom divorce petitions came, the institution of the family was affected in two ways. Walter Sickert pursuing his art at the expense of his family presents one extreme — but many others demanded more, not less, from their spouses. These individuals, putting more into their families, inevitably would include a few disappointed souls. From among them come the suits where collusion was practised; wanting much from a marriage and not finding it, they then wanted out of the bond so as to try again. Adultery was not their interest or their style, so divorce bore the stigma not of adultery, but of failure. Moreover, as had long been recognised by divorce practitioners and poets, marriages under these circumstances did not contain guilty and innocent parties. Rather than move away from the adversary process at this point and dissolve a broken marriage, the law remained unchanged. This forced the partners to return to each other and try even harder and demand more; the Divorce Act continued doing its work — keeping families together — despite the new ideas swirling around it. Eventually, one spouse would break under the pressure — adultery became the easy way out — or the pair agreed deception — collusion, 'hotel evidence' — was acceptable to end the marriage. Respectables could, under such difficult circumstances, become hypocrites.

The 'woman problem' reappeared in the 1870s. Feminists, after the setback of 1857, disappeared until they reformed in the 1860s around the new problem of the Contagious Diseases Acts, the old problem of women's property, and the long-debated problems of women's suffrage and education. In 1868 Barbara Leigh Smith Bodochon (a veteran of the agitation of the 1850s), Josephine Butler (a leading opponent of the Contagious Diseases Acts), and Elizabeth Wolstonholme (who soon took the lead), formed a Married Women's Property Committee. A much bigger movement than that of the 1850s, the drive combined feminists with many Liberal politicians such as John Stuart Mill, Sir

Charles Dilke and Jacob Bright. The resulting struggle which culminated in the passage of the Married Women's Property Act in 1882 attracted much discussion of the inferiority of women. Following the notion of separate spheres, opponents claimed woman was 'naturally inferior' and anyway men had the necessary experience with financial matters. Religion and the common law were rolled out, just as they had been in 1857, to maintain the status quo. What opponents most feared was that giving wives' property such protection would set husbands and wives against each other within marriage. To make husband and wife equal would increase the strains on the marital bond, equal authority providing scope for dissent in decision-making. Also wives, entering the business world, would be exposed to the lower morals of such a world, in both sexual and financial matters. Practical objections about the potential for fraudulent dealing by couples also were thrown into the scales. As often, however, the instance of abuse could highlight the injustices of the existing system better than theoretical arguments:

> Susannah Palmer was imprisoned in 1869 for stabbing her husband. He had, for years, mistreated her and their children by violence and throwing them out of the house periodically. He also brought prostitutes into the house and may have committed incest with his daughter. Susannah left with the children and set up another house but he reappeared and seized all of her belongings. Attempted murder was her response.[6]

Brought to the public's attention by Frances Power Cobbe in the *Echo*, this case had elements similar to reports appearing regularly about the divorce court. The Married Women's Property Act of 1870 resulted, but it satisfied few as it was designed largely to help working women, not Respectable middle-class women. Protecting earnings, the Act gave little protection to inheritances and did nothing to encourage women to enter trade or business. The injustice of Susannah Palmer's plight met, legislators did nothing to upset the marital arrangements of the day.

Twelve years later the same alliance of feminists and Liberal politicians finally achieved the goal of marital equality, at least as far as property was concerned, with the Married Women's Property Act of 1882. Not in response to any particularly scandalous event — Caroline Norton's experiences were still held up as the example — the final push came when Gladstone's Lord Chancellor, Lord Selborne, committed himself to the change. Like the Law Lords discussing divorce in the 1850s, Selborne saw the Bill as a tidying-up of confusion, confusion growing out of the union of the common law and equity in the 1870s, and not as a revolutionary step for women. The Bill passed through Parliament with remarkably little opposition, the arguments had all been made in 1870. Anyway, its immediate practical impact on middle-class families was minimal. As to the sense of independence, the new equality within marriage, the increasing individualism of women — these were part of the new spirit of the 1880s. A consequence of the Act was that a woman might remain in a shattered marriage — to avoid scandal — but no longer be forced to watch her husband dissipate her funds. Was that woman a hypocrite?

The original justifications for the double standard, another alleged element of Victorian hypocrisy, had largely disappeared by the end of Victoria's reign. The fear of 'spurious issue' being introduced into the family by the wife's adultery declined with the spread of birth control practices, which also reduced the threat of venereal disease. Social science brought forth challenges when John M'Lennan, in *Primitive Marriage* (1865), discerned patterns in early societies suggesting that monogamy and the fear of 'spurious issue' did not inhere in the constitutions of society. W.E.H. Lecky's *History of European Morals* (1869) found no constant or universal customs in European history; everything was relative.

Feminists' success in remedying the inequalities in the law made the remaining differences more anomalous. The growing education of women and the spread of ideas of equality generally meant the notion of the older, wiser master teaching the younger, more innocent novitiate fell by the wayside. What remained was the belief, already common in the eighteenth century, that for men intercourse precedes intimacy while for women intimacy precedes intercourse. This belief received regular reinforcement from divorce court suits as wives almost always were alleged to have committed adultery with one lover over a period of time while husbands occasionally were portrayed committing adultery with prostitutes, servants and other 'passing' attractions, not with a long-standing mistress. More often, however, the divorce proceedings revealed that the grounds, in essence, were the same — the marriage was broken and one spouse had found another partner. Adulteresses usually were living with their lovers and sinning husbands either were living with their mistresses or sinned so often as to leave no doubt about their feelings towards their spouses. However, the similarity of husbands and wives as to the grounds was obscured by the additional legal requirement that a wife should prove the husband's cruelty or desertion, even though such action by a husband almost always followed his adultery. Therefore the situations of spouses, in divorce court if not in marriage, were nearly identical. That all this was not easily explained and — in days of increasing individualism and desires for equality — not always believed meant more than a few saw the differing standards as male hypocrisy.

Late in the century the Moral Reform Union sought abolition of the double standard in all future legislation, and legislative attempts began in the late 1880s to give wives equality in grounds for divorce. Bills brought before the House of Commons in 1889, 1890, 1891, and 1892 failed of passage because they sought to abolish the double standard and, by including desertion as a separate ground, they would make divorce easier. It is doubtful whether easier divorce — other grounds besides adultery, or diminishing the stigma attaching to adulterous husbands by removing the cruelty and desertion requirements — would have been a boon to women in 1857. Many women, Respectable and middle class, had few alternatives outside marriage as the professions were not very open to them and other jobs populated by women in the twentieth century did not exist or were all male. On one occasion, in 1892, a Bill led to a debate in the House of Commons about giving wives equality in divorce, a debate which produced the old refrain that a woman's reputation suffered more than a man's when an adultery was proved. No rationale for this difference then followed. Instead, the discussion hinged solely on appearances — the eighteenth century revisited — not the substance. As the intention of Victorian divorce law had been to deter adultery by punishing with opprobrium its practitioners, appearance had soon overshadowed substance — the sin came to be detection and exposure, not the adultery itself. The stigma of adultery had, in 1857, been attached to divorce court proceedings and already by the 1870s, it was those proceedings as well as the adultery which conferred the stigma. That women had more opportunities for self-support by the 1890s also did not appear in the debate. As certain groups, including the upper reaches of society, came to fear the actions of the court, hypocrisy flourished, and appearances replaced substance. The double standard, symbol of male dominance, lived on in divorce law until 1923.

If the patriarchal family existed — and many speakers and writers claimed it did — the Divorce Act was popularly thought to reinforce that partriarchy. Adultery was to be deterred, especially adultery of wives, as the double standard was written into the law. Equality, not patriarchy, emerged, however, as it turned out that many men would be cruel to or desert their wives — the double standard was not as distinct as initially thought. By writing into statute law the double standard, reformers, though seeking only to codify what had been the practice all along, opened the door to attacks on that double standard. Josephine Butler and others, in their campaigns against the Contagious Diseases Acts, sought to raise men's standards of behaviour, not lower women's. Domestic affection, always present in many Victorian marriages, was not directly affected by the Divorce Act though it might change its nature as husband changed from patriarch to lover.

Wives' role as mother was emphasised throughout the century and one of the strongest deterrents to wives became the knowledge that their children would be taken from them. Caroline Norton, not a stereotype as to motherhood, voiced this fear, and *Englishwoman's Domestic Magazine* echoed Norton, conjuring up images of the wicked step-mother of children's stories. Generalisations such as these, however, are vacuous when divorce court practices are examined because the wives in the 'top 10,000' did not always participate directly in their off-spring's raising. The effect, if any, was further down the economic scale and, if realised, would keep the wives from ever turning up in divorce court in any case. Statistics did suggest this worked, as the proportion of couples in divorce court who were childless was far greater than in the population as a whole.

The changes in the laws and attitudes about women bore fruit in marriage, just as had been hoped by supporters and feared by opponents of such changes. By 1900 divorce petitions reveal that women occasionally exercised their powers of the purse and men were less ashamed to attempt to extort funds from their monied wives:

Margaret Lodge brought £500 a year to her marriage in 1865. After living with her husband in Bruges, she returned alone to England and then, when her husband would not join her, discovered his adultery. She thereafter kept him on a small allowance in Bruges which forced him to seek to rejoin her.[7]

Mr Swift sought restitution of conjugal rights in 1890, largely in order to force his wife to give him separate maintenance. He had only £45 a year and, as their joint income was £865, the court gave him another £243 yearly.[8]

The Hon. Wilfred Brougham, the great law reformer's nephew, continued his uncle's interest in things Italian by marrying an Italian wife in 1863, but they separated in 1870. In 1877 he obtained an order from the divorce court for restitution of conjugal rights and his wife paid him £600 a year not to enforce it. When the money ceased to be enough, he sought a divorce in 1893 but the Queen's Proctor thwarted the final decree, arguing successfully that the whole mess had been delayed too long.[9]

During the debates of the 1850s the English became aware of the status of divorce in other countries, and the divorce court made those differences more evident as it began receiving petitions involving the laws of other nations, especially the United States.

The Palmers married in 1848 and went to the United States. In 1856 Mrs Palmer obtained a divorce in Philadelphia and Mr Palmer remarried. In 1859 Mrs Palmer, upon her return to England, sought another divorce from the divorce court but the judge ruled the US decree enough. One suspects property problems lay behind her petition.[10]

The Yelvertons married once in Scotland and later in Ireland with Roman Catholic rites. Their marital troubles and their efforts to use English courts focused much attention on the fact that the three parts of the realm had three separate laws about marriage and divorce. Nothing, however, was done to harmonise those disparate laws.[11]

The Hydes, after converting to Mormonism in 1850, emigrated to Utah and married in 1853. During missionary work in the Sandwich Islands, Mr Hyde renounced Mormonism and was excommunicated. The marriage was then voided in Utah and Mrs Hyde married Joseph Woodmansee. Mr Hyde returned to England and sought a divorce in 1866 but the judge would not issue a decree.[12]

In 1861 Henry Brougham Farnie, a Scot, married a woman in England. They returned to Scotland where the woman obtained a divorce in 1863. In 1865 Henry ventured south again and married Miss Harvey who sought, in 1880, to have this marriage nullified in the divorce court. Miss Harvey (or Mrs Farnie) reasoned that the Scottish divorce was not valid in England, so Henry's marriage to her was bigamous and void. The judge rejected her argument.[13]

These petitioners sought various remedies from the English divorce court, but all called attention to the variety of divorce laws in other countries and helped undermine the certainty that many had in the uniqueness or value of the English solution to marital problems. After 1885 many MPs with experience or knowledge of Scottish society sought to amalgamate the divorce laws of the two parts of the United Kingdom. This usually meant adding desertion to the English grounds and removing the double standard. While these efforts failed, they emphasised that the two laws were different at a time many people believed citizens of the two areas were not very separate or distinct. Despite the easier grounds for divorce in Scotland, the Scots character and culture had not fallen. Doubt about the English law was engendered again.

This awareness joined the new attitudes to all sorts of traditions, easily typified by the appearance of American heiresses marrying English aristocrats. *The Times*, already in 1884, believed (wrongly) that the aristocracy was reappearing in divorce court for the first time since the new Act of 1857. And in 1889, just before the Parnell divorce case burst upon the united kingdoms, W.E. Gladstone wrote an article in the *North American Review* on the effects of divorce, asserting that the sexual morality of the upper classes had declined since 1857. Certainly, the big cases, the well-reported trials, always involved the rich and the titled. To combat this image, the divorce court judge said that the parties in divorce were usually poor, in which category he apparently included the lower middle class. *The Times*, building on the judge's statement, reinterpreted history by announcing 'The Divorce Court was avowedly established for the benefit of the poor.'[14] Whether these statements fooled anyone is doubtful; rather, they emphasised the problem that the Divorce Act created an expensive procedure. Money and the problems of class became concerns in the late 1880s and, combining with new attitudes to women, challenged the divorce law. As the family, however, was a valued institution, breaking it up should be costly. When people came to disbelieve the basis upon which the divorce court had been built, hypocrisy ceases to be the issue: such people are merely evading something they do not accept anyway. Nevertheless, Respectables still saw those evasions as hypocrisy.

The role of royalty in English history has come to be unfashionable with historians. Political history displays the lack of influence of monarchs, and efforts to reassert any such aspects meets overwhelming evidence and opinion. However, in matters of 'society' the monarch has long been a strong, even dominant, force. George III's domesticity restrained the public behaviour of some, while his son's antics and attitude combined to encourage Regency rakes. No one believes that monarchs controlled even the royal court absolutely; but, in a hierarchical society, access to that court kept some from marital philandering and forced others to hide their sins. Neither George III nor Victoria would receive the divorced; Victoria even refused the separated. Did the Marlboroughs reconcile in 1878 to obtain readmittance to their monarch's graces? Nothing better contrasts the tone of Victoria's and her son's courts than that Edward, in 1902, should have conferred a baronetcy on George Lewis, the solicitor who knew and kept the secrets of the country house crowd. The great actress Ellen Terry — divorced, separated, mother of illegitimate children — received the Dame Grand Cross in 1926 from Edward's successor. A fast set had existed throughout the nineteenth century, but when the Prince of Wales joined it in the 1860s his example undoubtedly led others to follow. Royalty, far from being the mere constitutional symbol depicted by Bagehot, had much influence on the public behaviour of Victorians, and Edward's activities did count.

Interest in royalty was part of the interest in aristocracy long taken by social reformers. Early in the Evangelical movement Hannah More had argued that the reformation of society would be best accomplished from the top down: change aristocratic habits and others will follow. If aristocrats set the pace and determined the tone, their activities in divorce court were particularly troubling. However, as that concern came after 1880 when the aristocracy had lost all of its power and privilege, in theory if not in fact, Respectables could take comfort in the knowledge that Respectable society now controlled England. With that in mind, we, and they, might see aristocratic high jinks as the occupation of the useless.

While various developments pushed certain Victorians in directions which led to charges of hypocrisy, a few things can be said in mitigation of those charges and in favour of the Victorian manner of doing things. Silence about matters of sex gave fuel to charges of hypocrisy. Imaginative literature, along with the examples of the titled, while giving Victorian society its hypocritical reputation, was unrepresentative. Much writing, by emphasising the sexual ignorance of the characters, pandered to the feelings of superiority of the readers — and the author. Too many late Victorian writers believed that the sexual ignorance of an Annie Besant — who knew all the writers of the day — was typical of the young woman of her day. Since the Divorce Act — and long before

— to be unusual in matters of sex had been a badge of the artist: Morris, Millais, Watt, Collins, Butler, and others give ample testimony to that fact. But Victorian literature and art were not the whole of Victorian life. Moreover, Victorians set up a code which limited public discussion of certain things though permitting private action — silence was a convention to protect the young and the masses. Also, believing that some problems were intractable, Victorians saw that public discussion served no legitimate purpose:

> In H——, falsely called C——, *v.* C—— in 1860 Miss H. sought a declaration by the divorce court that her marriage with Mr C. was a nullity by reason of his impotency. They married in 1834 when he was 28, she 18. She testified that 'Ten months after the marriage I discovered what consummation should be'. This had all come out when her mother had questioned her about her failure to become pregnant and this led to a fuller discussion of married life. The mother then talked to Mr C, and his distress over the disclosure broke up the marriage.[15]

> Ellen Terry, the great Victorian actress, at the age of 16 had thought that a kiss could make her pregnant. Writing this much later, she may have been exaggerating for effect — it helped explain why at 16 she married the painter G.F. Watts, 30 years her senior.[16]

That such silence produced ignorance cannot be doubted. But divorce court regularly revealed that Victorians — both men and women — knew much about the facts of life. The first divorce court judge, Sir Cresswell Cresswell, though a bachelor, understood sexual desire in its many ramifications. Ladies did move, and some ladies knew about 'French vices', 'German tricks' and three-in-a-bed. Not writing about a topic or not talking of it in front of the children should not be confused with ignorance of the matter. The children, who came to believe that sexuality contained the truth of the human experience, misunderstood their parents, who sought such truth through religion, moral earnestness and the family. Not talking about it to the children was merely a convention; it did not mean that it did not exist.

What is to be said, in fine, about Victorians, divorce and hypocrisy? Throughout the last half of the century, unRespectables obtained divorces. People beyond the pale — publicans and sinners, bankrupts and fortune-hunters, drunkards and seducers — all used the divorce court without much concern for shame or scandal. The actions of these cannot be imputed to Respectables, and it is Respectables who are the object of the charges of hypocrisy. The desire to be shed of a shaming spouse remained a goal of all Respectables who sought divorce, though the fear of scandal remained as high in the 1890s as it had been in 1860. Perhaps higher:

> In 1901 William Johnson sought a divorce for his wife's adultery in 1888. He explained his delay, to the judge's satisfaction, as caused by his wife's insanity (she had been in an asylum since 1890 due to venereal disease) and he thought all along she would soon die. He delayed as he wished 'to avoid scandal'.[17]

> Evelyn Matilda Georgiana de Vere Beauclerk, whose husband's life of adultery began with 'Skittles' in 1862 (see page 113) justified the delay of 20 years between her separation from her husband and her petition for divorce by saying that she had been waiting for their only son to grow up, to avoid the scandal.[18]

Separation deeds remained common after 1857 as couples used them in order to live separately without going through the scandal of divorce court; before 1857 separation deeds had to suffice because of the expense of divorce. Because Respectability, after half a century, included people further down the economic ladder than it had when Victoria became queen, expense did reappear as a problem needing attention before the end of the century. The growing number of maintenance orders given in local courts in the 1890s, however, wore down the barriers as national publicity was avoided and a separation had less moral and religious stigma attached. The half-way house of separation bridged the awful gap between Respectability and sin; the door was ajar for change.

The growth of volunteer associations, especially of women, gave other opportunities to wives which touched the relationships of husbands and wives, but which, like much of the development of separate spheres and the idealisation of domesticity, is beyond the history of divorce. The history of the family reveals a variegated pattern and the Divorce Act, as symbol and as reality, is the core of the changes in that institution.

These developments fade in significance, however, because Respectability itself, like all such governing ideas, began to show the strains of its diverging tendencies. So often gauged by appearances, Respectability lost its inner qualities for some:

In 1882 Mr Dagg sought a divorce from a woman he had married in 1867. At that time he had been a porter, she a cook, in a hydropathic establishment; she was also pregnant and Mr Dagg claimed he married her to help her avoid shame. At their marriage they signed a document that stipulated they would not live together as she lacked 'accomplishments' in 'piano, singing, reading, writing, speaking and deportment'. They agreed in the document that the marriage would be void after the baby's birth.[19]

After 1857 every effort to strengthen the safeguards and standards of Respectability also had a side that either undermined Respectability or contributed to charges about hypocrisy. Many reforms — temperance, for example — can be seen as efforts to further the purification of family life begun by the Divorce Act. Publicity and legislation, those stalwarts of divorce, often failed to further Respectability and occasionally they even damaged it.

The year 1886 — with the Campbell and Dilke scandals — produced another of the periodic revulsions against all the publicity attendant upon divorces. *The Times*, after gleefully reporting the details of the Dilke case — the paper was no supporter of Dilke's politics — and even more gleefully covering the Campbell divorce, wondered why divorce court 'let loose this flood of filth upon the public'. Early in 1887 a letter appeared, signed by such Respectables as W.E. Gladstone, Thomas Huxley, Cardinal Manning, J.F. Bright, and the Duke of Westminster, seeking less press coverage of divorce because of the bad influence on the young and the unwholesome effect on the many. The Home Secretary considered a Bill to restrain publication of evidence until the end of the suit, but such a law appeared only in 1926. The newspapers, however, responded with some self-censorship and reported fewer cases.[20]

Although the success of publicity through the divorce court encouraged imitation, few of the problems after 1857 lent themselves to publicity as a continuous weapon. The Criminal Law Amendment Act of 1885, attacking child prostitution and male homosexuality, produced an occasional sensational trial — Oscar Wilde for one — and also heightened the charge of hypocrisy. In 1885 the content of W.T. Stead's exposé of child prostitution ('The Maiden Tribute of Modern Babylon', in the *Pall Mall Gazette*) offended many while others still celebrated the cleansing effect of publicity in destroying the traffic in children.

Hypocrisy came occasionally from Respectables. More often, however, the activities which led to charges of hypocrisy came from people who rejected the code of Respectability. The Honourable Wilfred Brougham and Aubrey de Vere Beauclerk, among others, did not worry about Respectability so their lives were not ones of hypocrisy, and they made no great efforts to hide those lives. Yet divorce court, with its attendant publicity, was the forcing-house for the seeds of hypocrisy. Though the standards codified in 1857 were too rigid for some, the overwhelming consensus about adultery corralled the few potential wanderers.

Despite the changes in attitude to women and class relations, divorce court remained unaffected, churning out a few hundred examples of adultery annually. Adultery often appeared silly when exposed to the bright light of publicity and, to take an easy example, the activities of the Prince of Wales looked as ridiculous and juvenile as they did unRespectable. While adultery may have been a game to entertain the idle rich — passing the time with Byzantine sexual intrigue just as in centuries past they had filled their lives with Byzantine political intrigue — the Act of 1857 was the victory of another group, the Respectables, and thereafter public life lay in their hands, be it through voting or buying books.

The wonder is that so many for so long feared the divorce court — such was the desire for power, profit and perquisites by the intellectuals, the aristocracy and the professionals: therein lay hypocrisy. For such people, the poet Clough caught the mood: 'Do not adultery commit; Advantage rarely comes of it.'[21] Additionally, the problems of class — first in the Contagious Diseases Acts and then in child prostitution — revealed divisions in politics not appearing in divorce proceedings until the later 1890s.

The 1890s were not the 1850s — increased laws did not bring increased seriousness. Rather, increased laws and publicity only highlighted the magnitude of the problem, as the divorce flood of 1858 appeared to have done to contemporaries. Whether society had more vice and less virtue in the 1890s than the 1850s may never be known, but the increased awareness of the problem made it seem so. The greater willingness to talk and write about the topics further magnified the perception. Appearance and reality were not easily separated and, with a few in fact manipulating appearances, many believed hypocrisy rampant — the society was tarred with the brush of the few.

Divorce laws were not challenged. Indeed, by the standard of stability in an era of continuous change, the Divorce Act of 1857 was the most successful piece of legislation in the nineteenth century — the first and only effort endured. The greatest obstacle to any efforts to change the divorce law came from the fact that in England divorce so clearly meant adultery. No one — individualists, feminists, or radicals — ever felt secure enough or strong enough to praise adultery or even justify it very much. Hence, all efforts to amend the law were doomed. Those few who sought to change things faced, after 1889, the argument that this would mean different rules and different rules meant more divorce. That way lay disaster! Only at the very end of the Victorian century did the divorce court judge begin, in a series of small steps, to make divorce easier but, the steps necessarily being so slow and depending on a particular type of case appearing, he soon moved to calling for total reformation of the system. The Gorell Commission of 1909 resulted, but its recommendations disappeared into the darkness of the First World War and nothing was done until the 1920s. For 40 years after 1857 English Respectables had prided themselves on their 'middle way' in divorce, between the 'licence' of the United States and the French Revolution and the rigidity of the Roman Catholic countries. Upon this rock of moderation foundered the efforts to give wives equality of grounds in the early 1890s, as well as efforts to change the law in the early years of the twentieth century.

Divorce court continued working for Respectables, just as it had since 1857. It deterred adultery and encouraged forgiveness because the scandal of divorce was too much for any but the most infatuated, such as Lady Aylesford, to seek willingly. When disaster struck a marriage, few went to the divorce court, and to Respectables, therefore, the fabric of society remained unrent. That this group, the one with political power, refused to permit changes in the law argues persuasively that the law, on balance, worked to their satisfaction.

Respectability was a path taken by many people in the nineteenth century. Affection between marriage partners and issues of class become *questions mal posées* when confronted with Respectability — all could exist together and Respectability dominated. That the code of Respectability, judged, by its own standards, worked, cannot be doubted — drunkenness became less common (following the introduction of licensing laws and the like), violence rarer (the English became the wonder of Europe in this regard), and promiscuity reduced (Frances Place testified to this in the 1820s and Hippolyte Taine in the 1860s). Certainly the divorce court performed a major role in the history of Respectability. The history of Respectability, and divorce, touches areas other than merely husband and wife, however. Respectable society supported novelists who wrote about issues of concern and many nineteenth-century novels hinge on the possibility of adultery. In two eighteenth-century divorces the wives wrote letters referring to themselves as 'Leonora', a woman with a disastrous marriage in Henry Fielding's *Joseph Andrews*. Blanche Chetwynd and Mrs Robinson both kept diaries which mirror nineteenth-century romantic fiction. When Respectability thrived, so did the Liberal Party; when Respectability died, so did the Liberal Party — the coincidence of time suggests connections beyond the scope of this work. Similarly, the history of the novel follows the history of Respectability. The dark side, however, involved the increasingly hostile feelings towards those who were unRespectable — part of aristocratic society wrecked itself on the rock of its own fecklessness (and the First World War), workers became a separate species. Society survived, though some Respectables today might question whether that survival is civilised. Respectability taught one group to dislike, to feel superior to, another and the divisions of modern England originated in the history of Respectability more than in class struggle. Respectability, in its death throes, gave way to another conflict, one still lingering.

Marriages lasted longer in the late nineteenth century than at any time in history as mortality declined, and divorce rates did not increase until the twentieth century. Moreover, Victorians continued heaping more responsibility on the family. That institution, Victorians believed, gave stability to society while, somewhat inconsistently, it provided a refuge, a private garden, a sanctuary from the rigours, the pell-mell of that society. Even without religion, communion with eternal verities remained possible through the love between spouses and the education of children, and poets routinely celebrated that communion. Marriage changed between 1857 and 1900 as divorce and contraception turned the family into a union of affection as well as, with women's opportunities for jobs and control of property, a choice, not an inevitability. Respectability reigned, the family ruled, and divorce court, after initially establishing the rules, executed the deviants and released the unbelievers. The Divorce Act was the bulwark of the Respectable family, that most distinctive aspect of Victorianism.

Notes

1. Hippolyte Taine, *Notes on England* (Isbister, London, 1957) p.80.
2. 32 *Law Reports* 146.
3. 33 *Law Reports* 141.
4. *The Times*, 26th September, 1878.
5. 45 *Law Reports* 70.
6. Lee Holcombe, *Wives and Property* (University of Toronto Press, Toronto, 1983).

7. 59 *Law Reports* 84.

8. 60 *Law Reports* 14.

9. 64 *Law Reports* 125.

10. 29 *Law Reports* 26.

11. 29 *Law Reports* 34; *The Times*, 5th March, 1861.

12. 35 *Law Reports* 57.

13. 49 *Law Reports* 33; 50 *Law Reports* 17.

14. *The Times*, 5th April 1884, 26th April, 1882; W.E. Gladstone, 'The Question of Divorce', *North American Review*, 149 (1889) 641-4.

15. 29 *Law Reports* 81.

16. Terry caught on quickly. After leaving Watts, she lived with E.W. Godwin, an architect, and had children. After Watts divorced her in 1877, she married Charles Wardell, but they separated four years later. Wardell died in 1887 and she then married James Crow, a man 25 years her junior, in 1907; they separated in 1909. She was created a Dame Grand Cross in 1925.

17. 70 *Law Reports* 44.

18. 60 *Law Reports* 20; 64 *Law Reports* 102.

19. 51 *Law Reports* 19.

20. *The Times*, 21st December, 1886, 3rd January, 4th February, 14th June, 1887.

21. F.L. Mulhauser (ed.), *The Poems of Arthur Hugh Clough* (2nd edn.) (Oxford University Press, Oxford, 1974) p.205.

Appendix: The Literature of Divorce and the Family

While divorce has been a topic in English history since Henry VIII, the period since the Second World War has seen divorce become one of the most popular topics in scholarly and popular literature, as well as on television. The history of divorce, however, has not been examined closely as most works give a brief discussion of pre-First World War numbers, grounds and costs before moving on to current concerns. Even royal commissions, beginning with the one appointed in 1850, are skimpy on history, each gathering material from its predecessor and adding data from developments in the interval. O.M. McGregor in *Divorce in England* celebrated the centenary of the Divorce Act with the most complete study of Victorian divorce yet available. While most of his concern was with the twentieth century, he gave a responsible discussion of divorce in the nineteenth century along with a balanced description of family attitudes. Typical of mid-twentieth-century social scientists, McGregor sought to gather only 'facts' about the history of divorce, thereby ignoring any moral aspect of the matter. Most unVictorian. He saw the Divorce Act of 1857 as merely making the old procedures more widely available and, due to the double standard, for husbands. Once he arrived at the twentieth century, he provided much information not readily available elsewhere and his description of the Victorian family fitted in with historians' notions of the importance of that institution. Since McGregor's book, no sustained analysis of the history of divorce has been published.

Contemporaneous with McGregor, Griselda Rowntree and Norman Carrier, interested 'in problems of marriage breakdown', undertook a statistical analysis of divorce. Inasmuch as all of the divorce court records were closed to them under the 100-year rule, they obtained special permission to compile numbers in various categories in one year — 1871 — in order to make comparisons with twentieth-century divorce figures. Their comparisons of 1871 with 1951 left them unsatisfied because the data of the earlier year lacked enough 'flesh' to help them study 'marriage breakdown', while they believed that the latter year was distorted by the presence of large numbers of people using the newly introduced Legal Aid scheme to obtain a divorce. The bulk of the article is devoted to the twentieth century and worry about current trends.

Margaret K. Woodhouse in her article 'The Marriage and Divorce Bill of 1857' (1959) gave a narrative, marred by some factual errors, of the reform of the 1850s, based on *Hansard* and the report of the royal commission. Woodhouse, like legal historians generally, follows A.V. Dicey, himself a late Victorian, and sees divorce reform as an inevitable cleaning-up of the old system of privilege and tradition. Brian Abel-Smith and Michael Birks, studying lawyers, notice the passing of the civilians, the church lawyers. Histories of legal reform, always Whiggish, never discuss the possibilities that divorce might have been abolished in 1857, alternative procedures might have been chosen or religion played a major part.

More recent work involving Victorian divorce has focused on the limited part divorce, and especially the Divorce Act, played in the history of women. The legal status of women and wives — at common law, husband and wife were one, and the one was the husband — has supplanted suffrage as the item of interest for many historians. Mary Lyndon Shanley, in '"One Must Ride Behind": Married Women's Rights and the Divorce Act of 1857', well typifies this historiography. For her, the Divorce Bill was a step, a very small step, in the history of legal reforms of the nineteenth century. Lee Holcombe, most recently in *Wives and Property*, pursues this approach. For Holcombe the Divorce Act, with its few clauses concerning property rights of the divorced and the separated, 'took the wind out of the sails' of agitation to give women more legal rights. Holcombe examines the efforts of Barbara Leigh Smith and her committee, as well as Parliamentary efforts to obtain a separate Bill for women's property rights. A third work touching the history of women's efforts in the nineteenth century, Dorothy M. Stetson's *A Woman's Issue: The Politics of Family Law Reform in England* approaches the problems from the perspective of a political scientist. Analysing the techniques and forces behind each piece of legislation affecting family law, Stetson finds the Divorce Act to be a result of pressure by law reformers, some of whom were responsive to women's concerns over property, the Parliamentary process and the efforts of a few feminists. Common to all of these works is a lack of interest in the problems of the Church of England and a downplaying of traditional interpretations of law reform, though all three authors accept the general drift of law reform as a theme of the nineteenth century.

Finally, divorce pops up in numerous works which emphasise the scandals of the nineteenth century. No sustained analysis is ever made; rather, evidence is gathered from the trials of the aristocracy to illustrate the theme that not all Victorians were Victorian and that hypocrisy was rife. Christopher Simon Sykes's aptly titled *Black Sheep*, which includes much about the lives of Lord William Paget and the fifth Marquis of Anglesey, is the most recent in this genre, while Ronald Pearsall's *Public Purity, Private Shame* and Duncan Crow's *The Victorian Woman* are typical in that no change is noticed in the course of the century. The mid-Victorian decades of the 1850s and 1860s are almost entirely ignored, examples usually being chosen from left-over Regency rakes or late-century rebels. Not informed by any social scientific theory or historical interpretation, these works maintain the traditions of the antiquarians.

Another large English-speaking country has produced more work about the history of divorce from colonial days to the twentieth century. The well-studied inhabitants of colonial Massachusetts produce material as their divorces, though few in number, confirm historical understandings about their society. D. Kelly Weisberg shows that the greater equality of women in divorce proceedings arose from a desire to keep the community together and drive out the wayward. Single adults, especially women, posed a threat to the close-knit society the settlers sought, and divorce was a remedy for the deserted as well as the disciplined. Studying the eighteenth century, Nancy Cott, in two articles, discovers women gaining equality in divorce proceedings and affection appearing in marriages. Moreover, she sees a shift in the attitude to woman from temptress to saint, evil to pure. Another article, comparing Massachusetts, Virginia and South Carolina, by Michael S. Hindus and Lynn E. Withy, draws several conclusions about the role of divorce. In a state without divorce (South Carolina), people devised alternatives, though the authors in their haste to find the similarities tend to ignore the fact that no alternative ever fully replaces divorce. Mid-nineteenth-century America is the Dark Ages of divorce history until William O'Neill's *Divorce in the Progressive Era* follows the debate over changes in the divorce laws at the beginning of the twentieth century. O'Neill finds the clash of religion and individualism, of conversatives and liberals, generating the struggle. Elaine Tyler May in *Great Expectations* compares two states, California and New Jersey, in the years around the arrival of the twentieth century and also discerns the growth of individualism with its attendant great expectations about marriage being the cause of divorce increases. Carl Degler's *At Odds* briefly discusses divorce in nineteenth-century America and he too comes to the conclusion that individualism, this time of women, was the force behind rising divorce figures.

A study by Roderick Phillips of French divorces in Rouen during the revolutionary period produces conclusions not at variance with those of my text. Finally arching over all nations and all times, Max Rheinstein's *Marriage Stability, Divorce and the Law* attempts to examine every study of divorce to find what common themes emerge, and in particular how changes in the law affect divorce. His conclusion is that society, not law, determines divorce though his few efforts to develop a control situation for his theme are unconvincing; no two nations or parts of a nation have ever had the identical characteristics which permit the introduction of an easier divorce law in one to be studied in isolation.

Once studies of divorce reach the twentieth-century they are dominated by social scientists, not historians. Moreover, the volume becomes so great that discussion is difficult. Individualism, feminism, post-industrial society, sexual freedom, and myriad other explanations crowd in to dominate a story of ever-increasing numbers combined with ever-increasing worry over the numbers. Historical studies remain few, however. For instance, a recent survey of the literature of anthropological studies by David Kertzer has little touching divorce and history. The general theme of social scientific works has been that divorce is a problem and that when we examine the tracks by which we walked into the desert, we will be able to find the way out. Whether that path is to continue in the direction we have started, go back the way we have come, turn right or left, is unclear. But then historians are often sceptical about the theories and predictions of social scientists.

The other type of twentieth-century study involves the religious examination of divorce. And this area has been remarkably sterile. Largely a matter of intellectual history, biblical arguments have not changed since the nineteenth century and, for Protestants, that ends the discussion. Similarly, Roman Catholics have stuck to their tradition. Many churches have come to accept the divorced as members but it has been a recent development as, in England, the divorced, not being Respectable, were not around the churches in the first place. The bulk of the writing comes from sources within the Church of England which, almost annually, wrestles with the problem of the divorced, not the rules of divorce. A.R. Winnett's *Divorce and Remarriage in Anglicanism* and Hugh C. Warner's *Divorce and Remarriage* typify these works. Royal commissions and Convocation still regularly rehash the arguments about divorce and religion.

Related to the history of divorce, the history of family, marriage, and sex (or sexuality) has been one of the growth industries of the discipline of history and one where much borrowing from social science has occurred. Yet most of these histories fall into the traditional English category of 'Whig histories', the general drift being the same whether the author chooses a historical or more overtly social science perspective. At its crudest, family history follows a theory of 'modernisation' which originally meant that the family, as an institution, changed from a large, extended family to a small, nuclear one, and marriage from an economic arrangement to a romantic (or affectionate) connection. Edward Shorter's *The Making of the Modern Family* attempts to convince that the working class led the way in the growth of affectionate marriages, though he may mistake lust for love. Patricia Branca in *Silent Sisterhood* follows the history of lower-middle-class women and their success story in the nineteenth century as she argues things got better and better all the time. Randolph Trumbach, adopting the approach of the social anthropologist, studies the aristocracy in *The Rise of the Egalitarian Family* and finds romantic marriage becoming the rule by the latter third of the eighteenth century. Finally, the most magisterial of the works, Lawrence Stone's *The Family, Sex and Marriage*, traces the growth of affectionate sex in marriage and elsewhere. In true Whig fashion, Stone sees sexual freedom widening down from precedent to precedent, climaxing presumably on the East Coast of the United States in the 1970s. Many of these writers see divorce as a natural development in the pursuit of the affectionate marriage — when love dies, divorce arrives — and Victorianism as regressive in the grand movement from the past to the present. Both Trumbach and Stone find divorce in the eighteenth century as part and parcel of the development of the aristocratic affectionate marriage. However, one is left with the feeling that divorce should have arrived sooner in larger numbers. There seems to be a very serious lag — nearly a century — in historical development.

Since 1970 or so, the studies of marriage and the family have opened a can of worms. The title of Brigitte and Peter Berger's recent work, *The War Over the Family*, well expresses the situation. The Bergers examine contemporary issues, but their first chapter discusses the many works on the topic as seen by these two sociologists — writers with excessively American ethnocentrism. In a recent historical collection, R.B. Outhwaite nicely analyses the divergent approaches of demography, economics, feminism, anthropology and law, and also lists some of the vast gaps in our knowledge of the past of the family. Nearly every recent book on the family and marriage commences with a survey of the literature and most say more or less the same thing.

Recent studies, collected by David H. Olson and Brent C. Miller, about American divorce are also inconclusive. The United States, with the 50 separate 'laboratories' where many social 'experiments' occur, does not produce any insights about the effect of changes in the law on the numbers of divorces.

The present state of historical understanding about the English family in the nineteenth century begins with the loss of the economic function of the household as factories replaced home workshops. Then commenced a process whereby the genders move into separate spheres, the husband at work and the club, the wife at home and visiting. (That this scheme describes only the wealthier sectors is a problem rarely confronted.) With the decline of the traditional functions of economic activity and children's education, wives were left with less to do. Parallel with these developments was the increasing interest in marriage as a union of a loving couple, not an economic alliance. Whether feminist studies of women change this interpretation is unclear, because separate spheres can be seen as an opportunity, not a prison, for wives. Victorian divorce, seen in this context, came after the conquest of the family by affection. That so little divorce occurred despite the emphasis on love is rarely examined.

Examination of the condition and status of Frenchwomen conforms to this, as the bourgeoisie — growing in numbers and perhaps in wealth — followed or duplicated the path of their neighbours across the Channel. One of the rare works to touch both countries, Mary Hartman's *Victorian Murderesses*, argues that the similarities were far greater between the two nations than English Victorians would ever have thought. Divorce made its second arrival in France a quarter of a century after England as political, not social or economic, forces were different in a country of Roman Catholics and revolutionaries.

Another recent development in historiography has been the application of psychological insights, particularly Freudian analysis, to the past. This has been only lately applied to Victorians, which is surprising as Freud derived his theories from study of late Victorians. Peter Cominos's provocative argument linking the thriftiness of Respectable men to sexual restraint, while fitting our prejudices about the Victorians, has not produced much interest and, to the extent information about such matters can be found, appears wrong. Moreover, historians usually reject arguments exhibiting such present-mindedness as that of Cominos, who argues that the Victorian family was based on 'immature love'. The most recent, and most complete, effort in this vein is Peter Gay's *The Education of the Senses*, a study of the society whose members Freud was analysing. Gay alternates between analysis of individuals, using several private, and erotic, diaries and letters, and general assertions about society. Moreover he crosses the North Atlantic repeatedly with information from the United States, England, France, and Germany. He believes the United States was two decades in advance of Europe; what Americans were doing in 1880 would be duplicated by Europeans only in the twentieth century. In so far as much of his evidence comes from late in the century, his insights help little on Victorian divorce or even the Victorian family of which divorce is a part. For Gay, divorce, with its double standard, is part of the power of husbands over wives though, true to Freud, he sees the law as part of the defensive male's reaction to fears about the aggressive female.

Class has been a popular topic in English historiography and especially in the studies of the nineteenth century. However, the working class is the usual focus of efforts and whenever the scope is broadened, writers get bogged down in disputes about a society of three or five classes and the nature of class consciousness. One dominant theme paralleling this has been that of the development of a literary culture as a response to industrialism, a culture which was heavily upper middle class in its support. Family has never been a major interest in this branch of historical study, though the changing means of production — seen as so important in the development of separate spheres — is the cause of much change. Divorce, first for the very rich and then, after 1857, only for the well-off, has little attraction. Moreover, connecting behaviour to consciousness dogs all studies of class and marital behaviour frequently fails to fall into neat categories based upon class. One issue — whether the working class originated the affectionate family or love filtered down the social scale from the top — entertains, but rarely edifies.

Making of the English Working Class, what was needed was a book entitled *The Making of the English Middle Class*. As yet, 20 years after Thompson's work, the companion volume has not appeared. In all probability, it never will though G.M. Young's *Victorian England: Portrait of an Age* has long been a close, though unintentional, approximation. Perhaps Respectability, sometimes seen as an aspect of class, provides a key. Certainly Respectability, unlike class, connects behaviour and consciousness easily as Victorians knew and acted upon the term. If the title of the unwritten work could be revised to *The Making of Respectable Society*, various parts of it have already appeared. J.A. and Olive Banks in their work on birth control have made many suggestions about Respectability in connection with sexuality. Jeffrey

Cox in his recent study of religion in late-nineteenth-century Lambeth well illustrates the activities which made up such a large part of the Respectable life. And Brian Harrison's examination of the problems of drink fits this theme too. Going further back in time, Ford K. Brown's *Fathers of the Victorians* documents the moral intensity and its origins which are so much a part of Victorian Respectability. Finally, W.E. Gladstone's diaries provide a nearly infinite number of examples to illustrate the work. Divorce is another chapter in this history, not the history of class. Perhaps the book is taking shape.

Two final historiographical dimensions of a study of Victorian divorce come from the dreaded direction, at least to Victorians, of France. Recent suggestions that the nineteenth century is best seen as the gradual intrusion of the state into all aspects of the individual's life bear examining in the light of divorce history. The mere existence of divorce means an important aspect of the human condition, the marriage, can be terminated only by permission of, and under the rules established by, the state. The English divorce law went even further with the introduction of the Queen's Proctor, an official of the state charged with the responsibility of examining a couple's behaviour during marriage when they sought divorce. *The History of Sexuality*, Michel Foucault's masterful but short work, illuminates another aspect of divorce history. Foucault interprets the last three centuries as a steady progression of sex permeating everything. Certainly *Victorian Divorce* and the fact that you read it illustrate Foucault's insight; but the English historian has trouble in fitting the Earl of Rochester and Samuel Pepys into the scheme of development posited by Foucault, which is also undermined by evidence uncovered by a group of writers brought together by another Frenchman, Paul-Gabriel Bouce, in *Sexuality in Eighteenth-century Britain*. Measuring quantitatively the differences in interest in sex between centuries, like measuring differing responses to pleasure or pain, may not be possible. All that it may be possible to say is that we write more about sex than did the Jacobeans. Whether we talk more about it may never be known; certainly whether we think more about it cannot be known. Despite these limitations, Eric Trudgill's *Madonnas and Magdalens* and Jeffrey Weeks's *Sex, Politics and Society*, relying on 'public' information, are reliable guides to matters of sexuality in the nineteenth century.

All of these approaches to divorce suggest that divorce ends unhappy marriages and relates to marital breakdown. And that the introduction of divorce is merely one more step on the path to the present, to modernity. The approaches to Respectability and the French interpretations of the past point to another possibility: divorce is for the married. Long ago Brian Harrison, in 'Underneath the Victorians', suggested superior morality, not tradition, became the measure of privileged social status in the nineteenth century. Divorce, therefore, is not merely the legal end of a marriage as well as the break-up of a family; it influences that marriage and family long before the judicial event. While this interpretation stands many views on their heads, it addresses the problem of why so few Victorians divorced after the new procedure of 1857. Did the elephant labour so long and hard to bring forth only a mouse? Something else must have been operating when the Divorce Bill was debated and enacted and when so many divorces were reported in newspapers. That something is the subject of *Victorian Divorce*.

Select Bibliography

Material on divorces comes from two major and several minor sources. The *Law Reports* contain evidence beyond the minimum requirements of the lawyers, and *The Times* gives good summaries of most divorces and much coverage when the aristocracy is involved. The records of the divorce court, preserved in the Public Record Office in Chancery Lane, contain information not found in the two previous sources, though rarely anything of earth-shaking importance. For divorces involving the 'top 10,000', letters, diaries, and biographies often have bits of gossip providing insights not apparent from the official or public sources.

Manuscripts

Materials from the following repositories were used:

Bristol Library
Bristol Record Office
House of Lords Record Office
Public Record Office
Somerset Record Office

Parliamentary Materials

Hansard Parliamentary Debates
House of Commons Parliamentary Papers
House of Commons Command Papers
Journals of the House of Lords

Nineteenth-century Periodicals

The following periodicals have been cited in the notes:

Englishwoman's Domestic Magazine

The Examiner
Gloucester Journal
Law Reports (see Abbreviations, p.X)
Law Times
Monthly Repository
The Nonconformist
Punch
Quarterly Review
The Times
Westminster Review

The following periodicals have divorce materials in them, often reports of suits or comments on Parliamentary debates, but have not been cited in notes:

Blackwood's Edinburgh Magazine
Chamber's Journal
The *Eclectic Review*
Frazer's Magazine
The *Guardian*
John Bull
North British Review
The *Solicitors' Journal and Reporter*

Books and Twentieth-century Periodicals

Abel-Smith, Brian and Robert Stevens, *Lawyers and the Courts* (Harvard University Press, Cambridge, 1967)

Ansell, Charles, Jr, *On the Rate of Mortality, the Number of Children to a Marriage, the Length of a Generation, and other Statistics of Families in the Upper and Professional Classes* (National Life Assurance Society, London, 1874)

Aspinall, A. (ed.), *The Letters of King George IV* (Cambridge University Press, Cambridge, 1938)

Astell, Mary, *Some Reflections upon Marriage, occasion'd by the Duke and Duchess of Mazarine's Case* (J. Nutt, London, 1700)

Awdry, Frances, *A Country Gentleman of the Nineteenth Century* (Warren & Son, Winchester, 1906)

Banks, J.A. and Olive, *Feminism and Family Planning in Victorian England* (Schocken, New York, 1964)

Benson, A.C. and Viscount Esher (eds.), *Letters to Queen Victoria* (J. Murray, London, 1907)

Berger, Brigitte and Peter Berger, *The War Over the Family* (Anchor, Garden City, 1983)

Birks, Michael, *Gentlemen of the Law* (Stevens, London, 1960)

Blunden, Margaret, *The Countess of Warwick: A Biography* (Cassell, London, 1967)

184   *Bibliography*

Bossy, John, 'Challoner and the Marriage Act', in Eamon Duffy (ed.), *Challoner and his Church* (Darton, Longman & Todd, London, 1981)
—— *The English Catholic Community 1570–1850* (Darton, Longman & Todd, London, 1975)
Bouce, Paul-Gabriel (ed.), *Sexuality in Eighteenth-century Britain* (Manchester University Press, Manchester, 1982)
Bowman, W.D., *The Divorce Case of Queen Caroline* (George Routledge, London, 1930)
Branca, Patricia, *Silent Sisterhood* (Croom Helm, London, 1975)
Brown, Ford K., *Fathers of the Victorians* (Cambridge University Press, London, 1977)
Burke's Genealogical and Heraldic History of the Peerage Baronetage and Knightage, various edns (London)
Burn, W. L., *The Age of Equipoise* (George Allen, London, 1964)
Burnet, Gilbert, *History of My Own Time* (Clarendon, Oxford, 1897)
Cecil, David, *Lord M. or the Later Life of Lord Melbourne* (Constable, London, 1954)
Churchill, Randolph S., *Winston Churchill* (Harper, New York, 1958)
Clarke, J.S., *The Life of James the Second* (Longman, London, 1816)
Cokayne, G.E., *The Complete Peerage* (St Catherine's Press, London, 1910–59)
Cominos, Peter, 'Late Victorian Sexual Respectability and the Social System', *International Review of Social History*, 8 (1963) 1-63
Cott, Nancy F., 'Divorce and the Changing Status of Women in Eighteenth-century Massachusetts', *William and Mary Quarterly*, 3rd series, 33 (1976) 586-614
—— 'Eighteenth-century Family and Social Life Revealed in Massachusetts Divorce Records', *Journal of Social History*, 10 (1976) 20-43
Cox, Jeffrey, *The English Churches in a Secular Society* (Oxford University Press, New York, 1982)
Cranfield, G.A., *The Press and Society* (Longman, London, 1978)
Crow, Duncan, *The Victorian Woman* (Allen & Unwin, London, 1971)
—— *The Edwardian Woman* (Allen & Unwin, London, 1978)
Crowther, M.A., *Church Embattled* (Archon, Hamden, Conn., 1970)
Davies, Horton, *Worship and Theology in England* (Princeton University Press, Princeton, 1961–70)
Davies, W.M., *An Introduction to F.D. Maurice's Theology* (SPCK, London, 1964)
Degler, Carl N., *At Odds* (Oxford University Press, New York, 1980)
Dicey, A.V., *Lectures on the Relation between Law and Public Opinion in England* (Macmillan, London, 1952)
Dibdin, Lewis and Charles Healey, *English Church Law and Divorce* (J. Murray, London, 1912)
Duffy, Eamon (ed.), *Challoner and His Church* (Darton, Longman & Todd, London, 1981)
Earl of Ilchester (ed.), *The Journal of Elizabeth Lady Holland* (Longman, Green, London, 1909)
East Lynne (Dicks' Standard Plays, no. 333, 1883)
Eden, Emily, *Up the Country* (R. Bentley, London, 1866)
Fredeman, William, 'Emily Faithfull and the Victoria Press', *The Library*, 5th series, 29 (1974) 139-43
Foucault, Michel, *The History of Sexuality* (Pantheon, New York, 1979)
Gay, Peter, *The Education of the Senses* (Oxford University Press, New York, 1984)
Girourard, Mark, *Return to Camelot* (Yale University Press, New Haven, 1981)
Gladstone, W.E., *Gleanings of Past Years* (J. Murray, London, 1879)
—— 'The Question of Divorce', *North American Review*, 149 (1889) 641-4

Grey, Architell, *Debates of the House of Commons* (D. Henry & R. Cave, London, 1763)

Hardcastle, Mary S. (ed.), *Life of John Lord Campbell*, 2nd edn (J. Murray, London, 1881)

Harries-Jenkins, Gwyn, *The Army in Victorian Society* (Routledge & Kegan Paul, London, 1977)

Harrison, Brian, *Drink and the Victorians* (University of Pittsburgh, Pittsburgh, 1971)

—— 'Underneath the Victorians', *Victorian Studies*, 10, 3 (1967) 239-62

Hartman, Mary, *Victorian Murderesses* (Schocken, New York, 1977)

Hayek, F.A., *John Stuart Mill and Harriet Taylor* (Routledge & Kegan Paul, London, 1951)

Hibbert, Christopher, *Edward VII: A Portrait* (Allen Lane, London, 1976)

—— *George IV: Prince of Wales* (Longman, London, 1972)

Hindus, Michael S. and Lynne E. Withy, 'The Law of Husband and Wife in Nineteenth-century America: Changing Views of Divorce', in D. Kelly Weisberg (ed.), *Women and the Law*

Holcombe, Lee, *Wives and Property* (University of Toronto Press, Toronto, 1983)

Howell, T.B., *Cobbett's Complete Collection of State Trials* (R. Bagshaw, London, 1809–26)

Inglis, K.S., 'Patterns of Religious Worship in 1851', *Journal of Ecclesiastical History*, 11 (1960) 74-81

Jenkins, R.H., *Sir Charles Dilke* (Collins, London, 1958)

Kertzer, David, 'Anthropology and Family History', *Journal of Family History*, 9, 3 (1984) 201-16

Killham, John, *Tennyson and The Princess* (Athlone, London, 1958)

Kriegel, Abraham (ed.), *The Holland House Diaries 1831–1840* (Routledge & Kegan Paul, London, 1977)

Lyons, F.S.L., *The Fall of Parnell* (University of Toronto Press, Toronto, 1960)

McClain, F.M., *Maurice* (SPCK, London, 1972)

McGregor, O.R., *Divorce in England* (Heinemann, London, 1957)

Macqueen, John, *A Practical Treatise on the Appellate Jurisdiction of the House of Lords & Privy Council. Together with the Practice on Parliamentary Divorce* (A. Maxwell, London, 1842)

Maison, Margaret M., 'Adulteresses in Agony', *The Listener*, 19th January, 1961, pp.133-4

Maurice, F.D., *Sermons Preached in Lincoln's Inn Chapel* (Macmillan, London, 1891–2)

—— *Kingdom of Christ*, 2nd edn. (Rivington, London, 1842)

Maurice, Frederick, *Life of Frederick Denison Maurice*, 3rd edn (Macmillan, London, 1884)

May, Elaine Tyler, *Great Expectations* (University of Chicago, Chicago, 1980)

Menefee, S.P., *Wives for Sale* (Blackwell, Oxford, 1981)

Meredith, George, *The Ordeal of Richard Feverel* (Constable, London, 1914)

Morley, John, *The Life of William Ewart Gladstone* (Macmillan, London, 1903)

Mulhauser, F.L. (ed.), *The Poems of Arthur Hugh Clough*, 2nd edn. (Oxford University Press, Oxford, 1974)

Muscott, Edward, *The History and Power of Ecclesiastical Courts* (J. Snow, London, 1845)

Olson, David H. and Brent C. Miller (eds.), *Family Studies* (Sage, Beverly Hills, Calif., 1983)

O'Neill, William, *Divorce in the Progressive Era* (Yale University Press, New Haven, 1967)

Outhwaite, R.B. (ed.), *Marriage and Society* (St Martin's, New York, 1981)

Page, Frederick (ed.), *The Poems of Coventry Patmore* (Oxford University Press,

London, 1949)

Pearsall, Ronald, *Public Purity, Private Shame* (Weidenfeld & Nicholson, London, 1976)

Phillips, Roderick, *Family Breakdown in Late Eighteenth-century France* (Clarendon, Oxford, 1980)

Pickering, W.S.F., 'The 1851 Religious Census — A Useless Experiment', *British Journal of Sociology*, 18 (1967) 382-407

Plowden, Francis, *Crim. Con. Biography* (London, 1830)

Radzinowicz, Leo, *A History of English Criminal Law and its Administration, from 1750* (Macmillan, New York, 1948)

Rheinstein, Max, *Marriage Stability, Divorce and the Law* (University of Chicago Press, Chicago, 1972)

Ridley, Jasper, *Lord Palmerston* (Constable, London, 1970)

Roberts, David, 'The Pater Familias of the Victorian Governing Classes', in Anthony Wohl (ed.), *The Victorian Family* (Croom Helm, London, 1978)

Robbins, Sir Alfred, *Parnell* (Butterworth, London, 1926)

Rowntree, Griselda and Norman H. Carrier, 'The Resort to Divorce in England and Wales, 1858–1957', *Population Studies*, 11 (1958) 188-233

Rowse, A.L., *The Churchills* (Harper, New York, 1958)

Shanley, Mary Lyndon, '"One Must Ride Behind": Married Women's Rights and the Divorce Act of 1857', *Victorian Studies*, 25 (1982) 355-76

Shannon, Richard, *Gladstone* (University of North Carolina Press, Chapel Hill, 1984)

Shorter, Edward, *The Making of the Modern Family* (Basic, New York, 1975)

Stanford, J.S. (ed.), *Ladies in the Sun* (Dent, London, 1962)

Stephen, Leslie and Sidney Lee, *Dictionary of National Biography* (Oxford University Press, London, 1917–)

Stetson, Dorothy M., *A Woman's Issue: The Politics of Family Law Reform in England* (Greenwood, Westport, Conn., 1982)

Stevenson, Lionel, *The Ordeal of George Meredith* (Scribner, New York, 1953)

Stone, James, 'More Light on Emily Faithfull and the Victoria Press' *The Library,* 5th series, 29 (1978) 63-7

Stone, Lawrence, *The Family, Sex and Marriage* (Harper & Row, New York, 1977)

Sykes, Christopher Simon, *Black Sheep* (Chatto & Windus, London, 1982)

Sykes, Norman, *Church and State in the Eighteenth Century* (Cambridge University Press, Cambridge, 1934)

Taine, Hippolyte, *Notes on England* (Isbister, London, 1874)

Tantum, Lance, *The Ames Family and The Divorce that Shocked Bristol* (privately printed, 1983)

Tennyson, Alfred, *The Princess* (Ticknor & Fields, Boston, 1868)

Thackeray, William Makepeace, *The Works of William Makepeace Thackeray* (Scribner, New York, 1903–4)

Thomas, Keith, 'The Double Standard', *Journal of the History of Ideas*, 20 (1959) 195-216

Thomas, W.M., *Notes and Queries*, 2nd series, 6 (1858) 361-5, 385-9

Thompson, David M., 'The 1851 Religious Census: Problems and Possibilities', *Victorian Studies*, 11 (1967) 87-97

Thompson, E.M. (ed.), *Letters of Humphrey Prideaux, sometime Dean of Norwich* (Camden Society New Series XV, London, 1875)

Trials for Adultery (Bladon, London, 1779)

Trudgill, Eric, *Madonnas and Magdalens* (Holmes & Meier, London, 1976)

Trumbach, Randolph, *The Rise of the Egalitarian Family* (Academic, New York, 1978)

Vincent, John (ed.), *Disraeli, Derby and the Conservative Party, Journals and Memoirs of Edward Henry, Lord Stanley 1849–1869* (Harper & Row, New York, 1978)

Wagner, Peter, 'The Pornographer in the Courtroom: Trial Reports about Cases of Sexual Crimes and Delinquencies as a Genre of Eighteenth-century Erotica', in Paul-Gabriel Bouce (ed.), *Sexuality in Eighteenth-century Britain* (Manchester University Press, Manchester, 1982)

Walkowitz, J.R., *Prostitution and Victorian Society* (Cambridge University Press, Cambridge, 1980)

Warner, Hugh C., *Divorce and Remarriage* (George Allen & Unwin, London, 1954)

Weeks, Jeffrey, *Sex, Politics and Society* (Longman, London, 1981)

Weisberg, D. Kelly, 'Under Great Temptations Here: Women and Divorce Law in Puritan Massachussetts', in D. Kelly Weisberg (ed.), *Women and the Law*, 2 (Shenkman, Cambridge, Mass., 1982)

Winnett, A.R., *Divorce and Remarriage in Anglicanism* (Macmillan, London, 1958)

Wood, Mrs Henry, *East Lynne* (Dent, London, 1984)

Woodhouse, M.K., 'The Marriage and Divorce Bill of 1857', *American Journal of Legal History*, 3 (1959) 260-76

Wyndham, H.A., *A Family History* (Oxford University Press, London, 1950)

Young, G.M., *Victorian England: Portrait of an Age,* annotated edn. (Oxford University Press, London, 1977)

Index

Couples seeking divorces are usually listed under the husband's surname only unless significant reference is made to one of them elsewhere than in the divorce litigation.